Thank you.
for playing
your A game.
Bill & Carolyn

# PLAYING YOUR
# 'A' GAME

*Inspirational Coaching to Profitability*

BY
## DR. WILLIAM A. BLATCHFORD
AND
## CAROLYN PASLEY BLATCHFORD, MST

MAVERICK PUBLICATIONS
BEND, OREGON

ISBN: 0-89288-288-3

Printed in the United States of America

Book design and photo shoot concept by
RocketDog Dental
Call for your consultation today.
1.877.869.2293
www.rocketdogdental.com

Other publications by Dr. Bill Blatchford:
*The Blatchford Dentist's Mighty Guide Book,*
5th printing 2000

Blatchford's Block Booking video, 1999

For ordering:
(800) 578-9155; www. blatchford.com
P. O. Box 9070; Bend, OR 97708

# WE DEDICATE THIS BOOK TO:

Ruth Lundgren Pasley, Carolyn's mother
for her love and life lessons of time, patriotism and spirituality;

to Lennox and Ruth Blatchford, Bill's mother and father
for their love and lessons in math, responsibility and faith.

And to our two daughters, Christina and Tiffany,
the most loyal, loving and fun friends,
we dedicate "Playing Your 'A' Game.

# PROCEEDS

Thank you for purchasing this book.

While you are learning, proceeds for "Playing Your 'A' Game"
will be divided equally within two Blatchford causes.

Oregon Health Science University has a promising student,
Christina Blatchford and half of the proceeds of "Playing"
will help pay her four year dental school tuition.

American Diabetic Association (ADA)
where time and money are needed to make stem cells available to
average Americans, well, exceptional Americans
as Tiffany Blatchford Evans, a Type 1 diabetic
and Nanci Granahan, our Blatchford consultant,
a juvenile diabetic since age 11.

# CONTENTS

## ACKNOWLEDGEMENTS:

We want to acknowledge all the many mentors enjoyed by the Doctors in "A" Game. Many of these technical mentors have taken great risks over their careers to teach and share what they know. A dental school's mandate is to have students pass the state board, nothing more, nothing less. Upon graduation, continuing education choices are made and these impact a person's life as never before. Thank you Drs. Rosenthal, Dickerson, Kois, Nash, Spoor, Hornbrook, Jackson, Pankey, Strupp, Baird, Spear, Mopper, Farran, Trinkner, Nixon, Reed, Eubanks, Dorfman, Barnes and so many more. You help Doctors play their 'A' Game and keep moving forward.

We want to thank the many people along our life's path who have made significant differences, our Blatchford Solutions staff of Carol Bogner, Jeanne Swenson, Nanci Granahan, Kaye Puccetti, Peter Munton, David Kury, Sherran Bard, Janis Summerlin, Nanci Huston, and Drs. Robert Pierce and John Miner.

# PLAYING YOUR 'A' GAME

*Inspirational Coaching to Profitability*

## BY WILLIAM A. BLATCHFORD, D.D.S.
### AND
## CAROLYN PASLEY BLATCHFORD, M.S.T.

# INTRODUCTION

Our purpose is to provide inspiration, education and motivation for dentists and teams to achieve their dream practice. The business of dentistry provides many unparalleled qualities of independence, entrepreneurial leadership, teamsmanship, total control and so many choices.

In North America, we were fortunate to be born on the right side of the planet. People do have discretionary income, their smiles and teeth are important to them and you are respected and valued as that messenger.

I enjoy the challenge of dentists who feel frustrated, unfulfilled, overworked and underpaid as well as underworked or out of control with debt and worry with business decisions. The successful business of dentistry is not complex or a secret. The real challenge is the owner and leader is also the top highly skilled mechanical operator; the only licensed diagnostician. The owner also wears a team hat and letterman's jacket. The team owner is also the head cheerleader. The dentist wears every hat and must know every position played on the team. It is easy to get lost in the crowd and not see the score board.

Herein lies the challenge and work: to help the dentist find themselves, define their standards and values, help them discover and define clearly the practice of their dreams and help them create a plan to arrive there. Using basic business principles of vision, goal setting, leadership, budgeting, communication, sales, and marketing, I coach them to achieve their dream.

As a practicing dentist for twenty years, I understand and appreciate the science and technology. I also understand the debt burden of a young dentist, business choices in partnerships and associateships, as well as the real love many dentists feel for the actual practicing along with the extraordinary generational relationships that make a practice special.  Then there is the distinct dental opportunity to continue to practice as long as you are able and have desire.  There is not another profession like it.

In looking back, I can see I was always drawn to organization and efficiency.  Time management skills have been important all along.  I negotiated to have my college summer job be based on a salary when all the tasks were complete, rather then hourly and trying to "stretch" the job.  In dental school, I worked several jobs and was aware of time efficiency and value/result.

I started from scratch in Corvallis, OR and was discouraged from doing so by some dentists.  Dr. Charlie Stuart was most encouraging and let me work in his office on his off-days as my office was being renovated.  My first team member was a dental veteran of 17 years experience.  Lynn Borden taught me to throw away the alginate mixing bowls and quit waiting for "room temperature water." Have pre-measured baggies of alginate powder, mix with always room temperature water in pill viles, mix the two, squish around, cut the corner off the baggie and fill the alginate tray.  I employed our daughters to measure alginate into baggies.

Another veteran assistant, Ruth Calligan taught me about treatment room efficiency and having the assistant lead the room.  Her motto: once an instrument was used, Doctor lays it down and it is gone. Do it once and do it right. Her purpose was to have the doctor be focused, precise and efficient.  No dawdling with Ruth on board.

Other talented staff members encouraged me to apply the McDonald's philosophy of "Would you like fries with your burger?" to dentistry by asking patients, "Would you like to do additional treatment at this time?"

I learned the "60 second Crown Prep" from Dr. Omer Reed and that lead to a much greater efficiency as his technique was solid.  I always diagnosed a root canal and crown and was able to complete both in two appointments.  I was thinking not only of the patient's time from work and my time; I was thinking of the monetary results of being efficient.

Corvallis, OR is the home of the Oregon State Beavers with 4000 freshmen entering each fall. I saw 16,000 wisdom teeth needing my help annually. I liked oral surgery anyway but took more classes and my game was to have the first extracted while my assistant was in preparation.

Many dentists mistakenly believe if they open their office five or six days a week, this will make them more profitable. In my 18 years of dental business coaching, I see the opposite. Profitability actually increases by decreasing the hours in the office.

We have been practice management editors for Asia Pacific and Latin American Dental News for 15 years. I receive emails from all over the world saying "I am a new dentist. I want to set up a practice. What should I do?" Here is some business advice for the new dentist:

- Decide who you are, what kind of practice you ultimately desire.

- Do your demographics to find the desirable location and gamble it will be solid for next thirty years

- Ideal: find a practice to purchase in that area.

- Make sure you have your own representative looking out for you, your interests and your money. Do not believe the selling broker is your friend.

- Ask for tax returns, profit and loss, fee schedules, insurance collections, debt structure and staffing. Red flag—"I can't find it, you don't need to see all that," says the seller.

- Create a contract that the selling Doctor must depart immediately. There is no "indefinite departure" as selling Dr. will work on "his" patients. How can they be "his" patients when he just sold you the practice?

- Step up and be the boss, not just the person paying the bills. Staff is loyal to selling Doctor and you will need to work well at shifting their trust and loyalty.

- Make only positive statements about selling Doctor. You were not there when the work was placed.  These patients are loyal to the departing Doctor.  You cannot buy their loyalty.  Work at it.

- Do not long-term treatment plan at first hygiene visit.  Let patients become acquainted with you and approach them on the second visit.

Many times with young dentists, I see difficult situations after the fact.  Currently, a popular method is for a Doctor to have a younger partner buy in for 49%, the selling Doctor retaining 51% control.  Buyer beware:  Just because someone has been in practice for twenty years does not mean there is money to split the net in half.  The assumption is One Plus One equals Three which means not only did you purchase a minority share, you also now must create new patients and build your practice.  In some instances, the new Doctor does not see any hygiene patients for treatment.  By the selling Doctor retaining 51%, he is still the leader in the eyes of the staff and the 49% Doctor is the "interloper."  This is a challenging situation when one Doctor is unhappy.

There is joy however, in Mudville when a Doctor becomes again so excited about dentistry and does not want to quit.  When we are able to help create a "Retire As You Go" scenario with team and patients while the Doctor continues for as long as he is able or desires; this is very rewarding.

Our second purpose is to pay for our daughter's dental school education.  Christina Blatchford is entering her first year at Oregon Health Science University in Portland.  Happily married at 33, two bachelor's degrees and fully employed, she took a risk to complete her prerequisites in science.  She is delighted and will make a real contribution.  Our goal is to have her graduate tuition debt free.  Buy this book for your peers, your specialists, your children and grandchildren.  Inspire others to be part of this unique and very special profession.

# PROLOGUE

Dentistry can be so rewarding emotionally and financially if done well. Certain practices are very successful. They know themselves very well, they have standards and are able to communicate those values with passion and energy.

One thing is very clear, even with dentists—that behavior with its impending results, is a choice. We are at choice every minute of the day. What we choose to do with the paths presented us, is a choice. In dentistry, putting up with unskilled average staff is a choice, not being accountable for your own actions is a choice, having an overhead of 83% is a choice, selecting a poor quality laboratory is a choice, avoiding "expensive" continuing education courses is a choice, being frustrated in dentistry is a choice, trying to copy others instead of discovering yourself is a choice.

*The good news is you can change your behavior. You can change your choice.*

# WARNING!

These Doctors have shared their stories, ideas, worries and goals to help you. Their practices are unique due to their training, personality, vision, location, experience and marketing. There is only one Jay Neuhaus, Lori Kemmet or April Ziegele. You can use their ideas and it will be unique in your practice, but not exactly like theirs.

They have full time practices, just as you. Please respect this. We purposely did not list contact numbers. PLEASE DO NOT CALL THESE DOCTORS! If you have a question, please contact them through their websites. They may return your email inquiry.

Another avenue for information is to contact us at www.blatchford.com or Jeanne Swenson at (541) 389-9088, our Bend office.

# 1

## RETIRE AS YOU GO

## Dr. Barry Turner

Dr. Turner has always been on a mission to the edge, on the fringes where things are happening. A dedicated CE junkie who really does implement what he learns, Barry sees dentistry as a vehicle to live the kind of life of which he has always dreamed. At this point in his life, he is continuing to practice to support his volunteer work, contributions of time and energy to dental organization and be physically fit at age 63. His goal? Keep on keeping on. Not because he has to but because it is too exciting to leave and have a void in his life.

He was an Air Force navigator during the Viet Nam era. "Actually, I flew in the G Model of a B-52 which never went to Viet Nam. It was one month after I left to go to dental school the Air Force started cross-training G Model crews to go to Viet Nam to fly the older models of B-52's that were there. The closest I was to the Viet Nam War was to deliver a C-130 as far as Guam during my senior year of dental school." We all owe him a big "thanks" for his contribution to our freedom. As his fourth year was approaching, he wondered if he should continue in the military or try something in civilian life. An oral surgeon Air Force buddy asked him to scrub in for some procedures and encouraged Barry to do the dentist thing. Barry took prerequisites by correspondence, a semester of physics at University of

Pacific and summer school at U. C. Berkeley to barely complete the prereqs (his original degree was in Fish and Game) and started at Penn Dental in 1969. Dr. Turner arrived in Philadelphia without even knowing his final physics score. The Penn Director of Admissions thought that was very bold and Barry has followed that behavior pattern thoughout his dental career.

Always a hard worker, Dr. Turner just knew he would be a success. In the sixth grade, he picked prunes and delivered newspapers. He has always equated working hard with making money to do the things he thinks are important. Recently, however, Barry has had a shift in thinking. "Success" now is creating a balance of spiritual awareness, good health, good family ties, good friendships, a profitable practice, happy patients, happy staff and making a difference in local and world communities. Except for a certain comfort and mobility level, he no longer equates success to money.

Dr. Turner's desire to see the world and share his skill has led to volunteer trips with Northwest Medical Teams and Rotary in Mexico, Nepal and Uganda. He has become the expert in making use of Rotary Foundation to help fund predictably successful third world country projects. He has made several trips to Nepal where he established three dental studios in schools with the help of ADEC who gave Rotary big discounts on portable equipment. Their first trip was ten days after 9/11. In addition to doing dentistry, they gave polio immunizations. On the second trip, Barry and his son climbed to Camp One above the Tibet Everest Base Camp following the work project.

After a V. A. Hospital GPR, Barry was seeking an outdoor, hiking and healthy environment. He called an older Penn grad in Grass Valley who was busy enough to offer Dr. Turner a position on the weekends, then an associateship and eventual partnership. Barry sold his half back to the partner five years later and opened his own office in the same town.

Ten years into practice on his own, he realized he did everything at breakneck speed and was trapped in his own success. His motto at the time was "there is no amount of management shortcoming that can't be overcome by more production." He could see the next step was a practice sale. Could he keep up the pace to the finish line? He agonized over not being able to pay all his bills. Enter Dr. Bill Blatchford, speaking to his local dental society. He talked of the four day work week, six weeks off with pay, 180 work days with the same or higher production/collection. "My team loved the idea and I liked pegging the staff expenses at 20%. To me, the Blatchford bonus plan is what brought it all into line and created choices." Barry quit worrying about money and focused on the bigger picture.

Dr. Turner is an exciting, passionate leader who pulls people into his dreams. Earlier in his career, he was slow to let go of staff who were not good team players. "The Blatchford BAM bonus system made it easier to figure out the staff was not performing in proportion to their numbers. Missing bonus goals three months in a row, I immediately let go of the weakest team member. Always, this leaves a stronger staff."

He and his staff discuss all large cases in their weekly staff meeting. What made this guest feel trustworthy and what did we do well to completion? On others, what did we do to "drop the ball" and now set a different course? He had a staff of 12 starting with Blatchford and now has three team members.

As his staff really became a team and the practice grew with his leadership, his world vision grew. With profitability, he has fallen into a love of leading volunteer dental teams into third world countries. "The wealth that is not sitting in my retirement portfolio is resting nicely within my head from the experiences that I have had with this new-found passion." He has spent wonderful afternoons over campfires in Nepal villages talking with happy citizens whose annual salary is less than he nets in one morning.

Barry's team has participated four times in 1000 Smiles Cleft

Palate Clinic in Ensenada as well as two trips to Mexico City. His team is helping his Rotary club take over two Ensenada clinics. They also help strategize how Barry can take three weeks at a time to do volunteer work in Nepal and Uganda. He said "staff doesn't do tents," so they are happy to have Barry and wife, Sharyn do the more exotic trips.

Dr. Turner has become a featured speaker on the Rotary club circuit with a gripping PowerPoint presentation and will be speaking at the 2007 Anaheim California Dental Meeting. He makes a good point that he joined Rotary to help others. He was a member for six years before a Rotary patient came to him. The same has been true for his other activities like running. His advice is to become involved in projects because you are passionate about the cause or service. Do not expect patients to evolve from your interests. It will happen but that should not be the motivating factor.

Barry has an 88-year-old father as a great example of life and longevity. Thus, Barry has many interests to carry him that distance including sailing, marathons, ski racing and climbing with his son Brady. They have climbed in France (Mt. Blanc), Bolivia (Huayna Potosi), Mexico (Orizaba), US (Rainier) and Tibet (Everest Camp One). So, how much is enough for this man of many interests? He feels $2M is his retirement goal. Yet, he said "in a stretch," he could retire tomorrow in Shertung, Nepal and be the wealthiest person in a 100 mile radius.

Dr. Turner was serving as a Trustee to the CDA, a prestigious group making concrete decisions. No longer an insurance provider, except for the strong Delta in CA., he decided to drop Delta and the first person to shake his hand at that meeting was his friend, the President of the Delta Dental Board. Barry agonized over the Delta decision and it took time and effort to buck tradition in dental circles. He has no regrets. Because they are non-insurance, they have worked at communication. "We explain carefully most insurances do not

have 'lists' of dentists. We have the same guidelines for reimbursement as every other office. We submit the computer generated forms
just like every other office. The only difference is that we receive our
money directly from the patient and the patient receives the reimbursement from the insurance company. There are few misunder-
standings. It keeps us working harder to keep current patients happy
and to keep looking for new high quality patients to replace those
whose treatment is finished."

Barry attributes much of his clinical confidence to Las Vegas
Institute. As a leader, Dr. Turner has high standards. He knows he
will have to "exit" dentistry someday but before that time, he wants to
accomplish a couple dozen neuromuscular full mouth makeovers with
excellent results. In his path to retirement, he wants to have the funds
to take the upper end continuing education courses.

Realistically, he sees himself practicing until age 70. In the meantime, he is looking for potential opportunities in third world countries
with possibly World Health Organization or non-profits. "I have not
seen anything yet that would make me happier than doing exactly
what I am doing now. The mix of working hard at my regular practice in order to allow me the escape regularly to do my 'third world
thing' has keep the game interesting and fresh so I see no reason to
change that successful pattern any time soon."

He has grown his practice by marketing and practice purchase.
He has developed full page newspaper ads because that is what is available in his area. Six months later, he had his first patient and after
three years, half of his esthetic cases arrive from those ads. He is also
very current in continuing education and keeping his skills and clinic
current. He has all the "spa" things, fresh flowers, complete juice bar
and new LCD screens in each op.

His practice purchase of $115K was eight miles down the road in
a gated golf community. After establishing a strong presence in the
purchased practice, he was able to do twice the production in his

home office due to Myotronics equipment, laser, more equipment and more room. He completed the lease and will sell the equipment and leaseholds for $95K. "I have gained over 200 patients and learned from the experience."

Numbers: Grass Valley homes average in the $600K range. Aside from being a retirement area, it is a desirable place to live and work with some high tech firms. He is working five days a week, seven hour days when he works, with an annual goal of $830K. Daily hygiene goal is $700. Morning block goals are $1000 per hour. BAM is $4150 per day and staff exceeds BAM 80% of the time. Cosmetics are 25% of his production. He does some endo and dentures when he can be assured of success.

Dr. Turner takes a number of two to three week breaks to do volunteer Rotary trips and sailing trips this year, sailing from San Diego to Puerto Vallarta.

Staffing has moved from a high number of 12 to its present three plus Dr. Turner. Life is good.

www.turnersmiles.com

*Barry on 2005 medical-dental project. This is a cleft palate referral to an oral surgeon.*

*Dr. Turner's group of 23 volunteers at the 1000 Smiles Clinic, Ensenada, Mexico, 2004.*

*Barry, son Brady, and guide, Everest Camp One at 18,500 ft. after 2003 Nepal dental project.*

## Playing the Blatchford Game: Retire As You Go

Dr. Barry Turner has taken the concept of Retire As You Go and made a lifeskill out of it. He is in love with dentistry, excited about the new changes, takes excellent continuing education and can see he could continue to practice into his 70's. One of the main advantages is you can create this in any fashion you desire. You can take every other month off and work 15 days in between. Find a staff who sees the same thing and continue the income stream as well as the emotional joy of feeling needed.

Many important factors are creating an opportunity for dentists to practice their skills years beyond the normal retirement age. Because of changes in our demographics, economics, longevity and a renewed passion for dentistry, we have reached a new career opportunity in what I call the "Retire As You Go"program.

The factors making "Retire As You Go" a real force are:

Dental boomers are reaching retirement age at about 6,800 a year and dental schools are currently graduating 4,000 a year. Consequently, the dream of selling your practice for a bundle is fading fast. The formula for sale has been 1.5 times net. Keep practicing for 18 more months and throw the key in the river on the way home! You would be even, if you could sell.

Females comprise about 40% of graduating classes and statistically, are practicing 12 years. Many are associating so as to raise a family. A new dentist is likely married to a professional whose employment may be limited in your town. Consequently, dental graduates are forced to be more selective in location than 40 years ago.

Many dentists were depending on the stock market boom to retire early. For many, the retirement nest egg has a big crack.

We are living longer. How old are your parents? The self-employed American male dies within 18 months of retirement. Why? Because the status and structure of what has been the norm is gone.

It takes emotional and spiritual skills to retire well, psychologically. Why retire at 55 and become depressed?

Newer technologies in all phases of dentistry allow the passion to return within the profession. Sixty-five year old dentists are saying, "I wish we had these materials 30 years ago and that I was 30 years younger. This is great fun."

The paradigm can shift as to what constitutes a dental practice, when you work, who will work with you and what treatments you will render.

Every person's retirement dream is different. As with dentists, there is no set box you must fit. The true "Retire As You Go" program is filled with personal choice. As you reach middle age, you have earned a reputation of excellence and probably been a standard in a community for 25 years. Keep the same patient base who generally match your age.

If you continue practicing in some fashion, you need to revisit the vision of yourself and change your paradigm of practice. "Retire As You Go" means your days of practicing full out four days a week, ten hour days are over. Our longevity is not ours to choose, however, you can still make some smart choices and plans.

Ask yourself, for the future, three questions—Who am I, What do I do, For Whom do I do it? Then think long and hard about what patients you have enjoyed the most, what treatments still offer intrigue and what treatments you would most like to eliminate. Think of the offerings outside of dentistry and build your dental life around those. Would you like to take a month off at a time, would you practice three days a week with a week off every month? The choices are yours. If you are clear about your practice plans and have enthusiasm and direction, you will find teams who want what you want.

Your speaking to staff and patients is positive...."I am so in love with dentistry; the thought of fully retiring is appalling. What I am doing instead is staying in the field and continuing to be technically competent. Instead of rushing here and there to take continuing education, I will take a week to enjoy the museums, golf and dining."

You must continue to show enthusiasm and amazement with dentistry. You can create this any way you want. For it to be successful, you must communicate your love of dentistry rather than wanting to escape from it. Dr. Omer Reed is an excellent model. A curious bright man, he practices nine 10-day cycles annually. He and his wife attend continuing education and take notes like they are hearing it for the first time. Will Omer ever retire? I doubt it and you, too, can create your own "Retire As You Go" in dentistry.

Bill Blatchford, DDS

## From the Blatchford Play Book:
## Loyalty to Local Team

Dr. Turner is an international being. Yet, in Grass Valley, he is active in Rotary, marathons, civic groups and climbing. He and his wife raised their children in the area and she is a local school nurse. Being loyal to the local team makes a real difference.

>> Support the home town businesses and teams

>> Buy your cars locally

>> Gift baskets should include local products

>> Support local faires and events with your signature food booth and give money to charity

>> Know your local industries so you can ASK intelligent questions 'how's the soybean harvest?" "saw you won a contract," etc.

>> Buy products locally even if it costs a little more

>> We are global. Think how that product will help a local business person (that is what you are, too)

>> Select Christmas gifts from local industries

>> Be a "cheerleader" for your town, community. Attend concerts, sports events, openings, Chamber of Commerce Field Days, fund raisers, potlucks, high school art shows, etc.

>> Arrange for a local high school scholarship for entry in the dental industry, assistant, lab tech, hygiene or pre-dent.

# 2
## EYES ON THE BALL,
## ALL CELLS MOVING FORWARD

## Dr. April Ziegele

A successful balance was April Ziegele's desire when she began working with us. How to juggle a large fast-paced practice in a small Washington town, keep being a great wife and friend to her husband, be an integral and influential part of raising two toddlers, be a grateful daughter and spiritually active?

A graduate of Loma Linda, April wanted to associate for five years and then make some choices. In her first associateship, Dr. Ziegele saw beautiful dentistry being delivered in twelve hour days with everyone running ragged. She knew she was not giving her best and was very frustrated. She knew in her heart she had different goals of how guests should be treated and dentistry delivered.

After six weeks, the owner took her to lunch and offered her the practice. Yikes! April was just out of school and naïve enough to think $890K was the norm. Yet, she realized her payments would be $14K a month and she would be responsible for all bills, including staff. She had no idea how to make a practice operate with two full time Doctors and staff of fourteen.

"I was so afraid that I would end up bankrupt and my family would suffer for ten years. I lost so much sleep, my husband Jon was afraid for me and shared that he thought we should not proceed with the sale. I asked my professors from dental school and one said 'run for the hills' and the other said 'go for it.'"

A small, rural lumber mill town, Sumner (pop. 8,504 in 2000) is 35 miles south of Seattle and had tulip and daffodil farms. By a stroke of luck, in 2001, Sumner became the starting terminal for the Seattle commuter train. Sumner is now growing at 6% a year.

Yet, in 1997, four months out of dental school, running a huge practice with no leadership experience was agonizing. A big case was four crowns at a time. A/R reached $220K. In 1998, they sent 489 statements monthly which took three days to process. The computers crashed and they discovered the backup had never worked. Cry, cry, cry.

Dr. Ziegele went through four associate Doctors in four years. Each seemed to want to work for a year and run the practice how they wanted when April was not present. April made a real point to honor and compliment her staff but it seemed they, too, took more and more each day. Embarrassed to admit it, at one point she said to her staff, "Why don't you all just suck my blood out too, and get it over with?" She wondered why she didn't go into hygiene.

Dr. Ziegele took three weeks off to have Christopher in March of 1999. She was working 12 hour days and had an overhead of 78%. Patients and colleagues criticized her but the pressure was there. Her second child was born in 2001 when the associate was not a great producer. "He was content to the minimum and would send his patients home instead of doing the work." April was so frustrated as she was leaving for work before the babies were awake and arriving home when they were down for the night.

When April met Lori Huber, a Blatchford enrollment coach, April shared she wanted to spend more time with her two babies. It was a very emotional meeting and a turning point for her to enjoy dentistry, become more profitable and be a mother again.

Starting Blatchford coaching, Dr. Ziegele was producing $1M a year with a 73% overhead. She had two Doctors, two hygienists and a staff of 14. A/R was $195K and each of the 50 new patients a month were told they needed to first have a full new patient exam with the Doctor and they could eventually get their teeth cleaned. They were working 69 hours a week with one week vacation.

Now, they are attracting 30 new patients a month, work 28 hours a week and take eight weeks time off with pay, have one Doctor, one hygienist and a team of two with overhead at 48% and produce $1.8M.

Previously, April feels she selected her staff poorly and lacked leadership skills. As a new graduate, Dr. Ziegele was looking for skilled staff rather than attitude. This was especially true in hiring associates. April left leadership up to her "office manager" and then yelled at her when she didn't get "it" right (she deeply regrets those times). She was so busy in the trenches trying to find her way out; she had no vision that was clearly stated. Everyone just did the best they could and "obviously, this did not work."

April would go to a class and come home with great ideas. Monday morning she would tell her staff, "This is what we are going to do—do it now." They knew she didn't really mean it plus, they had no idea how to implement. "Often I would let staff say whatever and I would just avoid confrontation instead of handling an issue. This just made things worse."

Dr. Ziegele always felt she would be successful. Selecting dentistry in the medical field, she figured it would be a good income while being a mother, too. Her childhood dentist reminded her recently that at seven years of age, April said she was going to be a dentist and she never wavered from that goal. However, once she purchased this large practice, she knew she was in over her head. "I recently ran into a sales rep in our area who told me she could just look at me then and know I was just keeping my head above water."

Though her family moved all over, they always considered Seattle home. When April graduated, she and Jon looked for a "cosmetic practice" and found a great match as the dentist was AACD accredited.

In her transition from ragged to wonderful, she took the time to clearly write and express her vision. Her picture for her practice was always there but daily she was so busy staying afloat she never communicated it to the busy staff. Once the direction was clear of who they are and what they do, systems were put in place to create the results of which April dreamed.

Block booking was mandatory. A daily goal and bonus system were critical. Learning sales skills and offering comprehensive care was essential. Firm financial arrangements were made as well as clear communications of meaningful morning meetings, evening meetings to end the day, weekly staff meetings, and monthly training sessions called BMW 4 x 4 (Blatchford Motivational Workshop held for four hours every four weeks). Guest protocol systems were introduced as well as marketing. April stopped doing the treatments she disliked—extractions, endo and dentures. Crabbiness ended.

Simultaneously, April stepped up her leadership skills. When she made the decision to be coached by Blatchford, one of her fourteen staff said, "We can do this ourselves. I don't think we need Dr. Blatchford." April's new leadership response was "I have already decided the path we are taking. Your choice is whether you want to work here or not."

"I think it is really tough to be a woman in a leadership position. I struggle with it all the time. I want to be friends (April is a very high I on DISC test) with my team, hang out with them, etc., like they do with each other. I can, to some extent, but not completely since I have chosen to be the leader. This is hard for me. It is a very fine line. I really struggle with decisions that impact the staff—especially cutting positions. I am getting better and I have learned that once I am frustrated enough to think about letting someone go, I have already gone about eight months further than I should have."

"And I have a fabulous team who encourage me on a daily basis. For example, recently Jon and I purchased a new home. Five years ago, the staff comments would be "it must be nice to have all that money to do that kind of thing." Now I hear, "Good for you, we're proud of you to make the decision, we can hardly wait to see it, how can we help?" What a difference! I know the biggest difference was just deciding to be the leader instead of waiting to see if someone else would just do it. You should hear me on the way to work. I listen to Brian Tracy's Maximum Achievement. At the stoplight, I turn it off and say out loud, 'I am going to lead with compassion and empathy. I will make my team and guests feel good about themselves today and I will have a blast doing it.' I have to do this every single day. I have to."

Dr. Ziegele does not consider herself a natural leader. She does however, possess an extraordinary amount of enthusiasm, passion and conviction as well as a killer sense of humor about the world and herself. Her excitement is contagious. "Once I told them exactly what I wanted, we talked about it every single day at first, then every single week for a while and now once a month—they caught the vision. Now they are pushing all of us to improve. Other leadership skills she has learned:

Dealing with small things immediately, no festering of non communicated items. *April makes the final decision after asking her team's input. This is not a democracy.*

Communicate appreciation and celebrate their milestones. *Each staff member carries April's vision as if it were their own.*

She sees leadership as being the torch bearer for encouragement and optimism. "I cannot have my team see me freaking out," April confides. Some days when the morning blocks are not full, the team takes it personally. Instead of freaking out over an unfilled schedule, they practice their sales skills, transfers and role playing to increase "quality case acceptance."

Another area of leadership April struggles with is eliminating staff positions. Moving the team from fourteen to three was really difficult because she liked them all. "When I couldn't figure out what they were doing, I knew I HAD to do something." When she was down to four staff, she really struggled letting this person go. She had been an employee through the last four Doctors for 22 years. "I agonized for three months longer than I should have." The push for three members came from the team themselves. They came to Dr. Ziegele and said, "We think we can do the job with the three of us. What do you think?"

Since the Ziegele team is composed of four, including the Doctor, everyone is completely cross-trained. All can excellently answer the phone, change appointments, make financial arrangements, consult or do initial conversations, clean or setup a room and run instruments. "We will NEVER interrupt a member who is with a guest." April feels it is critical for Doctors to do whatever it takes to get the job done. Because they are cross trained, they all see the opportunity and do not have to be asked.

The hardest decision she had to make was to cut hours from 69 a week to 28. She still had practice bills and staff to pay, would she be able to make ends meet? Her goal was to spend more quality time with her family and that drove the decision with excellent results.

What has the Ziegele practice done to brand themselves, to make them stand apart?

Being an all women team, they genuinely enjoy each other. They think about the creature comforts which might be overlooked. For example, their post-op bags are stocked with items they would love to receive. Their environment reflects women and they have great empathy when women say "I don't want to look older."

Choosing to be excellent is everything they do. They do not compromise——ever. They are not trying to be everyone's dentist, just those in search of the very best.

Putting their families first, Dr. Ziegele has a family photo in the entry way to tell everyone right away what is Priority Number One. The Ziegele team puts their family first, too.

April feels her team of three is extremely motivated by several things: the bonus system is a monetary reward for being focused, skilled and going beyond ordinary. The team loves playing the game and checking daily to see how they are doing. Secondly, is the fact that April adores them and trusts them implicitly. "I talk about how great they are in front of them, each other and our guests. Wherever I go, I tell people how awesome my team is!"

When the Ziegele team is playing their 'A' game, there is no stopping them. "The energy is so contagious, it seems we can do no wrong. Treatment is accepted, we are having fun, it is almost like being 'high' on drugs, except we are simply high on life. We seem to gain energy as we go, no fatigue at the end of the day—we can hardly wait to get going again. The feeling seems to spread as our guests feel it, talk about it and even the mailman mentioned it."

April says, "My team rocks! They are simply amazing—they sell dentistry, make guests feel good, enjoy each other, lift each other up, laughing and smiling. I feel so blessed to have them enjoy this journey with me and I let them know that. I can't wait to write $6,000 bonus checks and hope to be writing $10K bonus checks each. The enthusiasm it generates just sells more dentistry. What an amazing gift to be working with such professionals on a daily basis."

Average bonus currently is $3100 monthly each. Goal is to double in next 12 months which means two more smiles per bonus time and equals talking with about ten guests of their dream smile. Team (April does not call them staff, as that is an infection!) is actively looking for the opportunity. "There is no more complaining, whining, or gossiping because we don't have time anymore. We now have a credit balance because the team recognizes that is their money. They have bought into the "ownership" of the practice due to bonuses and it makes my job so much easier."

Originally, April hated dentures. However, she is coachable and now has a cosmetic denture for $7000. She is learning to love them, do well with them and enjoy the response from guests.

Gathering thirty quality and curious new patients a month is done through marketing plans both internal and external. "We try to make our office as pleasant as possible." With a complete dental spa, they communicate their appreciation and ask for referrals. They communicate with email messages and updates (this is Seattle, remember). They give out flowers and cookies to every guest. April has created a drawer full of Starbucks cards, movie certificates, stickers and encourages staff to give to guests. "We treat them so well, they rave about us wherever they go."

April has found great success with her website www.aprilziegele.com She has three search engines hosting her website and the response in computer saavy Seattle area is most worthwhile. She posted a "temporary banner" on the roof of her practice, 'Accepting new patients—www.aprilziegele.com"

Externally, Dr. Ziegele focused on a yellow page ad and it worked because Sumner is growing rapidly. The team realized this golden growth opportunity to meet new people and joined networking groups of Chamber of Commerce, Lion's Club and Rotary. Every six months, they walk downtown in an afternoon to distribute information about their office, greet people, invite them for a tour and complimentary spa service. They dine in a different local restaurant once a week, in their uniforms and receive much attention. They have also networked with the largest bulb farm in the area to participate and advertise at all their events.

Beyond that, April has budgeted big marketing dollars and a long range plan with Hamilton-Saunderson of Seattle. Initially, Dr. Ziegele is on the Number One radio station on the South Puget Sound with five daily sixty second spots. April is a very polished announcer inviting people in with patient testimonials.  Results are happening.

Being ready for anything, recently the Ziegele group was on Bravo for Show Dogs Mom and Dads and the blurb was picked up by Access Hollywood and Extra.  Sumner locals called April's office saying they had seen them on television.

April feels she is profitable because her vision is so clear and she never wavers from it.  She has written goals, a team and family to keep her accountable.  "I am enthusiastic about my vision and can hardly wait to move forward.  Staff and guests are drawn to a winning combination."

April is a real fan of Dr. Rhys Spoor and has taken his anterior, posterior and occlusion courses.  She has passed the written exam and taken the courses for AACD accreditation.  She has a goal to produce and collect $2M by 2008 as well as reaching insurance freedom in 2006.  40% of her collections are from insurance and Delta is half of that.  In Washington, that is Microsoft, Boeing and school districts.  The Ziegele team is mentally free of insurance as they realize "insurance does not believe in the dentistry we believe in."

Dr. Ziegele is further branding herself by placing her photo studio in the consult room which was the first operatory.  Another "studio" is now for Zoom! and crown seats.  A second hygiene studio is fully stocked and ready should they need it.

April's closing comments:

"The very best decision I have ever made was to hire Bill Blatchford.  You may think I am just saying this because this is your book but I absolutely believe it to be true.  I would still be wandering about—doing one crown at a time, fighting with staff to appreciate each other and me, still talking about all the things we're doing wrong at staff meetings.  Instead, I LOVE what I'm doing, surrounded by a team who loves it, each other and all of our guests.  My only desire about the Blatchford decision is that I had done it earlier.  It was a bargain at five times the cost.  Once he helped me establish the blocks which were keeping me from getting what I wanted, I went forward one at a time. This is fun stuff!"

"I am still challenged by home and work life. I refuse to take one into the other. It really doesn't matter to my team or guests if I was up all night with a sick kid, or my husband left my car on empty or the cat threw up on the carpet. And my family doesn't want to hear about a whining guest we had today. They all deserve my undivided attention. In the back of my mind is always my family and my practice—it's what I decide to focus on that makes the difference.'

"I heard once in a movie someone complaining that something was too hard. The response (I will never forget) 'Of course, it's hard. If it wasn't hard, everyone would be doing it.' That is the way I look at it. I don't want to be like everyone else. I want to be extraordinary and have an exceptional life. So yeah, it's going to be hard. Bring it on!"

www.aprilziegele.com

*Team Ziegele*
*L to R:*
*Jennifer Warren, RDA;*
*April Ziegele, DDS;*
*Anne Medges,*
*Guest Concierge;*
*Helen Bechtel,*
*Hygienist.*

## Playing the Blatchford Game: Take Action To Sell

Dr. Ziegele was greatly inspired by hands-on participation in two of Dr. Rhys Spoor's cosmetic courses. April and her team could see the possibilities of becoming accomplished in cosmetics along with a steady general dentistry practice. Hands on cosmetic courses mix well with the Blatchford skills in non-pressure patient driven case presentation. Dr. Ziegele's team is mastering these skills and their numbers demonstrate their commitment.

The motivation and excitement generated when a Dentist learns modern ideal dentistry is the new high point in her dental life. The enthusiasm a "born-again" dentist exhibits is undeniably contagious. We have seen dentists, looking forward to retirement, take a live-patient course, and now become so excited about practicing dentistry again that they develop a "retire-as-you-go" program. Taking a live-patient course is a real renewal.

A gap occurs when the newly regenerated dentist returns to practice and finds for some reason, the patients are not eager to have the modern, ideal dentistry. Patients seem to respond with, "But do I need this?" "Will my insurance cover this?" "I don't really want to change things, I just want my teeth to look just like they do now." The dentist gets stuck, reverts back to education and pictures on the bracket table.

The patient's answer will probably be a stall, "I'd like to think about it," or "I'm not interested in cosmetics."

The gap occurs because we try to use the old, heavy pressure system of presentation, learned when needed dentistry was the answer to crisis-care. Dentists are slow to accept the paradigm that dentistry is optional, elective care. Patients know they do not need what we have to offer. Therefore, the old pressure system of technical education and "you really need to have this done" mentality needs to change. Because modern dentistry is a choice, an option, the sales approach needs to be one of creating dreams and offering choices. Education and technical drawings are not a part of the emotional sales process.

Because the old sales approach of technical education is used to present the new modern, ideal dentistry, patients are not wildly accepting of a new smile. What is needed here is a new action to accompany your new modern skills. Successful dental sales have moved into the ethical and emotional arena, leaving the technical area behind. The action necessary is advancing your skills in sales.

Frustration can occur when a dentist learns the modern dentistry and perceives he cannot sell this beautiful dentistry "on my patients, in my town, in this blue-collar area, in this heavy insurance town, in this college town," etc. Our own paradigms of years in traditional dentistry hold us down. Change comes slowly in dentistry.

Do you have modern dentistry in your own mouth to match what you are offering your patients? Does your staff believe in and have smiles, which match what you have to offer? Patients will wonder why you are offering them beautiful optional smiles when it is very apparent you do not believe in it yourself. Walk your talk.

Part of the action we need to take is a delving into our own mental psychology. We hold ourselves down with our own self-imposed lids to greatness. Fine dentistry will have a better chance of acceptance in your practice if you believe your patients deserve to know about these choices, that you are the dentist who has the technical skills to deliver, that it is all right for you to charge a fair fee. Another part of the mental game is for thirty years, we have allowed insurance companies to dictate our treatment, our fees and our return. Dentists have also allowed the insurance companies to do your marketing and sales. Insurance companies brought in new patients and patients learned about insurance maximums, accepting treatment to that limit. If you are fearful of breaking through the insurance barrier, not only is this a mental question but also, specific skills and financial considerations are essential to have in order before becoming a non-provider.

It is exciting to coach a Doctor who is taking technical classes in bonded dentistry to shift the paradigm from needed to optional and teaching scripts, which have the patient driving the conversation. We coach our doctors to concurrently take action in the live-patient process of learning. We can teach you how to sell the treatment of dreams. You must also be able to technically deliver what you can now sell.

*The action is concurrent: technical and the skill of selling dreams.*

Bill Blatchford, DDS

# From the Blatchford Play Book: Choosing the Team

Dr. Ziegele's team is the envy of many. She and her team of three have bought into the practice vision and are the messengers of that dream. Whittling the team from a high of 14, these people have selected each other. See Staff stories for Dr. Ziegele's team.

>> We want to fly with the eagles, no turkeys allowed

>> Select on a winning attitude, skills can be learned

>> If a team member says, "I don't do…," they cannot be on this team

>> Hire curious people who want to win

>> If the applicant asks about benefits early, it is a clue

>> Hire givers, not takers

>> In trying out for the team, offer an applicant a "working interview."

>> Set high standards for yourself and your team. Hire to those standards

>> Hire for a specific position

>> Hire people persons, look for healthy relationships in their lives

>> Acting together as a group, you can accomplish things no individual acting alone could ever hope to bring about

>> Great plays happen when unselfish and disciplined individuals are more concerned with end results than with personal ones.

>> The better the team plays, the better you play

>> Great teams do not do it for individual glory. They do it because they love one another

>> It's amazing how much you can accomplish if no one cares who gets the credit

>> Know that behavior is always a choice

# My Vision

## Atmosphere:

- Contagious enthusiasm and energy, individual time and attention for guests one at a time
- Each guest receives extra special attention, from the minute they walk in the door to when they leave - there is no question that this is a special experience that they will remember and rave about.
- We include coffee mugs, juice, water, warm blankets, massage pads on chairs, paraffin dips, and bags for our guests after long procedures which include Advil packets, water bottle, tissue packet with office logo on them, lip gloss, and mints.
- There is no yelling in the hallways.
- When somebody needs something, they simply get up and get it.
- Our studios are completely ready prior to bringing guests back.
- We work from a checklist to make sure we are prepared.
- BUSINESS TEAM - staff wearing uniforms. Look professional, clean, pressed -no bare legs or sandals. They are friendly to every single person, have time to chat with our guests, go over all financial options with each guest so that each one feels they can afford the very best dental treatment. They answer the phone with a smile in their tone, using our script.
- CLINICAL TEAM - staff wear nice clothing, such as:  Black dress pants with dark blue blouses. They have on white lab jackets. They are not stressed, but instead are relaxed with our guests, know that there is plenty of time to make them feel comfortable. We remember the important details of their lives. We offer each guest a blanket, massage pad, paraffin wax prior to treatment. We also have small gifts for our guests that we offer with their treatment. We let our best guests know that we appreciate them and request a referral.
- This is a group that enjoys each other. They are constantly "talking up" each other, including me. We spend time letting each other

know that we feel they are important. There is no bickering. There is no complaining.  There is no whining.

## Dental Treatment

- We are all up to date on the very best dentistry available. We let our guests know what's possible. We never offer less than the best because we believe our guests cannot afford it. Instead, we offer financial arrangements to make it comfortable for them.

- I know that my skill levels are superior because of the CE I have taken, and my staff knows this as well. They feel very comfortable recommending treatment to our guests. I will have the very best clinical and technical skills available and will actively seek out CE to improve even further. I will take one LVI, John Kois, or Rhys Spoor course each year.

- We spend quality time with each guest and they understand what we are recommending and how it will improve their smile. Our guests feel that we take time with them, they know that we care. We are known in town as the place to go for excellence.

- We work with a lab that cares as much as we do. The shades are right on the first try, and our guests are thrilled with their new smiles instead of aggravated that they have come back so many times.

- We will treat mainly adults, very few children, and will only treat the children that are well behaved. All others we will refer out to a specialist.

- We will stop advertising for all new patients and be more selective. We will become a word of mouth referral office.

## Misc.

- We work 3 1/2 days each week. Our schedule is easy to do, and everyone enjoys coming to work.

- The team feels they are well compensated and that motivates them to do even more. I want each member of our team to be compensated at no less than $50,000 per year. I want our team to be the best paid in our area and the best trained.

- We will be insurance independent by July 4th, 2008.
- By the year 2008, we will produce and collect a minimum of two million dollars, which will give each team member a bonus of $43,000 each year.
- Our team enjoys their job. They feel they have more responsibility, more control over their career direction. They are happy and enthusiastic because their environment is pleasant and low stress.
- The team all pulls together to make the office a success. The more successful the office is, the more successful each team member. We share our profitability.
- Our team enjoys fabulous vacations and time off with family. They are not worn out from working, but energized and ready to go at it again. We will take one week paid time off after every six weeks working.
- I enjoy coming to work because the stress level is lower. I know that we will meet our goals, and that we will collect the money from our guests.
- We will stop depending on insurance and instead concentrate on what is the best for our guests and what THEY want. We will give our guests what they want. We will never again say, "If we wait six months you'll have new insurance benefits."
- We will all enjoy our time off from the office. We will have the best-treated staff in our entire area, and they will brag about this at dental conventions.
- We will all attend CE and be excited about starting the new things we have learned about. Once each year we will attend the AACD convention as a team, traveling to fun and exciting locations together. We will bring the enthusiasm and team spirit back to the office.
- We will all handle problems in the same systematic approach. We

will be scripted and consistent. In spite of this, each person will know that they can do the job the best way that THEY can within the set parameters.

- There will be no associate doctor.
- We will no longer serve the guests that drive us all crazy. When we find that we have a person like this in our office we will take steps immediately to eliminate this problem. We will not "feel bad" for the people that are high stress for us. We will do what works to make us all happy and productive, including removing some guests from our office active files.

## Lifestyle

- Our team will enjoy their time off and be rejuvenated for the work ahead.
- Our team will have the finances available to do what they want to do and will have fun doing it.

## Office Hours

    Monday: 12-7
    Tuesday: 8-4:30
    Wednesday: 8-4:30
    Thursday: 8-Noon

# 3

# STARTING ALL OVER AGAIN

## Dr. Fred Berman

*"Starting all over again is going to be tough, but we're going to make it."*
—Israel Kamakawiwo'ole

Dentistry has allowed Dr. Berman to reinvent himself and flourish. He has experienced starting three practices from scratch, partnerships, volume practices, HMO's, a failed marriage and lots of worry about the future and present, mostly revolving around money. With all this life experience, he is now flourishing in W. Palm Beach in a successful solo practice, has a wonderful wife and life, all possible because of the portability of dental skills, his renewed confidence and embracing bonded dentistry.

An instructor at Rosenthal's Aesthetic Advantage in Florida, Fred now feels blessed with that opportunity to learn and share. All his skill building started upon his move to Boca Raton, Florida 21 years ago at the start of his reinvention. He studied with Peter Dawson, Frank Spear and the Pankey Institute. He had no extra money to take these courses but felt it was a must to be successful.

Originally and not very seriously, Fred thought medicine was his path. Then it was marine biology and he actually applied to the CIA. Fred's dad poured on the pressure—"ok, ok, I'll go to dental school."

Fred admits "I did not go for the reasons I now find so enjoyable in my profession." He is honored to be a graduate of Penn where so many legends in dentistry have studied.

Initially, Fred made a good choice of becoming partners with the best dentist in his hometown of Cherry Hill, New Jersey. Dr. Berman gained confidence and knew he would be successful. There was instant credibility by going in with the top crown and bridge man in town. The breaking point was when the Doctor hired another associate when there was work just for two. The associate contract gave them less income over a five year period and kept growing until they were equal.

When he went out on his own, he developed two high volume practices which attracted "You broke it, I'll fix it" patients with low expectations. Dr. Berman compounded the problem by starting a second practice and hiring an associate for each office. He was busy, making some money but with patients only coming for emergencies and lost teeth, his psyche was in terrible shape. He struggled with leadership. He hired dentists who wanted to work as little as possible until they could start their own practices. All this contributed to a failing marriage.

Moving to Florida to reinvent himself, he worked for six years in an HMO type practice. "That," said Fred, "was the worst experience ever." He feels he would have been better off to purchase an already successful practice. He saved enough to purchase a DOA practice in a great location. His present wife was running one of the top Palm Beach banks and was the source of some great referrals to revive that practice. He also ramped up his skills with quality continuing education. His new brother-in-law, Dr. Jay Lerner, could see Fred was professionally beaten down. Jay insisted Fred take the Rosenthal course and bring back the joy of practicing.

What has he learned from his bruises?

Follow the Pankey philosophy of balance between family, faith, work and growth. If all the corners are not working, it breaks down fast. "When my personal life broke apart, it affected everything," Fred shares. Some good advice from Fred:

- Invest in good continuing education and keep up. By instructing, being current is a must as your instructor credibility is on the line.
- Go solo in practicing dentistry
- You can bounce back. "It is a journey and Bill gave me the process to reach personal and financial goals."
- Life is precious and love is, also.

Dr. Berman's flourishing practice is located on Southern Blvd., a main E/W corridor on south border of West Palm Beach. He has questioned whether he should move to a more upscale part of the upper upscale W. Palm Beach. However, here are his numbers:

Purchase year of 1998, gross $380,000

2003: $584,841

2004: $724,005 (started the 12 month Blatchford Coaching Program) and two hurricanes*

2005: $425K for the first five months and projecting $900K for year. $6000 each staff in bonus for the first five months.

His early marketing effort in West Palm was advertising in the local newspaper for five months. Fred thought they were catchy, quality ads—without much success. However, by treating people with great care and special attention, the practice has grown to 14 new patients a month in season, up from eight. He also feels the monthly coaching call with Bill as well as the Dr. and staff conference calls share ideas and give him more confidence.

Dr. Berman has had good responses on his website— www.fredricbermandmd.com Both he and his wife are very active in Jewish Federation, Opera, Ballet and other charities. There are numerous black tie events in West Palm. He is out and about networking while pursuing activities of passion for him. They have a referral gift program with a handwritten note.

An interesting challenge in Southern Florida is "the season." Mainly from January 1 through April 1, snow birds nest in their second homes. All services experience the busyness of the high season and lows during the summer. This makes a huge impact on the business of dentistry where they produce half in the summer months what they produce in the winter. However, the lows of the off season for the Berman team are not as low because "we have a much higher success rate with our presentations and present more dentistry. And, we present more because we are much more comfortable with having good quality conversations."

Dr. Berman indicates "success now for me is not having to worry about the lows of the off season." He has better leadership skills, reads and applies sales books and uses all the resources Blatchford has available. One example of his leadership is an excellent morning meeting where he coaches staff to goal, looking for conversations, asking for referrals. "I set a positive tone for the day."

Dr. Berman feels at 57 years old that his profitability is also due to great effort and a great staff. When Fred started at age 50 to build success, "it is a leap of faith to make some of the changes." All has led to a practice where we all make more money, enjoy it more and work less." Fred and team have six weeks off with pay. Even in the very productive "season," they take two weeks in intervals to rejuvenate. More vacation is taken during the low season of summer.

It does take daily effort to implement new ideas. One word they do not hear anymore from patients is "no." Fred explains, "Mostly, if presented properly by listening well and asking proper questions, we may have to segment treatment in stages, but rarely is the answer 'no.' When patients see you have taken time to listen to them, they are impressed with your calm approach and sincerity. We did not change the treatment offered but we now present it in a different way that results in "yes" more often."

Realizing real leadership comes from the top, Fred feels the staff really appreciates honesty and respects the leader's convictions. He now has his systems in place and is committed to attracting more and better new patients. He wants to increase his production by 20% each year. He now actually feels this is achievable.

A perfect day in Dr. Berman's office is like being a part of a fine symphony with everything playing together. Smiles, enjoyment, confidence, comfort are all the factors which feed on each other.

It looks like the love of dentistry and life is even more fulfilling the second time around. Here's to many more years of success for Dr. Berman, staff and guests.

*In September 2004, Palm Beach area was directly hit with two hurricanes. It took two months for dentistry to be on people's priority lists. People had high deductibles for damage which left few expendable dollars.

www.fredricbermandmd.com

*Dr. Fred Berman enjoys the warm Florida waters with his weekly SCUBA dive.*

## Playing the Blatchford Game: Dental Mobility

Dental practices are available in the areas that you want to move. Dr. Berman is a prime example of dental mobility. It used to be your first choice for location was it. You planted your feet and stayed. Now, dentistry matches the transitions of America. Moving can be a renewal of energy and focus. Is it the right thing for you? Dr. Berman reinvented himself when he moved. He is in love with his wife, dentistry, the area, new activities and new friends.

One of the standards in dental practice has always been  decide where you want to live and hang your shingle . The set rule was that once a dentist established a practice after dental school, he was a definite fixture in that community through retirement years. This paradigm or way of looking at the world is now passé. One of the main reasons is that 44 states now have licensure by credentials. You can move!

Dentists can sell their dental practice and move to another area of town, another area of the state, another state. Dentists are not stuck in an area just because you own your practice, own your office and a home. Remember, all of these things were for sale when you established your practice and all will sell again.

I applaud situations where dentists have selected desired areas and after thirty years are still finding the population and economy is stable. Where I am encouraging change is when the dentist established a practice ten or twenty years ago and he feels it is no longer as desirable an area but feels stuck. The idea of utilizing his well-honed skills somewhere else wouldn't occur to him because of this old dental paradigm about moving.

Just as America is more transient than ever, dentists can move too. A variety of situations could occur:
  • population mix of the area is changing

- change in family situations requiring your presence in another area (like older parents)
- economic base is changing
- area of concentration (cosmetics or family practice) would be more successful in another area
- frustration, apathy and boredom are occurring in the practice because of the above
- desire to practice in a recreation area or new hobby

Benefits of moving could be finding a more promising economic situation where patients see value in your fine work, being close to family in times of need, and selling your practice to someone who now perceives value from his perspective. A change in scenery for a dentist who actually stimulates thinking, growth, and positive energy.

Mental barriers to moving are passing the state boards, selling your practice, finding a suitable practice in the desired area and the stress of moving. Passing another state's board seems like a huge barrier. In actuality, a competent practicing dentist can pass a board. Forty-four states now have licensure by credentials—a valid dental license in one state is acceptable in another state. In addition, there are five regional boards which create opportunity in other states. Feeling stationary or stuck is now a state of mind, rather than an actuality.

The whole transition from preparing your practice for sale to purchasing another practice can be nicely done in 24 months. It is important to know what creates value in your present practice and how can you prepare it for the best sale. A practice has more value when:

- the overhead is 55%, net is 45% or higher
- skilled stable staff
- lab bill of 10% or higher
- 50% case acceptance
- six weeks time off with pay

- treatment of choice
- nice facility
- change – bulk of the dentists are over 50, having graduated when dental schools expanded their numbers in the early 1970s. Some may be looking to retire, some may be wanting to add an additional smaller practice to their existing patient base.

You may perceive your present practice has a declining value because of a changing economic base or population mix. Just as we do not want to prejudge patients, do not prejudge the value of your practice. It is valuable to others for different reasons.

Just as you, practices may be for sale because the Doctor is going back to graduate school, has family needs in a different area or feels it is just time to sell. Some Doctors may be feeling frustrated at the changes in the dental marketplace and are unwilling to participate any longer. Some practices may be listed with a broker while others are not officially for sale. This is where networking with your peers works well as there are dentists who are either frustrated with the present system, nearing retirement or perceive a different practice environment would be best. A definite decision to sell has not been made. By lunching with possible candidates, you can offer your support should a decision be made. Be the first in line.

There are great success stories in practice sales and there are also horror stories. My purpose is to help the dentist who wants a move to avoid the heartbreaking pitfalls of some purchases. For help in structuring a practice sale, call Blatchford at (541) 389-9088. Learn how to avoid costly pitfalls in purchases and sales.

First, seek a professional broker both for selling your practice and purchasing a new practice. Have the practice appraised. Make certain you are being represented individually. Many times we find the purchasing Doctor becomes friendly with the selling Doctor's broker. They do not represent you, no matter how much you like them. Find your own representative to look out for you. Look for actual net of the practice by seeking recent tax returns along with profit and loss statements. Net and percentage of lab bill will indicate the real strength of the practice.

A successful practice purchase really requires the help of a smart practice broker. His goal is a win/win for both parties. We coach our Doctors to avoid the pitfalls of practice purchase with strong guidelines. A few are:

- purchase the practice outright and avoid a partnership situation
- seller leaves the practice with non-compete convenant
- purchase price is definite at time of sale
- financing is a complete package and a total buyout is best

A competant broker will help you structure a win/win contract. The selling Doctor wins when the financial structure of the sale supports his goals and is able to move into his next project. The buyer wins when the contract structures the sale so there is financial reward from the beginning. He must be in control and able to see benefits from the beginning rather than strictly a payback for the first five years.

## Pitfalls we have seen which you can avoid:

- A successful and mature Doctor sells and moves to a completely different area somehow perceiving his experience and reputation will be enough to make the new practice successful
- Doctor moving to escape problems in his practice must be aware those leadership, communication or self-esteem issues are moving with you. Seek professional help before taking them with you to the new location
- Moving is a very emotional decision. Doctor wants to move bad enough and does not do homework on demographics and where the transition areas are in the new city.
- Doctor purchases the practice and building. Best to let someone else be the landlord, especially in a transition area

We have seen some real horror stories in practice purchases. We have inherited situations where the selling Doctor stays in the practice for an indefinite period of time taking care of any patient he chooses. The purchasing Doctor in the meantime, is expected to produce enough to make a comfortable living and repay the selling Doctor. A single practice cannot instantly support two full time salaries. This dream can turn into a nightmare quickly. The contract needs to be structured so the selling Doctor receives his money and leaves with a non-compete covenant.

Once the practice purchase has been made, you have made the move from one area and successfully purchased in another area. The next immediate step is learning and mastering new skills in enrollment to make certain these new patients are asked questions to discover their needs, really listened to as never before and treatment is actually completed. This is the real value of purchasing a practice—how well you take an already successful practice and make it your own with excellent resulting numbers. Learning case presentation and closing skills are essential to practice success.

If you are not pleased for various reasons with where you are practicing, consider preparing your practice for sale and moving to an area with a fresh approach, new skills and new patients. You are not stuck where you are. You are free to move where ever you desire and take your valuable skills with you. You are at choice to make the new practice successful.

Bill Blatchford, DDS

## From the Blatchford Play Book: A Winning Season — planning, communicating, executing

Dr. Berman and his team want a winning season. This is appropriate as Florida has "the season," a major event from January to April. Because of the influx of "snowbirds" the challenge is businesses are seasonal. The challenge is to create for snowbirds a new paradigm of excellent service and care available in their "vacation" spot, not just in their northern home town.

>> Define "winning." Will you grow 1% or 10% in what areas?

>> What is the plan to achieve goals?

>> What is the benefit for team if we win?

>> Make available resources of new skills and capital to achieve a winning season

>> What skills or systems will you implement to make the numbers different from last year?

>> Make your team meetings effective

>> Everyone must be at the team meetings, even the kickers and special teams

>> Communicate the plan, asking for specific accountability from each team member

>> Break the annual goal into monthly and daily goals. Check at the morning huddle, "where are we, what do we need to do today, who will do it and let us know?"

>> Practice, practice, practice the skills. Consider a BMW 4 x 4 which is a Blatchford Motivational Workshop four hours every four weeks to master skills. Winning teams have drills again and again.

>> Can people trust me to do my best?

>> Am I committed to the dream?

>> Do I care about my team?

>> There must be loyalty up and down the line

>> What can we learn from this?

# 4
## GRANDFATHER, FATHER, & SON THREE GENERATIONS

## Dr. Carey Weatherholt

Being a third generation dentist is a sense of pride and confidence for Carey. Proudly displayed in his office are his grandfather's 1917 diploma from Indiana University and his father's 1948 diploma, also from IU. A senior at University of the Pacific, Carey was looking forward to "working with and learning from a very talented practitioner who had the love, and respect of his patients, staff and dental colleagues. Unfortunately, my father, who had been diagnosed with cancer three years earlier, died with ten months left of my senior year of dental school."

Professors at University of Pacific were so supportive. During his father's illness, he found a dentist to work the practice. He was a family friend and his younger brother was best friends with Carey. Just four weeks after the newly graduated Dr. Weatherholt arrived, the Doctor left to Saudi Arabia for a two-year tenure. The 23-year hygienist who had promised to be there for Carey left to follow her husband's work. The 13-year receptionist decided to retire upon his father's death. Carey was grateful for the eight year assistant of his father's to lead him and link his father's patients to him. She was positive and provided the visionary link in the practice. Let's hear it for strong assistants!

Most of the patients, out of respect for his father, decided "to give the kid a try." Carey was just trying to survive and hold the practice together. Determined not to fail, "I woke up each morning, took a deep breath and off I went." After six months, the new Dr. Weatherholt started to see patients returning in hygiene. "That is when I knew I was going to be successful."

There was no pressure to be a dentist but Carey did odd jobs and rudimentary lab work just to be around his dad. He saw the quality of life it gave and his father daily expressed the joy of the profession.

Carey's original goals were to keep the existing patients and develop relationships with them. Money was not the issue but "I wanted to make the practice mine." His father had said his practice would be Carey's for $1 as his sister was not interested in the practice. With his father's passing, his mother was concerned about financial security and asked $150,000 for the practice. Carey gladly paid and that actual purchase benefited him in many ways. It legitimized his ownership with staff and his family and allowed him to be a more effective leader.

His bold move was to relocate the office after six years as he was bursting at the seams. "By zip code, I identified the home location of my existing patients. I decided to move my practice to a rejuvenated upscale area of San Jose which was convenient to my existing patients and smack in the middle of Silicon Valley."

Highlights for Dr. Weatherholt have been:
- Completing his first year and the practice was still alive
- Completing an implant case in 1984 when University of the Pacific Prosth department said they would never work and twenty years later, the case looks great
- Patient's tears of joy over a new smile
- Building an accountable and open-minded team
- Working with Bill and Carolyn Blatchford and putting bonus system in place

- Eliminating annual raises and having staff compensation linked to performance

"The most significant loss I hope I ever endure is the loss of my father." Similarly, Dr. Weatherholt lost exceptional individuals who could not keep the hectic pace prior to being coached by Bill Blatchford in 2003. The hardest decision he ever had to make was to eliminate the assistant who saved his life his first year in practice. "She took advantage of personal time and became very territorial when a second assistant was needed in the practice. She sub-grouped and became a destructive influence."

Here are some numbers to contemplate:

|                   | 2002     | 2004                                       |
|-------------------|----------|--------------------------------------------|
| Annual collection | $1,050M  | $1,180M                                    |
| Annual production | $1,050M  | $1,200M                                    |
| Overhead %        | 65%      | 60%                                        |
| Annual NP         | 156      | 132                                        |
| Staff             | 7        | 5.5 with 4 additional weeks of time off with pay. |

Dr. Weatherholt and staff have eliminated all insurance contracts except Delta (35% of his collections) which is strong in California. His best decision was moving his practice and having the building match the quality of his work. "I just wanted to be the best dentist I could be and I value quality. When insurance companies were signing up dentists to contracts with ridiculous compensations, I simply said 'no.' I had great fear my patients would leave. I stuck to my guns and continued to promote quality. Most patients stayed and many returned. I made the choice to either practice the right way or not at all."

Dr. Weatherholt had a sound generational practice when the dot.com boom occurred in his front yard of Silicon Valley. "During the boom, new patient numbers were up and more were interested in elective cosmetic procedures. The Valley was hit very hard and many patients lost their jobs. I find they are still very cautious and continue to express concern. For this reason, Bill is supportive of me continuing as a Delta provider as our pre-pay numbers increase. Our conversations about insurance emphasize insurance companies are interested in the least expensive and this office is about providing quality irregardless of insurance coverage." His current unit fee is $1150 and Delta pays $905. Being a Delta provider also causes him to have accounts receivables with a goal of being a non-provider and a credit balance.

Technically, Dr. Weatherholt has completed all of Peter Dawson occlusion and management courses and has started classes at LVI in cosmetics and occlusion. He feels "about 15% of his production is truly elective cosmetic and cosmetic dentistry plays a huge role in the other 85%. Much of the routine quadrant restorative dentistry is presented on a cosmetic theme."

To Carey, who married beautiful Kellie at age thirty-three and now has two grade school children, success encompasses the quality of one's life. "Bill tossed me the possibility of taking all of August off and it nearly brought me to tears." To that end, Dr. Weatherholt's group has set an eight week vacation goal to match the $2M production goal. Success is providing for family, comfortable retirement and a full, rich life the entire way.

Dr. Weatherholt feels relationships with his patients are the key to profitability. The deeper the trust factor, the more they value your work and your word. "We care about our patients and take the time to do things right," said Carey. They work on the "wow" factor, the creature comforts and the technology. What makes them different is the deep level of caring and this is demonstrated by working on their listening skills. They have developed a motto, "We Listen, We Care, and We Deliver." They strive to do each of these things thoroughly and very well.

Carey feels one of the most important pieces of the puzzle is the quality of team. "A wrong staff member can hold an office back more easily than any other factor." People with positive attitudes and curious minds can learn the skills. Attitude is key. Meeting resistance to change and unlearning old habits is a leadership challenge. Carey said he had to learn communication skills to be an effective leader. He had to place his vision into words and speak with passion and conviction with staff. He feels he is not a "natural." Listening is not just for patients but to listen and understand team as a leader is key to earning their respect.

His smaller team is now motivated by increased time off with pay and bonuses. He feels they take pride in the quality of work. The biggest struggle towards profitability was "taming the beast," says Carey. He was doing the Bigger Is Better model with staff salaries over 30%, too much hygiene and too little diagnosis. With Bill's coaching, they placed computers for hygienists and assistants to schedule, produce insurance forms and collect. This reduced by 1/3 the staff hours at the front desk, freeing them to have right-brained conversations with guests. They also reduced their hygiene days from a high of eight to six as the hygienist's skills improve in discussing client dreams and desires.

The Weatherholt "A" game? Everyone, including the patients, is having fun. There is confidence and conviction in communication. There is no fear. "When you are unafraid to hear a patient say 'no' to treatment, staff will usually get a 'yes,'" Carey observes.

Marketing has mainly been internal with evening calls to patients, completion letters with hand-written notes, quarterly newsletters, theatre passes for referrals, block time in hygiene and Dr. time for new patients. Externally, they have met local businesses on their block with bagels and invited them to the office, column in the neighborhood newspaper, Chamber of Commerce and attend events as a group, some speaking and a guest on cable access show. The internal building of long lasting relationships is their most successful marketing.

Carey has planned well and by 2015, he will have the choice to

continue or retire. He would love to work 2-3 days a week. "I desperately want to be there for my children as they enter adulthood." He is involved in the community and consistently gives back. A goal is to pay for grandchildren's education.
www.SJSmiles.com

*1964, Three Weatherholt generations at Clear Lake, CA L to R: Carey, Carey's father, Carey's grandfather and Carey's sister.*

*Dr. Carey Weatherholt*

*Carey's father, Dr. Howard Weatherholt*

*Carey's grandfather, Dr. James Weatherholt*

## Blatchford Game Plan
## Assessing Your Insurance Dependence

The Silicon Valley has experienced incredible peaks and valleys in the last decade. Dr. Weathetholt has a solid second-generation general practice with cosmetics. He has rid the practice in being dependent of all but Delta which is very influential in California. Blatchford is coaching Dr. Weatherholt to continue to change the mix of treatment, reducing dependence on Delta and watch the numbers as San Jose recovers economically.

Continued profitability is important. It is one of the main reasons you chose dentistry. In changing economic conditions, is it feasible for a dentist to become a non-provider of insurance? If you continued to be a provider during the last ten years of boom economy, are you forever tied to insurance? If I make changes, how will it affect my profitability?

Insurance decisions are emotional. And yet, it is fiscally irresponsible to make a decision, strictly on an emotional level, which will greatly affect your profitability. It takes an emotional and financial assessment and a solid plan of action.

On an emotional level, you need introspection to discover why you want to be a non-provider. Know these reasons. What is the purpose of coming to work each day? What are you and your staff trying to accomplish? If words arrive like excellence, results, choices, freedom, responsibility, how then does insurance support fit for you? In your opinion, how can you best provide excellence, freedom of choice?

You decide, for that decision is based on your own ethical standards. The financial assessment is simply numbers. Find out your percentage of collections from insurance. It does not matter the number of patients on insurance. You need to know the amount of treatment being accepted in your office and supported by insurance. If you have over 50% of your collections coming from insurance, you still have several choices. You need to plan for the worst. If 50% of your practice left, would you still be operating?

One choice is to continue as you are and keep challenging fees and diagnosis. Another choice is to establish an "insurance independence" date several years from now, like July 4, 2008. The goal is to change the mix of treatment being offered in your practice from the present "Crown of the Year" Club, "just fix the worst one," or "just do what my insurance will cover." Moving from Crown of the Year Club to offering more optional treatment requires new sales skills. This is no pressure sales where you ask the patient questions. If you have a 50% insurance collection, you and your staff, as well as your patients, are mentally tied to insurance. It is on your mind all the time and you are aware of each patient's insurance, thinking there is no other path.

As you change the mix of treatment offered, your goal is to show a decrease in insurance dependence. You need to become more skilled in relationships, selling rather then telling and attracting patients to your practice who see value in work beyond their insurance maximums. Learn how to create value for treatment not covered by insurance. Ask your patients what benefits or advantages they see in healthy teeth and smiles.

If you choose to become a non-provider of insurance, your plan for profitability must include the increasing of your marketing and sales skills and budget. You must fill the void for insurance companies have marketed for you by signing with employers who encouraged their employees to seek your regular care. Insurance has provided your sales. If you use the same sales technology when selling optional care, it will not be successful. An insurance sale is "let's preauthorize this," "let's fix the worst two" with the expected response of "I'll do what my insurance covers."

Evaluate your ability to become a non-provider by examining your own numbers. Plan for that percentage of your practice to leave. If that percentage of treatment left your practice, where would you be? Change the mix of treatment to more optional care and make a plan for learning marketing and sales.

Bill Blatchford, DDS

## From the Blatchford Play Book: Creating A Fan Club

Dr. Weatherholt has a second generation practice and has had to continue to build on this own through changing times in San Jose. His internal marketing is especially important in building relationships and trust. Here are some things you can do to form a Fan Club.

>> Doctor and hygienist call your patients at night

>> Respect your guest's time, in on time and out on time

>> Develop deep relationships with your patients which creates trust

>> People will buy from you because they trust you. Show your guests you care, an important element in building friendships

>> Ask questions of them; make them the focus of the conversation. Sadly, people aren't really interested in you, your political opinions or your cat

>> Be generous, give guests a good looking bag of "goodies" from their dental visit

>> Think of guests often on birthdays, different holidays like Thanksgiving, New Years, Flag Day

>> Create email newsletters to continue contact with your guests

>> Fill newsletters with human interest stories, not about your new laser

>> Have all creature comforts of spa by visiting www.yourcomfortsolutions.com

>> Have a full complement of juice, coffee, soups, teas

>> Think about an espresso with hot cookies

>> Know the latest events in guest's lives like graduations, births, travel, etc.

>> Photography is a real practice builder. Create a photo studio in one operatory or consult room.

>> Learn case presentation skills to involve your guests in sharing their dreams

>> Have latte gift certificates

# 5

## MERGERS AND ACQUISITIONS

## Dr. Tom DeLopez

For Dr. DeLopez, an aspiring clinical speaker and author, the business of dentistry is a numbers game. He is a perpetual student and keeps pushing himself to see how much he can learn and apply. Earning is not the game as he has enough. He is a talented clinician with a penchant for teaching, wants to go out on top and be remembered for excellence.

Tom and his wife Sandy have traveled the world and are real goal setters. Dr. DeLopez says, "set your goals with the knowledge you have now. As you progress, make alterations. Be firm in your core beliefs but flexible as external situations change." Good advice.

Although a business major on a football scholarship at Florida State, Tom really majored in football until mid-sophomore year, injuries dictated he was not going to be a famous football star. He liked biology but wanted a better than average return. At age 19, he watched a local surgeon at a 6 AM lung surgery and realized real Doctors worked 12 hour days plus emergency call and people died. Tom shadowed his dentist and was surprised at the variety of treatments, out by 5:15 PM and no one died. To cement his choice, at age 19, he was invited to the local dental Christmas party with drinks, hors d'oeuvres and lots of pretty staffs. Dentistry became the choice.

Raised in Miami in the idyllic '50's with college at Florida State in Tallahassee, dental school at Emory and three years in the Army, he selected Tallahassee as his home. It was small with oak-treed rolling hills, four seasons, two universities, an airport and interesting things to do. The upper income area was the northeast side where most dentists had their offices. After an associateship, he wanted to go solo.

In 1976, he built a duplex with an optometrist and did two mornings of pediatric Medicaid for cash flow. The hardest decision he had to make in dentistry was in 1984 to give up Medicaid as it was a guaranteed source of income and kept him busy.

The rest of the time in his new office, he built a quality fee for service practice. Several events and people made a difference in his growth:

- A mentor, Dr. Enwood Ashmore showed him how to present cases (1979)
- He purchased a friend's practice (1982)*
- Walter Hailey's Boot Kamp helped boost sales
- Bill Blatchford's coaching and purchasing a friend's practice will double his 2004 production

*His friend moved to the mountains and was grossing $150K. Tom paid $75K and produced $150K more the next year.*

Technically, Dr. DeLopez has taken all of Pete Dawson's courses on philosophy of practice, occlusion, esthetics and technique. Starting 1999, Tom participated in four Frank Speer courses and Dr. DeLopez shared, "his concepts for creating teeth in harmony with the individual's face and occlusion are very insightful and inspiring and it applied new technology to Dr. Dawson's principles."

He knows perfection is not possible but there is a real difference between excellent, good and fair. "Learning the difference was not an easy task. Striving for excellence and constantly improving the care provided is a stimulator for me but often the staff does not see the subtle differences." Tom observes, "a dentist who has great clinical skills and average communication skills will not be as successful as an average dentist with great communication skills. A financially complacent dentist with a staff who is satisfied with the status quo, prevents changes from sticking and the staff offers resistance to new ideas. I read constantly and attend a significant number of meetings. I bring new ideas to the office several times a week only to meet with resistance to any improvements." This has frustrated Tom and this is not unlike many dental personalities.

Dr. DeLopez is a high "C" on the Disc test and is a self-proclaimed perfectionist. In the past, he realized he was a task-oriented personality and tried to lead by example. "Left brained communication with a staff of right-brained thinkers is not as efficient or successful as intended." Being left-brained, he has struggled with communication, motivation and excitement. Thus he has made a point to hire staff with very out-going personalities.

As a leader, Tom walks his talk, provides very high quality patient care, keeps his word and treats staff fairly. Yet even this is frustrating to Tom. "What motivates staff has always been a mystery to me," Tom says. Up until now, it really has been a benevolent dictatorship. Communicating with very right-brained staff when I am very matter of fact in my thinking and speaking is a challenge. Often my ideas are not well received initially but after a day or two, are accepted."

Now, "the Blatchford coaching has been the best motivator and specifically, more time off without a decrease in income is a great motivator. Having everyone on the same page, reaching for a similar goal is the best motivator." Tom sets the standards, vision and delivers world-class dentistry. His team does the rest and it works.

In 2004, Dr. DeLopez' practice produced $800K. He is debt free and financially independent. He could retire in three years but making a difference is important to him. He has ideas and techniques to share with dentists. Since 2002, he was published nine times and honored twice with covers. It is a thrill for him to think a patient he never saw might have the end result of a technique a dentist learned from his articles or speaking. He also was a speaker at 2005 Chicago Midwinter.

Over the years, he reinvented his practice by eliminating treatment of pedo and dentures, extractions and endo. He feels it makes the schedule very predictable and eliminates emergencies. This is really Pareto's 80/20 principle in play. By eliminating the bottom 20% of patients or treatments, you erase 80% of your headaches and concerns, allowing you more quality time to devote to the top 20% of your patients who see value in you.

With the May 15, 2005 addition of the practice across the street, Tom expects to produce $1.4-$1.8 in 12 months and continue to refine the patient numbers, eliminating the bottom troublesome 20% of each practice. By combining these practices, his hygiene has doubled. Busy he is and we are thinking of an "intern" dentist two days a week to do single crowns and fillings.

All patients in the purchased practice have received several letters, one from the selling Doctor extolling the virtues of Dr. DeLopez, another from the DeLopez team inviting them in so they are part of the communication loop. When a "new to Tom" patient meets Tom, the patient is sitting up in the chair and Tom likes to "meet and greet, knee to knee, eye to eye." They want to make it easy. "Do you have any questions you would like to ask me?" An almost too powerful question to ask in a three minute hygiene exam is "If I see any work you might need in the next five years, would you want to know about it?" Powerful because the answer is almost always 'yes' which at this point of busyness in merging the two practices is time he does not have. A very relaxing statement from Tom is "You have the option to choose—to do all the work, some of the work, none of the work or have someone else do it." This is the way to build trust and new relationships.

As a perfectionist, he has had to learn to not beat himself up. Everyday he schedules something he enjoys like tennis, a swim or coffee with a friend. At 30 years, they wanted to medicate his blood pressure. Making an effort to change his lifestyle and demeanor and accentuate choices rather then "need to," Tom has had normal blood pressure for 25 years.

The 'A' Game for the DeLopez team is smooth flow with profitable procedures in the morning. Staff is involved in sales with unhurried right-brained conversations and all the Doctor has to say is "We can do that, would you like to?" There is a very relaxed and confident feeling when playing our 'A' game," said Tom.

Dr. DeLopez tries to deliver the end result of patient dreams with a minimum biologic cost. If he can create a beautiful smile with five veneers rather then ten, that is his path and he is passionate about it. "I understand the difference between aesthetic and cosmetic dentistry and am capable of delivering treatment that makes a patient look like they were born with naturally beautiful teeth, not like teeth made in a dental office." Currently, he is wanting to find a vehicle to market to this niche in dentistry.

Internal marketing has been the primary vehicle in DeLopez' practice. Externally, they have good signage outside the office, a good website: www.smiletallahassee.com, photo albums to specialists books and staff lunches with specialists. His external marketing, especially in 2005, has been the guaranteed new patient flow of purchasing a practice equal or larger in size than his present practice. Any good marketer will share there is a gamble in marketing. There is no sure thing, In addition, he became an "advertising sponsor" on NPR at $260 a month for which he has received much feedback.

For Tom, a recent shift has been new patients arriving in his office knowing what they want. "I want seven crowns on the lower and a new partial." "All my teeth are deteriorating and worn down, I want them fixed." "I am tired of my mouth, I heard good things about you." Is the *Tipping Point* happening to Dr. DeLopez?

Tom wrote goals when he was 18 and has achieved most of those goals. His life has been far more successful then he ever dreamed possible. "I love my practice and profession. I live in a dream house with my soulmate. We have traveled all over the world many times and we both drive Mercedes with big engines." Travel and photography have added depth and variety to his life. He and his wife, Sandy, are enjoying the challenge of planning their financial distribution. With no children, some will go to relatives and because they both have been active with their alma maters, they are endowing professorships and chairs in studies which interest them.

Dr. DeLopez' advice is to "set goals with the knowledge you have now. As you progress, make alterations in your course as needed. A travel analogy; life is like an uncharted river with places you will want to visit on both sides. As one looks and plans ahead, they can easily glide from on side of the river to the other going with the current. It is difficult to paddle upstream and it wastes your time and energy. Set goals. Be firm in your core beliefs but flexible as external situations change."

www.smiletallahassee.com

*Tom and his wife, Sandy enjoying the SPHINX and other Egyptian wonders in their many travels.*

## Blatchford Game Plan
## Pareto Principle—The 80/20 Rule

Dr. DeLopez is using this statistical analysis to merge two practices. He wants to watch the top 20% of his patients emerge during this year. Pareto's Principle is most useful in dentistry as the result is greater efficiency in concentrating on those who enjoy you and your services as opposed to crying over those bottom 20% who cause 80% of your headaches. *

Pareto's Law (the 80/20 Rule) has been effectively used for years by big business in marketing and sales. The 80/20 Rule is a fascinating percentage which applies to so many areas of our lives and which nobody can explain why it continues to occur. It really is the secret to success by achieving more with less.

We coach our Doctors and staffs in sales, ask questions so your guest or patient speaks 80% of the time. Conversely, if staff and Doctor are "educating" 80% of the conversation, you will talk your way out of a sale 80% of the time.

We receive 80% of our headaches, complaints and cancellations from 20% of our patients. These are patients who don't see value in what we have to offer. We create "office policy" for all because of the problem few. Your worst patients have then helped you create a pessimistic practice, rather then one of optimism and trust.

A computer survey will show you produce 80% of your production from 20% of the patients. Look carefully at the top 20% of those patients last year. Who are they? What did they elect to purchase in your office? Why are they attracted to you? What can you learn from this exercise? Be curious and study this magic 20%. Focus and concentrate on replicating that behavior.

The 80/20 rule of marketplace consumption is in every industry. Airlines know they make 80% of profit from 20% of fliers. These business travelers and frequent fliers are awarded with extra perks, bigger seats, upgrades and service. Airlines know they do not make their profits from a family traveling to Disneyland once a year.

Dentists tend to ignore the 80/20 rule because we are trying to please everybody all the time. Our percentages are reversed. We want patients to accept what we feel they need. We work hard to reverse the thinking of the emergency patient who is demanding of our time every three years.

We struggle to diagnose above insurance maximums. Frustrated, we quit trying. We fill our hygiene schedule with any "meat in the seat." Upon cancellation, we give them other immediate choices. We devalue our own work to cater to the 80% who are not our best patients.

In our Custom Coaching Program, we designate patients as A, B and C. The majority of your patients are A patients who faithfully remember your birthday, bring tomatoes from their garden, keep their appointments, pay on time and refer people just like them. Conversely, C patients are the unfaithful who have no tomatoes, only come when it is convenient and refer friends just like them. These are the bottom 20% who create practice pain.

B patients just take up space. Their attention is sporadic. We want all A patients but tend to create policies and treat people as if they are C's.

Watch for indications you and your staff may be catering to the B and C patients.

- Is insurance mentioned by you in the initial phone conversation?
- Health history in mail prior to first appointment relationship opportunity?
- Is money mentioned in the initial phone call?
- Is respect for time a problem in your office?
- Does a new patient sit alone in "waiting room" completing forms?
- Is one of your first questions, "do you have any concerns today?"

- Is finding insurance information a priority before Doctor sees a patient?
- Are you insurance experts on codes, fee structures and maximums?

If you answered yes to above, you have geared your practice for average. In order to cater to the top 20%, a clear sense of leadership and passion for change must be communicated and demonstrated. Stop doing the things that make you average and shift to being extraordinary. Attitude is a big factor. If you see yourself in the average 80%, unable to break out, stuck in a scheduling quagmire and insurance diagnosis paralysis, you will stay in the 80%.

Find yourself a coach who can turn that attitude into winning. As Lou Holtz says in a commercial, "Son, there is no such thing as just a sales call. You need a fight song."

*Another way to discover the top 20% of your patients is to ask each staff member to list their 100 favorite patients based on attitude, relationship, fun, commitment, etc. Then merge the list into the team's 100 top patients. Check this 100 list against your computer survey of the top 20% who account for 80% of your income. There will be a great correlation of the two lists. Then study those people. Who are they? Where do they work and live? Why do they see value in your services? These are the top 20% of people who make your life wonderful. How can you thank them and honor them? Also, how can you duplicate them? How can we attract more of them?

Bill Blatchford, DDS

# From the Blatchford Play Book: Winning Play

Dr. DeLopez was a football player at Florida State in Tallahassee. Winning teams practice for any possibility and go full out all the time because they never know which one of the 100 plays or more in a football game will be the deciding play.

>> There is no such thing as a "sure thing."

>> Play hard and focused on every play; this may be the one.

>> Hard work makes dreams come true

>> Time and efficiency is important, time your procedures, learn efficiency

>> Practice, practice, practice

>> Let staff enroll the dentistry

>> Doctor tells the patient the fees

>> Stop blaming others, take responsibility for your life.

>> In learning new skills, it will always feel downright phony at first. Stick with it and it will be uncomfortable sometimes, then comfortable and finally integrated

>> Put strong systems in place in your practice which will tide you in good times and not so good times

>> Staff for what you are presently doing, not what you hope to do in five years

>> The important thing is to know you've tried your very hardest, have given 100% on every play.

>> Being successful is doing your best

>> Don't be known as the one who could have or should have but as one that did.

>> A great player must rise to the occasion and turn the game around on his own

>> Choose winning players based on attitude

>> Winning teams practice harder than they play

# 6

## STATE OF GRACE

## Dr. Jim Elias

"God put us here for a reason and in our office, it is the positive difference we can make in people's lives. We do "missionary dentistry" here and our mission is to help our patient's feel important, help them overcome fear, be a positive in people's lives and really listen to them," says Dr. Jim Elias, an accredited member of AACD in 1989 and a Creating Restorative Excellence mentor with Dr. John Kois.

Jim feels dentistry is in such a good place right now with many advances in materials, techniques and delivery. Cosmetics is his niche to complete dentistry in Independence, MO. He and his partner, Dr. Kirk Opdahl will produce $2M this year working three to four days a week.

Even though his father was a physician in family practice, the road for Jim was not always smooth and he chooses to see them as gifts for learning and growing. His mom had counseled him to go into health care and choose dentistry instead of his father's medicine as the hours were more controlled. Jim was married twenty days after high school graduation and six months later had a baby girl. He worked full time and went to school full time. By his own admission, he was obstinate and didn't get very good grades. After three years of college, he applied to dental school and was rejected.

Bummed, he decided to graduate from college in economics, find a real job working at First Federal Savings and was promoted to head of the electronics funds and transmatic department (a new thing in 1973). One day, lunching with the vice president, Mr. Carl Wicktzig, he asked how Jim got into banking. The story of dentistry was revealed and the coaching he received was, "are you going to wonder about this for the rest of your life?" Jim decided to get serious, retake classes and was accepted as an alternate but didn't get in. He got real serious, quit his job and learned how to study. As a full time student, he was accepted on his third try to dental school. "I made a pact with myself that I would take my grades each semester to Dr. Butterworth, Dean of Admissions, to show his coaching made a difference." Jim ended freshman year at the top of his dental school class and a baby boy.

In 1979, after a year's association elsewhere, Jim found a practice for sale in Independence at the Blue Ridge Bank Bldg. where 23 other dental practices reside. In asking around, almost all dentists told him "there are too many already." Jim's father, who had a large following with a good reputation, counseled him,"if you are fair, honest and do a good job, you can practice anywhere." The practice was for sale from a charismatic person having licensure problems being too familiar with staff. Other dentists said, "do not buy for it is the kiss of death." Jim did purchase (even qualifying for the loan without a co-signer) and it went well. He ran yellow page ads saying, "we cater to cowards" and "emergencies welcome" and "we take all insurances." He did not realize this would make him "Dr. Everything to Everybody at Any Time and for Any Amount."

Jim created a huge practice and he didn't know anything about business. He knew he wanted to be the best, not the biggest. Yet, he still equated being busy with being successful. His practice pitfalls include:

- Trying to do something for everyone. Now, he sees dentistry is so vast, you must decide your own path and brand.

- Trying to grow too fast which meant hiring more staff where selection is tough. He wanted to find people with "heart" who wanted to help others and also be accountable for results and their actions.
- Being a leader and a friend. Recognizing there is a fine line in relationships where you can be too close with staff. You want to lead but still be a part of their lives.
- Trying to teach communication to others.

Early on, Dr. Elias became a dental partner in using Mirage porcelain with Roger Sigler of Myron Dental Laboratory. Roger was at an Idaho mountain lodge and met Bill Blatchford who in turn introduced Bill to Jim. "Before I met Bill, I felt stuck in a rut. Bill taught me a lot—that bigger wasn't better, decide what you are good at and get better, eliminate the unprofitable or unfun things in your practice. I really enjoyed the cosmetics and got rid of ortho and endo and cut back on emergencies. He helped me see the path to profitability."

"My definition of profitability is living within your means, doing what you like doing. My parents taught me the only times you really should have loans is for a home, car and practice purchase. For 'luxuries,' you save and pay. Success is the freedom to treat people as you like, whether they pay or not. Being financially free is to be able to help others. I am not really driven by numbers and I feel if you treat people right, they will come."

Dr. Elias feels he has a reputation of being a "people pleaser." He and his team like to help patients who are scared to death, to restore hope. He feels relationships are the key.

When he met Blatchford, his overhead was 80% and producing $1M. Bill showed him if he reduced his overhead to 60%, he could produce half as much and still take home $200K. Now he and his partner, Kirk Opdahl are producing $2M and Jim works 3 to 3.5 days a week. His collections are the same as production. In the old days, he was attracting 120 patients a month and now sees 15-16 new patients a month.   In the old days, he had four assistants and 2-3 hygienists and now two assistants and two hygienists are shared.  Just for Jim, he had 11-12 staff and now has 5-6 team members.

"I was able to do this by changing the mix of treatment offered. Now I work on fewer patients, doing more work.  We quadrupled our production with more comprehensive treatment planning.  Bill taught me what patients want is 'look good, feel good and last a long time.' He said 'it is not an accident people are coming in.  They want something.'"

Dr. Elias became labeled as a cosmetic dentist is 1989 and has taken Pankey, Dawson and CRE courses with Kois and Speers. Cosmetics is combined with a total treatment plan.  "Cosmetics gave me the avenue to do total dentistry."

When Jim first started, he was bothered by his team's bickering and the underlying chaos.  He could not tolerate it.  His Number One Rule in leadership was to declare a state of enjoyment, being positive and helping patient's overcome fear.  The last thing a patient needs or wants is for staff upset.  In his role as leader, he gives his team lots of credit, sharing all patient cards and telling them "it is all to their credit."  We do not subgroup.  Bottom line, "God put us here for a reason and that is the positive difference we can make."

Jim feels internal marketing is the key as the team works on building relationships and real listening.  He writes a handwritten note to every new patient and also to referring patients.  He has had many patient appreciation parties and the latest features hot air balloon rides. He also has a $25 Care to Share credit for referrals.  He keeps relationships current with all specialists and general dentists.  He works especially with their staffs (Jim says "this is the key") to "help them provide the best service for their patients."  Thinking of people with congenitally small teeth, as an example, he works with periodontists, oral surgeons and orthodontists to create an awareness of dentistry.  He provides before and after picture books for all specialty offices.

Dr. Elias does feel internal marketing is the biggest source of dentistry for them. Recently, however, Channel 4 in Kansas City, on their "Problem Solvers" program featured a successful result of a young girl shot in the face during a drive by shooting. Doctors saved her life and now, after six years, she desired to look pretty. Dr. Elias became the dentist and it turned into a three part series. Let us share the story of how this opportunity evolved. A television station had a two to five minute health tip years ago. Jim let the station know he could help as a dentist. For eight years, Dr. Jim Elias was the "noon-day dentist" and taped a message once a week. People responded and a television reporter became one of his patients as a program called "Problem Solvers" evolved. Out of this relationship, she suggested an opportunity to help a young girl who had been shot in the face and though she lived, no one had helped repair her beauty. She wanted to look better and had no revenge in mind. Jim agreed to do it for only one purpose—"God put us here to help one another." Jim contacted a plastic surgeon, learned a lot about creating lips and prosthesis, now she has MDI implants. Recently, another patient emerged who will be the next "Problem Solver" and Dr. Opdahl will do the case of a 15 year old who was abandoned, stayed active in her church and will be an honors student at MU.

The hardest decision he made was to become fee-for-service, no insurance. At the end of one year, he noticed a write off of $150K. He asked his receptionist what this was. "Dr. Elias, it represents the amount we write off for Blue Cross/Blue Shield insurance patients." Because the team treats each patient equally, they did not want to go broke working their tails off for insurance companies. They decided as a staff, they did not want to have a two-tiered system and did not want to have treatment dictated by insurance. Scripting to patients included, "to take your insurance, we would have to cut corners. What corners do you want me to cut on your family? We will not compromise your treatment and what corners would you like us to cut?" They all were concerned about patient reaction and retention. Some left, most came back and some asked if they could come back.

Jim is a multi-faceted man. He has made three trips to Zambia originally to help teach the Bible. In restoring a migraine patient with occlusal rehab who happened to be a missionary in Zambia, she convinced Jim he needed to come. He took his first two-week vacation in twenty years, brought some dental instruments for their staff and actually spent ten days teaching a local how to do extractions. At lunch, they would have anatomy lessons. The Chief of Lamba (a very poor area) committed to having a permanent facility. Jim and friends raised money, drove the donated equipment to Gulf Port, MS for customs. A permanent hospital, medical and dental clinic is being built for $200,000 with the idea of Doctors, students and interns to come and give help year round. This is through IAM (International African Missions) Ministry, a non-profit through Rochester, NY. (www.iamministries.info). On some of the information Jim shared, "AIDS has lowered the life expectancy from 72 to 39....More than 75% of children live below the poverty line....In Zambia, more than 100 people die each day from AIDS." After Jim's first visit, he wrote, "I first went to Kafulafuta Mission in 1997 to help teach kids. I ended up teaching a clinical officer how to remove teeth. The medical needs are incredible. I have never seen the need and opportunity to help improve the quality of so many lives." In addition to nurses, Doctors and dentists to help with time and skill, they could also use donations of updated machines, playground equipment and furniture.

Another part of Jim's life that is important to him is physical fitness. Being a slightly competitive personality, Jim's events are triathlons with swimming, biking and running. When in training, he has been known to swim his Lake Tapawingo at 4:30 AM; how else do you train?

One of the things that makes Dr. Elias different is he has a most successful partnership with Dr. Opdahl. Jim had several partners over the years and was not looking for another. A friend said he had met "a young Doctor just like you who is appreciative, loving and honest." Jim met with him and told him he would be very successful on his own. They did find they had much in common, sharing faith and talked of partnership possibilities. Jim feels the key to great partnerships is to take it like a marriage—they are equally responsible. They plan, talk and pray together. Jim has learned a lot from Kirk and there is joy in sharing. They do have fun competing on quality.

In closing, Jim feels dentistry is an awesome profession as there are so many areas to choose. "God put us here and together, not just my partner but our team as well. There is stability and peace."

Though the next story has nothing to do directly with dentistry, it does have to do with the person, quality of life and why Jim's practice is a cut above. Jim is one of five, the only son. His father was a successful physician and his mother, a nurse. She was "the Queen of faith, trusted God and kept the family close with celebrations and gatherings." All five siblings lived close to the parent's home on Lake Tapawingo. As the parents aged, others urged the family to put them into assisted living. Jim asked his mother what she wanted. "We want to stay here." Jim said, "how long?" And his mom said, "until we die." That was the mandate then, for the five "children" to care for their parents at home. Two were nurses, one lab tech, one dentist and a home economics teacher. One sourced meals, another paperwork, Jim in charge of finances and so forth. For 12 years, they took turns actually doing the care. As care needs increased, they hired grandchildren and nephews to spend the nights. Jim said, "these are the people who gave us life and all it's lessons. This is what we do."

www.smiledrs.org

*Dr. Jim Elias, AACD accredited and Mentor with Dr. John Kois' Creating Restorative Excellence. Speaking of his recent trip to Zambia, Dr. Elias shared how great it was to have wife Sharon help at the new dental clinic. In the past, "we had to have a make-shift clinic, but now we are ready for any of the profession who would like to come see Africa and help at the same time. These people are so caring, warm and appreciative. This is a place that possesses all understanding of 'you will gain more than you give.'"*

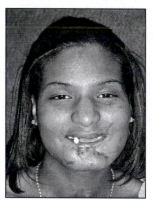

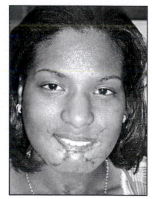

*The before and after surgeries of a well-publicized drive-by shooting victim at age 17 in Kansas City. This was a three-part television program called "Problem Solvers." Dr. Elias orchestrated the interdisciplinary case with an oral surgeon and plastic surgeon.*

## Blatchford Game Plan: Romancing The Patient

Drs. Elias and Opdahl make a real point of developing trust and relationships as an important part of their internal marketing. Both being people-persons, these relationships are vital to their emotional well-being as well as practice vitality. They are skilled at genuinely romancing people.

In changing times, people are seeking security. They want to feel known, needed and that you care about them. Building these relationships is a factor of caring, time and respect. In a way, building a relationship with patients is like a romance. Relationships are the most important quality, which keeps clients and friends mutually attracted. It is that element of trust which bonds two people together.

Because each being is so precious, high priorities should be placed on building solid relationships. Many books have been written about romance and attracting the positive attention of that special someone. To be an interesting person, very simply you must be interested in others. Ask questions. These social skills, communication and curiosity can be learned.

Because 20% of Americans move each year, your new patient goal needs to replace that 20% plus a factor for growth. When we find a practice gathering five new patients a month, the question is, "What are you doing to keep people away?" Where is the romance in your dental office?

Demonstrating genuine caring, quality time and real respect can start with the initial phone call. This is where the romance starts. A warm personal response before the second ring will gather notice. STOP whatever else you are doing and focus on your new friend. Though you answer the phone two hundred times a day, recreate newness. Try, "Thank you for calling Vitality Dental. It is a great day to be pampered. This is Toni and I can help you." This is a surprising and excellent way to start a new relationship.

Your job is to find their name early and use it often. Upon making a timely appointment (within the next several working days), ask of their expectations for the appointment. As in a romance, a definite "no-no" would be to ask, "When was the last time…?" or "Do you have insurance?" Ask your new friend, "Who may we thank for referring you?" Have printed directions to your office ready to fax or email. In preparation for the appointment, invite the patient to visit the office's website. To further enhance the new relationship, you can ask them for a favor. The response is always positive. Your question might be, "Between now and next Tuesday, will you think about what you like best about your smile and what you dislike about your smile?"

Upon arrival at your office how would you like to be treated on a blind date? How do you make them feel important? How do you acknowledge them for their brilliance in calling your office? When your new friend arrives, greet them at the door by name with a warm handshake.

On a first date, you would not want to gather information, which sounded like you were interested in their financial history or family medical secrets. Ask person to person only the medical information you need to complete a prophy in hygiene. They have not asked you for any other treatment at this time.

You can create a practice culture where strangers become friends, and friends become clients, by enveloping them in a sincere and immediate friendship. You are the receptacle for their thoughts and feelings. Very little is shared about yourself.

In demonstrating care, time and respect, create new agreements for patient protocol, which are akin to rules of romance:

- Never leave your guest alone
- Follow-through by doing what you promised you would do
- Create a renewed respect for time with patients being seen and able to depart on time

Think of these first appointments as opportunities to romance your clients. Review the atmosphere and logistics to shift from clinical order takers to an atmosphere of romance. Make people feel needed and wanted as a person, not just a set of teeth.

Bill Blatchford, DDS

# From the Blatchford Play Book: Leave Something Behind

Drs. Elias and Opdahl see dentistry and their lives as "givers." Yes, they are profitable and are grateful. They are also conscious they have skills and financial abilities others do not possess. Dentists and teams can make a difference for others by being a mentor, creating a better opportunity for someone less able and to have choices for themselves and others. Consider:

>> Help young people get started

>> Be a mentor in something you have passion

>> Share your knowledge and experience

>> Helping others helps yourself

>> Consider teaching in some form

>> Be a giver, not a taker

>> Be a hero to someone

>> Set a lofty example as a rich bequest of scholarships, endowments, trusts

>> Do something meaningful for others

>> Look for ways to share your skills in the community of man

>> Encourage your team to volunteer

>> Establish quarterly "giving days" to do dentistry for those who are in the gaposis between insurance and welfare

>> How much is enough?  How will you give back? What is your plan?

# 7
## LEADERSHIP REVISITED TECHNICIAN, MANAGER OR LEADER

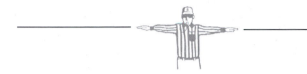

## Dr. John Kelly

During John's sophomore year of college, he needed to make a decision regarding his curriculum. Still undecided, he attended an orientation meeting for medical school. The room had 800 students. "If all the students and I would be looking toward the same thing, then this is not for me." As he left the building, he saw another meeting with 30 students which turned out to be the dental orientation. They spoke of the variability and control in dentistry. He asked his dad not to throw away his old dental texts. The other motivating factor was John's desire to be his own boss and then there was the factor that his father already had a successful practice where he wanted to live. John greatly admired his father and was proud of his success in supporting his family. The decision was made.

One goal John had in starting his practice was to change the way dentistry was perceived by the public. He was disturbed by "hate the dentist," or how dentists appear to be the center of many fear and pain jokes. He wanted to make his guests comfortable and offer dental treatment in a relaxed environment.

In dental school, John worked in his father's practice by assisting. The new Dr. Kelly then did hygiene and small restorative cases. His father's unhappy partnership was coming to an end as father and son built a new facility in a nearby neighborhood. Staff and patients easily moved and he and his dad worked together for several years as his hours lessened and he eventually retired for good.

Initially with his father, his goals were undefined and he just wanted to start working and making money. Thus, he enjoyed his few years with his father. Now on his own, John discovered he owned a successful practice that just wasn't him. He wanted to run it differently. He wanted to be recognized throughout Chicagoland as providing exceptional aesthetic and neuromuscular dentistry. Being competitive, he wanted to do the best he could or why bother? He needed to take some steps in his own direction.

When he began his advanced technical education at Las Vegas Institute, he brought the staff he inherited, wanting to make them his own. He joined Blatchford Coaching to help him clarify his vision, communicate, learn sales skills and get results. John shared with the staff how he wanted to change the practice, to communicate with patients differently and to set new standards. John communicated his vision and the office goals daily and at weekly staff meetings. They worked on sales skills, communication and systems to allow great patient experiences. "I knew change was necessary and difficult for some. I gave them every opportunity to embrace change. What I saw was indifference and lack of enthusiasm. I still persisted."

The staff still saw him as the son of the father they adored. He was the pseudo-leader. He wanted and needed them to be on board in reaching his goals.

John's toughest decision was to let go of the staff he had inherited. He had taken them to Las Vegas Institute to help with their clinical training and the Blatchford Management Program to learn business accountability and skills. "I told them of the changes and invited them to change with me. They felt the practice was already as good as it could get. They were blind to the possibilities of providing exceptional care. It became painfully obvious to me the staff was not on board and was holding me back. The frustration of the situation finally became greater than the fear of letting them go. With great counseling from Nanci Granahan of Blatchford, I let go of my staff effective immediately. I had to deal with the inconvenience of having no staff but that was easy as compared to keeping them on and going nowhere."

"After the initial shock, I celebrated. I felt free, refreshed and ready to move forward. I took on the hygiene and made do with temporary staff. I looked for people who would 'get' what I wanted and where I wanted to go. I rescheduled a lot of people. It was a difficult time but I was free to start fresh."

"I hired winners because I knew exactly what I wanted. I wanted a positive attitude, thinking for themselves yet following direction, willingness to accept change and try different things. I wanted accountability and respect. I wanted people who were motivated to do better and liked the idea of monetary incentives. I specifically looked for people outside the dental arena. I even applied the DISC test to figure out who would best fit in their respective job and with me."

"I have not had to replace any of my team. They understand the drive to move forward and are ready. They all want the best for themselves and their lives. It is a real pleasure to work with our team. We all understand who we are, what we do and for whom we do it. The accomplishment and achievement are there."

The Kelly team is motivated by the bonus system. They are very aware of the numbers and have actually taken on enhanced roles to improve collections. They also have generous time off with pay, light work hours, pleasant work environment and pride of working in an exceptional office. In playing their 'A' game, there is a sense of freedom from worry, happiness and an overall energy. The team sees what they can do and want to perform at that level every day.

His father had wanted to carry accounts receivables in the $150K range because he said it was good for "PR." They were also an insurance practice. "When I joined Blatchford, Bill helped me create a different system for financial arrangements. It took about 18 months to rid of the A/R and we now have a credit balance. We also became insurance independent."

"My final hurdle was the old philosophy of helping every patient entering our door. I worked through the idea that as a dentist, I also have a choice as to whether I will treat them. I want to work on select patients who see value in what I am doing. This was a real challenge for me with my father's long-established patients. However, with time and my continued devotion to create a new practice environment, many patients have seen I am not my father and have either changed with the practice or drifted away."

"I used to offer treatment that wasn't ideal—patching fillings, large buildups, etc. This is what the patient said they wanted because:
- I wasn't listening to what they wanted, or
- They did not see the value in ideal dentistry, or
- Patient and I were influenced by their insurance to make dental decisions

Numbers: Production has increased accompanied by a decrease in overhead.

|        | 1999   | 2004   |
| ------ | ------ | ------ |
| Prod.  | $323K  | $635K  |
| Coll.  | $299K  | $655K  |
| OH     | 79%    | 63%    |
| NPts   | 145    | 166    |
| Staff  | 3      | 3      |

In marketing his vision, John has tried many avenues. Chicago is an upscale and huge area to market with numbers of other health care providers in the mix. Some ideas actually produce patients and some continue the 'branding' process. He was on "Unsung Heroes," a television segment featuring people who help others live a better life. John had written a press release a year before about his involvement with AACD Give Back A Smile. During a slow week, the producer called and in a five minute segment, the patient graciously shared her wonderful story and nervous John felt he did rather well. The story then went national and has been played numerous times.

Externally, John is in glossy magazines, does public speaking twice a month, local newspaper ads, business networking, open houses, and his website: www.johnjkellydds.com, PR consultant and LVI branding. Currently his glossy ad in the highly niched group is targeting professional trumpet players (see his website). Most of his marketing brings in people who are in the $2K to $4K result. The best external response is from website and LVI branding which result in larger cases.

The hardest thing John had to do was let go of his father's staff. The best decision he made was to work with Blatchford. "I may have achieved the same technical skill level, but I would be trapped in an unhappy office, with little use for my skills and without any significant profit, progress or change."

www.johnjkellydds.com

John's story about the husband and wife team:  "My first full mouth restorative cases were on this couple.  The wife originally wanted to have her mouth restored but was scared because of past dental treatment.  Her husband wanted his smile to look better and said he would go first to show her how comfortable it is.  As we went through treatment, the husband shared past symptoms of sleep apnea and neck discomfort.  I took he and his wife to LVI for the full mouth course.  While arranging for the trip, she mentioned she was looking forward to seeing her Vegas friends from her dancing days.  She shared her stories of her dancing days and how she met her husband.  His results were great and his sleep apnea and neck discomfort were resolved.  She was grateful because now she could sleep without worrying about his apnea or snoring.

The husband became a great communicator for the practice as he was the director of audio/visual production for the Chicago Midwinter Dental Meeting for the last 20 years.  At the convention, he would immediately identify me as his dentist.

After seeing his results, she was able to get past her anxieties and decided this was the type of care she wanted also.  She actually had more symptoms of discomfort and overall oral breakdown.  Although her case was more difficult, in the end, she received an even more life changing result.

These two people have become a strong part of the practice and are constantly speaking to others about the types of things that are possible at my office.  They were fun to work with and we enjoy their entire family.

*Don and Camilla —*
*beautiful guests and loyal friends*
*both aspiring for the best in life.*

*Dr. Kelly and his father, always*
*working together with influence*
*and support.*

*Dr. Kelly's wife Maribeth*
*and two boys Jack and*
*Will, the priorities of his*
*life.*

*Dr. Kelly's staff – "a smiling combination."*
*Top: Angelica, Geri, Kate. Bottom: Maribeth,*
*Dr. Kelly, Mary.*

## Blatchford Game Plan: Two Hours to the Future

Dr. John Kelly epitomizes the necessary change from dental technician to manager and then the struggle to really lead. You can taste his struggle and see his emergence as a strong winner who knows what he wants. Reading _E-Myth Revisited_ by Michael Gerber demonstrates many of us in dentistry are stuck at the technician level and are frustrated. Life can be different.

We have all made a choice to be in dentistry. For many of us, the fulfillment of our days is in the intricacies of developing the perfect treatment plan, the challenge of creating a dazzling smile, the reward of the radiant result.

These are the technical skills at which some dentists excel. This is what dentists love to do. That is why the decision was initially made to become a dentist. In dental school the techniques and skills were taught so that upon graduation, the new dentist could immediately begin helping mouths to become healthy and smiles to be beautiful. Upon graduation, many thought that their skills and a sign on the door would be enough to gain patients. For many, while their technical dental skills were excellent, their ability to run a dental practice would become a continual struggle.

Statistics show that 95% of businesses fail when technical skills alone are relied upon. In this era, good, or even outstanding, technical skills are not enough to ensure success.

Merely fixing teeth for 40 hours a week will give a dentist a slim chance at financial success and a rewarding life.

This grim statistic is balanced by a simple solution. Choose to do treatment 28 hours a week and spend an additional four hours per week on management. Staffing, budgeting, brainstorming and training with the team, scheduling for profitabilityand associated factors, all play a vital role in the success and profitability of the practice. These four hours are well spent as they can actually double the gross of the practice!

## The Four Hours

In these four hours the doctor performs as a manager. The time is spent on the needs of the practice—not the patients. As a manager, the finances would be reviewed, the profit and loss statements and monitors checked—what aspect of the practice is doing well, where is help needed? Team meetings would be prepared, who's in charge of the meeting, what is the topic, what areas are challenging and need addressing, what areas are doing exceptional and need recognition? Analysis of the marketing would be done, is it effective, are targeted patients being reached, does it need updating?

With good management, these four hours a week can result in an incredible increase in the annual gross. It can double! For example, "Dr. Technical" works 40 hours a week for a year doing the dentistry he loves to do. He grosses $125,000 that year. The doctor next door, "Dr. Manager" adds another four hours a week in efficiently managing the practice plus 28 with patients. This doctor is aware of his finances and is proactive with their information. The staff is competent and proficient. They work well as a team offering excellent dentistry. The patients are scheduled profitably. The marketing is successful and up to date.

"Dr. Manager" earned $250,000 working 32 hours. These four hours doubled the annual gross.

"Dr. Manager" is feeling pretty good! His additional four hours have really made a difference. Not only did he make more money, he has a competent staff that schedules well, leaving him time to spend with his family. Life is good. But with a mere two additional hours per week, it could be even better.

## The Two Hours

"Dr. Leadership" spends an additional two hours as CEO in the practice. He is a visionary who looks into the future and develops the dream. He is the leader. It is his vision that inspires the team. He communicates it clearly so that all can see it, communicates it enthusiastically so that all believe in it, communicates it with such inspiration that all want to share in it.

The CEO is the master of the future. These two hours bestow the possibility of earning substantially more. What is the goal? 500K? A million? 3 Million? More? The clarity of the vision and the ability to communicate it well are the key to attainment.

A leader's job is providing the vision. That can be a difficult task in dentistry as most dentists are more comfortable in "left-brain" activities. Most gravitate to the technical, the "how-to" of things. To develop a vision, the right side of the brain needs to be fired up. A CEO focuses on the future. To facilitate future focus a leader answers these questions as if it was now 10 years into the future:

- Where are you? What city? Where is your practice? What is its atmosphere? What equipment is being used?
- How many days a week are you working? Which days? How many hours?
- What is your net income?
- What is your mix of treatment?
- What is your overhead?
- How many staff do you have? What are they like?
- Who are your patients?
- What type of marketing do you do?
- What are you "known as"?

The answers to these types of questions define the vision. The more detailed the vision, the more clearly it is communicated, the more it is shared with enthusiasm, the greater the possibilities of attainment. The team is completely enrolled in the vision. That is leadership. That is what propels the "Dr. Leaderships" to where they are.

Who do you choose to be? Take action in the development of your dream. Hold yourself accountable for the future and it will be the future you envision.

Bill Blatchford, DDS

## From the Blatchford Play Book: Team Pitfalls

When a group of individuals fail to form as a team, there are some reasons. Dr. John Kelly discovered the staff he inherited from his father was unable or unwilling to shift their trust and loyalty to John. He had to make some uncomfortable choices and is now the better for his courage.

>> Having the wrong team and not recognizing it

>> Having a micro-manager as the leader belittles team and no one wants or needs to step up

>> Failing to communicate the vision or hold it as your own

>> Subgrouping or gossiping about other team members, Doctor or patients

>> Failure to form a real team

>> Becoming stuck in tasks by loosing sight of the bigger picture

>> Allowing an attitude of mediocrity to prevail rather than one of winning

>> Forgetting who we are serving

>> Not having an effective bonus system

>> Failure to learn and apply new technical, sales and marketing skills

>> Not having regular morning meetings or weekly staff meetings

>> Working overtime and blaming it on someone else

>> Continually running late in hygiene and Doctor schedule will decrease new patient flow

>> Allowing personal issues to pervade the practice

>> Allowing non-professional behavior to be the practice norm

>> Super-stars are generally not great team players

# 8

# MENTORS WITH COMPASSION, GRACE AND COMMITMENT

## Dr. Jim Birrell and The Birrell Brothers

Throughout Jim's life and dental career, he has been open to meeting people with different ideas. He has taken the opportunity to engage himself with others, books, experts and courses who challenge his way of thinking. And he has the grace to continually acknowledge others for their guidance.

This is the guiding principle of The Birrell Brothers concept. When we first heard from Jim, "The Birrell Brothers thank you. You are one of the Birrell Brothers," I thought, "How nice. I did not know Jim had a brother who practiced dentistry with him." He doesn't have a dental brother.

The concept of the Birrell Brothers is unique to Jim. "The Birrell Brothers are those individuals who allow me to deliver the level of quality dentistry I demand in my Vision and Purpose. They are often unknown to my patients, but they are known and valued very much by me. I wish to dedicate my entire story to the Birrell Brothers, for I would not be here without you." It is an honor to be a Birrell Brother.

As a USC undergrad Biology major aiming at a career in medicine, Jim envisioned prestige and earning potential. His organic chemistry professor, Dr. Bill Weber urged Jim to consider dentistry with the benefit of more time for his family. "I think he had foresight on the path of medicine." When Dr. Birrell's oldest daughter was at USC, Jim reconnected with his early mentor and told him how grateful he was. They still are in touch and Dr. Weber is a Birrell Brother.

Everyone told Jim his choice of Marin County was overcrowded, too many dentists and tough to start a practice. In Jim's senior year at U of Pacific, Dr. Jim Pride taught an 8 AM Monday morning practice management course. Less than half the class attended the 8 AM class but "I would meet Dr. Pride at 7 AM and he guided me in analyzing my future practice. I negotiated the purchase of my Marin practice prior to graduating University of Pacific." Dr. Pride is a Birrell Brother.

Jim associated briefly with the landlord of his building, Dr. Louis Geissberger, an excellent Marin dentist who welcomed Jim. Dr. Geissberger became a role model and the father Jim never had. This was a time of learning and hard work as Dr. Geissberger had a very busy practice with three hygienists and a lot of single tooth dentistry. "This was the beginning of a very close relationship with a new mentor who taught me the principles of integrity, high standards, morals and the importance of running a dental practice like a business. This gentleman also led by example, and early in my career I became aware of the importance of acute observation of the strong points of others and how to incorporate those points into how I conducted my affairs." Jim had ambition, did his research and had good role models. Dr. Geissberger is a Birrell Brother.

His Greenbrae practice is on the water with beautiful views of the mountains. Two U of Pacific graduates in the area encouraged Jim and are still friends today. To say that Marin was tough just challenged Jim more. "I didn't go to dental school to live somewhere I did not want to."

He modeled his practice the first year on the Pride Institute model. He wanted to be the best dentist he could be, be busy, have a nice car, buy a house and join a golf club. "Looking back, the goals were quite materialistic, really."

The selling dentist had joined the military. Jim discovered the charts were filled with inactive people and many Denti-Cal patients. Many local dentists sent a regular flow of patients.

Career highlights for Jim include:

- Practiced entire career in a desirable and affluent community, one where many urged against.
- Served dental community as president of Marin Dental Society, Peer review and Trustee to CDA
- Blatchford experience
- Mentoring with Drs. David Hornbrook, Mike Koczarski and Mark Montgomery of Pac-Live.
- Becoming an insurance-free practice
- Product evaluator for Ivoclar Vivadent and Discus Dental
- Participating fully in AACD.
- Dr. John Kois series, Creating Restorative Excellence
- Having had the joy to work with and lead many wonderful people
- To honestly feel I am living my vision
- Receiving Dr. Bill Dorfman's endorsement, not given lightly

Jim feels "you have got to have 'game,' that learning doesn't stop, that time is of the essence, that you have to be able to pay the fee for quality continuing education and that the outcome is directly proportional to the amount of mental and physical energy that is put forth. Bill, John, David, Mike and Mark are all Birrell Brothers.

Regrets? "We need a state of the art facility and not having met Bill Blatchford much earlier. Bill taught me to learn, grow and many people can contribute to that. Currently, I am also working with Fortune Management. My appreciation to Dr. Blatchford has been increased tremendously. He taught me the importance of goals centered upon personal vision, then putting these goals into action."

"Success is being the man God would have me be." Honesty, integrity, commitment, hard work, willingness to grow and change with a spiritual centeredness results in successful outcomes.

Profitability has a "deserve level" component. Bill talks about floors and ceilings, levels we will not go over or under. Dr. Koczarski asks, "Where, on the road to Paradise, is your train going to stop today?" This implies movement and growth, rather than attainment. "I am still in the process of profit and things are going well."

In a book called _Now, Discover Your Strengths_ by Buckingham and Clifton, I discovered my five talents are:
- Achiever–focused on attaining goals
- Discipline–orderliness and structure. This can also lead to perfection paranoia.
- Learner–I had 280 units of CE, when California only requires 50 units. I love learning.
- Empathy–seeing the world through the eyes of others. It is in the heart and it makes a good listener
- Fairness–we are all equally entitled. I am USDA Certified 'Fair.'

I am different because of what I have been blessed with, what I have done and how I have chosen to use my talents. "A real pitfall in my career was allowing drugs to become a part of my life. The wheels came off the car and spun out of control with no direction or purpose."

"Another important pitfall was if I hired someone less than stellar, I thought I could change them and make them better. It always ended disastrously."

Numbers:

|  | Before Blatchford | Today |
|---|---|---|
| Production | $42K mo. | $85K mo. |
| Collection | 92% | 103% |
| Overhead | 78% | 54% |
| New Pts. | 10 | 15 |
| # of Staff | 7 | 3 |

Jim started with a general practice and is now about 50% cosmetic with an indirect crown fee of $1300. His hygiene goal is $1000 per day. BAM is $59,900. He defines himself as the premier cosmetic dental practice in Marin County with a general practice base. His treatment has changed from single tooth dentistry to a more comprehensive, proactive form of dentistry. "Blatchford and Kois interface well in this regard. Systems such as block booking, scripted conversations and financial arrangements allow the desired mix to happen. Without systems, the result will be less than possible."

Dr. Birrell became insurance free three months before working with Blatchford. "We were only 12% Delta so the financial impact was negligible but heartfelt emotionally. You have to be prepared to say 'goodbye' to your insurance patients. Yet, it is the best decision I have made."

"When a patient said 'no,' it used to signify failure, negativity, doing something wrong. Today, I am happy with 'no' for several reasons:

- I know 'yes' is right around the corner
- 'no' could mean 'maybe' or 'yes' later
- if I live my Vision, 'no' is their decision, not my failure to do what is best

"I lead by example. I routinely say 'make an executive decision' which empowers a staff member and once they take risks without negative repercussions, they will learn to make more decisions with confidence and direction, dictated by Purpose. I never facilitate staff meetings. I give a compliment to each team member before going home. Be on time. Be you. Have fun."

Dr. Birrell's staff is motivated by seeing results, having things work. They also are motivated by knowing Jim supports them, respects and values them. They know Dr. Birrell's office is different than others.

Jim has struggled with:
- Finding and keeping a cohesive group of '10's.
- Budgeting dollars and time for continuing ed
- Holding blocks open long enough

Playing the Birrell 'A' game is a "refreshing feeling; palpable. Vision and Purpose are reinforced for collectively, that is what is happening. Team is lighter, happier, more energetic, more focused and certainly more united during those moments."

Retirement plans for Jim are vague as he is more excited about what he is doing in dentistry. He would continue to make a difference with his family, Habitat for Humanity, Tony Robbins Foundation and local volunteerism.

The Birrell team is very conscious of internal marketing—being able to deliver what is promised. Externally, they have a working relationship with RocketDog Dental of Seattle doing high end magazine advertising, radio, feature articles in SF magazines. He has a "classy" website: www.drbirrell.com created by Shelly Rager of HealthCareWeb Image who now is a Birrell Brother.

They are currently a sponsor for "Best of the Bay," a fund-raising event for Glide Memorial Church. Dr. Birrell networks at dinner with different dentists twice a month. They have developed a flip binder with rosewood cover for display in health clubs, spas and salons. Part of his marketing was a photo shoot of 800 pictures with four staff and eight patients. In Dr. Birrell's office, there are floating frames of large pictures, moved weekly. Dr. Birrell uses the photos to tell relative stories in case presentations.

With RocketDog Dental, they have a one year plan and the team is always focused on the next project. Staff is involved once a month and Jim communicates about twice a week. "Marketing is a continuous creative process for which help must be solicited. Becoming engaged in marketing it quite a fun challenge for me."

The hardest decision for Jim occurred recently when he terminated a wonderful, talented, bright dental assistant for substance abuse. "We were a great team together. She was a '10' with a problem. We parted ways amicably. My Vision helped me with this decision. I accepted that One greater than me was going to get her well and that was not my role."

The best decision I ever made (as corny as it sounds) was to be coached by Bill Blatchford for a number of reasons:

- Bill has developed systems for running and maintaining success
- Bill pushed me to enroll in PAC-live so I could deliver the goods I was learning to sell. I was the first dentist to complete that entire program in less than 11 months
- PAC-live led me to Dr. John Kois and RocketDog Dental as well as GoldDust Laboratory in Phoenix.
- All above have led to many life changes for my clients.
- Bill coached me to join AACD and begin the Accreditation process with huge benefits which are life-changing.
- Bill's coaching renewed an appreciation for books. I have consumed and applied many with pleasure.
- Bill's coaching has become tenants or tools I use daily

I want to thank Dr. Rhys Spoor for being such a 'light' in his kindness and encouragement, so giving, so positive and so humble. He is a Birrell Brother.

I also want to thank Dr. Fritz Meyer of Blatchford who took the time to meet me during a very difficult time in my life; his encouragement and guidance really were turning points. Fritz was kind and sincere; he held me in his arms and kept me from falling at just the right time. He is a Birrell Brother.

### Dr. Birrell's Personal Vision

It is my vision that my dental practice will forcefully and steadfastly be ever moving towards success. By doing so, the goals and desires of my patients, my staff and myself will be understood and achieved.

It is my vision the dental desires of my patients are being fulfilled with compassion, diligence, comprehensiveness and with a quality that are all sincerely the best they can be.

It is my vision my dental practice will be profitable for each team member and my self. Financial profit is important; equally is spiritual profitability. My practice will be an emotionally positive for all.

It is my vision that because everything counts, everyone will do everything they can to make a positive outcome.

It is my vision the purpose of my practice will serve as a light to guide and direct each team member, including myself. It is the destination.

It is my vision my dental practice will be the best it can be and be FUN!

### Birrell Office Purpose

It is our purpose to strive for and achieve, natural beauty and brilliant smiles for our patients in a compassionate and professional manner, in order to provide optimal oral health.

We support each other and value our patients. We actively utilize continuing education to incorporate state of art techniques and knowledge.

Our purpose is to provide a warm and trusting environment. We are committed to listening in order to fulfill all theirs needs, desires and dreams.

We want to make your experience in our office fun and enjoyable for you and for us.

www.drbirrell.com

*Dr. Jim Birrell of Birrell Brothers is awakening the giant within him for marketing his brand. In wealthy Marin County, he knows he needs to stand out. He is using Rocketdog Dental to position himself through advertising and other key marketing initiatives.*

## Blatchford Game Plan: There Is No Final Answer

A bright, curious and knowledge seeker, Dr. Birrell pushes himself to learn more and applies his new knowledge from many continuing education courses. Constantly reading and evaluating, he is a wealth of thoughts and ideas to implement into dentistry. For Birrell Brothers, there is no final answer.

Many dentists are comfortable with the status quo by clinging to traditional methods and ways of thinking, rather then seeking the possibility of a better result. Change is a challenge. We stay with the answers we know, rather than risking something new.

In _Who Moved My Cheese?_, Dr. Spencer Johnson shares some eagerly look for cheese in another spot, some reluctantly find cheese in another station and others would rather die when the cheese is not in the same spot.

In dentistry, the cheese has moved. New answers are available technically, in sales conversations and in marketing opportunities. Are you content or is there more "cheese" to be learned?

The top 10% of dentists know there can be no final answer. Approach the successful practice of dentistry as a constant work in progress. Are you part of the dental revolution or are you in the stands watching?

The most exciting aspect of the dental revolution is the technical advances. With bonded dentistry, new materials and techniques, you and your laboratory are able to deliver beauty, comfort and longevity. Your patients want to look good, feel good and last a long time.

The insurance game is another area where Doctors can feel trapped yet reluctant to change. Dentists, staff and patients have become willing partners for 40 years. We have allowed insurance companies to market and sell dentistry in your office. If your desire is to be insurance free, you must create a new image and become very skilled in sales and listening.

Dentists do have a clear choice to continue the same or become insurance free, mentally and financially. With any change, create a plan towards insurance freedom. Do the math, work with your staff on scripting and speak with every patient who is involved, sharing the benefits. Forever being a dental insurance provider is not necessarily the final answer.

Blatchford Coaching has led the way to another change—our patients do not NEED our services. Virtually everything we do is a choice. This coaching is different than taught and shakes the very core of insurance paradigms. When the NEED paradigm is resolved in dentist's minds, it creates the opportunity to help patients develop dreams of good-looking smiles. There is no final answer here, either, for as the marketplace changes, the skills and attitudes in dentistry will shift, too.

Learning sales skills is a real change. Stop the pressure sales of talking patients into fixing things. Learn to ask questions about their long term goals. Take a dental sales course like Blatchford Coaching. Have right-brained conversations. Start a sales library. There is definitely no final answer in the sales arena for just when you think you have it, the marketplace changes and dentistry takes a different position of choice.

In dental marketing, there is no final answer. Many dentists are slow to embrace the importance of marketing. The public recognizes dentistry is a choice and not a NEEDED service. Since dentistry is a choice, develop a niche and be the leader. Create a long-range plan, based on your personal vision and values and seek expert advice to position yourself as the expert in your area. Marketing in dentistry will never have a final answer as it is fluid and dynamic. Lead the marketplace, for if you wait for every answer, it is too late.

You do not have the final answer if your overhead is near 75% or higher. High overhead is a choice. The bigger, busier model of trying to be "everything to everyone" results in a higher overhead. It takes more staff for smaller procedures on many patients. Change the mix of treatment being offered to more optional services. Offer choices, not just the "patch-type" dentistry. Resign from the Crown of Year Club where the staff percentage is near 30% and the lab is under 10%. A lower overhead percentage means acquiring new skills and attitude.

Think of the passion in serving patients with beautiful, optional smiles. There is no final answer. Revisit your reasons for entering dentistry. Is there satisfaction in keeping things the same or is there a real possibility for you to take some risk, learn new skills and rekindle the excitement you first felt in being a dentist? The skills, knowledge and coaching are available to you. Take a chance. Give it your best.

Bill Blatchford, DDS

# From the Blatchford Play Book:
## Coaching the Team

Dr. Birrell is a strong people person, very introspective and sensitive. He is a good listener which is a fine quality for coaching a team to results.

>> Discover your vision

>> Write your vision

>> Communicate your vision to your team

>> Never compromise your vision

>> Keep your eye on the ball

>> There are no favorites on your team. Communicate equally

>> Praise often, in public and with specifics

>> Communicate what you stand for and what you don't stand for

>> Don't allow anything less than 100% from yourself or your team members

>> Don't let a bad apple spoil the team. Throw out the bad apple

>> Constructive criticism is done privately, timely and with specific requests for change

>> Make the hard decisions

>> Be the leader who walks the talk; team expectations of conduct are the same for you, the leader

>> Do not have any business dealings or loans with your team members

>> Dress appropriately, speak well and carry a positive attitude at all times

>> You must have respect. People do not have to like you but respect is an absolute

>> Allow staff to grab responsibility and run with it

>> Avoid "micro-managing" like the plague. Hire great staff and let them be accountable when it works and when it doesn't.

A World War II story showed President Franklin Roosevelt visiting an aircraft manufacturing plant and boosting morale. The first man, when asked what he was doing, he replied "Placing screws in the wing." The second man replied when asked, "I am cutting the sheet metal for the tail gunner section." The third man replied, when asked, "I am preserving our freedoms." Morale to the story, coach to the bigger picture. The details don't matter.

# 9

## PERFECT SMILE STUDIOS

### Drs. Rahul Doshi and Ashish Parmar
### London, England

Drs. Doshi and Parmar are true partners in the Perfect Smile Studios. Let's set the stage for Americans to recognize what a unique position Rahul and Ashi have created.

United Kingdom has offered dentistry on National Health Service (NHS) since 1947. Every citizen has free basic dentistry and over the years, the remuneration to the participating dentist has been reduced and reduced. Thus, several generations of Brits see free dental care as a right. This is much like PPO plans in US, only nation wide. Added to that is the recognition the English love their sweets and have one of the highest edentulous rates in the world. There is even a sort of pride in recognizing the oxymoron of cosmetics and English teeth. The actor, Hugh Grant laughs about his "English teeth."

Enter the technical revolution in dentistry, the appeal of global media with beautiful smiles and the threadbare existence of doing only what National Health Service affords, Rahul and Ashi saw something different for their path in dentistry.

They are not the first cosmetic dentists in UK yet, they have composed a package of beautiful smiles, service and marketing to bring awareness to the British public. They are becoming recognized for beautiful smile transformations.

Rahul and Ashi have been friends for 18 years, studied together at Guy's Hospital in London and qualified in 1991. Both their wives (Bhavna and Jyoti) are dentists also and work part time at The Studios, making this a unique team and workforce. Their first practice purchase was in Hornchurch with a 5000 patient list, 3500 of which were NHS. With just 1500 private patients, their aim was to make it totally private as the leading practice in the area, renowned for the quality of dentistry, for décor and service.

They wanted to purchase an existing practice which would be predictably successful. Hornchurch has wealthy homes with wage earners in the top 5%. The practice was on the main High Street yet on the second floor. It had antiquated treatment rooms (one of the dental chairs was 35 years old) and the dentistry delivered was simple— no crown and bridge or cosmetic dentistry, no endodontics and inadequate periodontal considerations. The scope to develop this practice was enormous.

Their second practice was started in Hertford with no existing patients. They purchased a shell and converted it into a Smile Studio with the help of a unique designer who used vibrant colors and fabric textures to make the establishment stand out in this growing wealthy town. They wanted it to be unique and different from all the others in the area. It is also the sight of The Perfect Smile Academy which host a number of aesthetic hands on courses.

Drs. Doshi and Parmar always believed they would be successful because they work hard and are determined with high aspirations. They entered dentistry because this healthcare field involved running a business and they knew dentistry would have a positive impact on changing people's lives.

Partnerships are challenging yet, Rahul and Ashi feel they have the same vision, drive and enthusiasm to succeed. "Our proactive and dynamic approach and using our individual strengths synergistically has helped in our progress."

Highlights on this highway to success include "setting up two stunning practices, establishing a successful teaching academy, lecturing internationally in India, achieving media publicity thorough television, radio, newspapers, magazines, being invited to speak to the British Dental Association and being features regularly on the Extreme Makeover UK television shows. They give technical credit on implant training to Dr. Hilt Tatum, having completed his one year training programme at The Tatum Institute in UK some years back. "Dr. Tatum is an inspiration to us as he is humble and has unparallel clinical skill, always doing what is best for his patients. The Perfect Smile Studio offers a comprehensive range of surgical care at The Studios including implant placement using bone expansion as well as conventional drilling techniques, bone grafting, sinus grafting and soft tissue surgeries.

In Smile Design, they credit their teaching and mentorship to Dr. Larry Rosenthal. "He has given us passion to enjoy dentistry, change the lives of our patients and allow us to change the face of dentistry in UK. This revolution in cosmetic dentistry started from Larry's first London presentation in 2001."

In addition, one of the main aspects of the Perfect Smile Studios which contribute to its individuality is the provision of the Facial Rejuvenation to its patients. This area has been the speciality of Dr. Bhavna Doshi BDS, Facial Rejuvenation Director of The Perfect Smile Studios.

Facial Rejuvenation is any treatment which contributes to facial enhancement by either sculpting or recontouring the face and its skin. Most treatments are non surgical and are provided in the form of an injection. These treatments include Botulinum toxin administration, Hyaluronic acid based gels, Poly-L-lactic acid formulations and injections of the body's own fibroblast cells for use in an autologous cellular repair system.

The massive boom in facial rejuvenation has until now been in the domain of aesthetic nurses and dermatologists. However the provision of facial rejuvenation has allowed The Perfect Smile Studios to grow in a 3-dimensional way by providing "mini" makeovers to those patients not wishing to undergo extensive surgery and lengthy post-operative recovery periods.

Dr. Bhavna Doshi believes it all comes down to looking at the face as we should have in the first place. The beautiful smiles that are being created are already creating enhanced facial features in the lip region; however the provision of treatments to enhance other aspects of the face into which these beautiful smiles fit gives our patients that much more in a stunning medical environment! This coupled with the fact that dentists are very articulate with their hands and administering injections is second nature makes facial rejuvenation a powerful tool in marketing a dental practice.

It tends to draw in the type of patients that are interested in improving their face—not just from a dental or smile aspect. Only too often patients are wanting facial enhancements but are only aware of improvements that can be made in teeth and feel any other aspect of their face would require surgery. The Perfect Smile Studios found facial rejuvenation to be a niche market in dentistry—one which not only drew in the right client base but one which set them apart from their colleagues.

As the cosmetic and pharmaceutical companies started to meet the growing demands of facial enhancement procedures that were non – surgical in nature, their marketing companies started providing opportunities to many clinicians. Bhavna had a personal interest in facial enhancements and started developing her interest in this field in 1999. She undertook extensive training and research in all aspects of facial enhancements including marketing, skin evaluation and con-sultation procedures, staff training and injection techniques. One of the obstacles that came in her way was the dental protection society did not recognize facial treatments as being in the domain of the dental profession hence an outside insurance company was sought to provide indemnity. Since, Bhavna has enjoyed all aspects of providing treatments which turns back the time on many a face.

Rahul and Ashi's greatest successes are being appreciated for the quality teaching academy and having the ability to provide stunning cosmetic dentistry.

Their regrets? "The greatest loss is the time we could have spent with our family during our initial years of establishing ourselves. Any successful and growing business requires a commitment of time from the leaders. We both married shortly after opening our first practice."

One goal of The Perfect Smile Studios is profitability. The partners feel they are "consistently hitting their turnover targets at both practices, staff is enjoying fantastic monthly bonuses as a reflection of team performance; overheads are within recommended averages and moving towards 45% net."

They have focused on particular skills and systems to make themselves more profitable. These include:

- Leadership
- Excellent selling skills by the Team
- Excellent case preparation and presentation ... allowing guests to say "yes"
- Team focus is motivated by Blatchford bonus plan
- Block booking for profitability and reduced stress
- Conversations with patients based on emotions, not logic (this is the single most important thing that Blatchford has improved in our performance)
- Offering unique services
- Doing high end dentistry
- Superb marketing with a professional plan, website: www.perfectsmilestudio.com
- Delegation of everything to Team except actual dentistry

- Dove-tailing (maximizing the use of treatment rooms and
  having correct staffing levels

Drs. Doshi and Parmar make a point to be different from other dentists. They have and continue to improve their own technical skills (they consistently travel to the top postgraduate training courses in the US having done most the courses in the UK), office décor, marketing and customer service. Their motto is "Changing Lives-Exceeding Expectations" and this is inherent in everything they do. They have the ability to carry out smile design, implantology and facial aesthetics and with one Team.

In their search for profitability, they spent years trying to reduce expenses rather then concentrating on increasing income. As Blatchford says, "income can be easily doubled with creativity but it is more difficult to halve the overhead." Ashi and Rahul agree "simplifying systems and looking at the major overhead variables is the key."

Some pitfalls on their path to excellence have included:

*Staff Selection*—"some of our biggest headaches and stresses have been selecting incorrect staff, even at management level. Blatchford has coached us to hire 'givers' not 'takers.' We want people to give us energy. Now we evaluate more critically who we recruit and make swifter changes if need be.

*Leadership*—we have spent a lot of time and energy this year becoming better leaders and being consistent in following rules, protocols and policies. We feel it is the single most important requirement to having a successful business.

*Communication*—Poor communication has led to dissatisfaction of some patients and staff. Clarity in everything we do has transformed the happiness between us, patients and the Team.

After 14 years in practice, the partner's idea of success is:

- Appreciation from clients when we positively change their lives

- Extraordinary and motivated team who share the business vision
- Leading a stress reduced life
- Having time off to spend with family, friends and to self-improve
- Be at leading edge of dental profession
- Having fun at work
- Reaching financial and professional goals
- Being respected by dental peers

They can be proud of production/collection at Hornchurch which has quadrupled while overhead has remained consistent. Their new patient numbers have been cut in half because of dropping NHS but the quality of patients has increased. Their fees have increased ten fold and certainly dropping NHS fees was a part of their path to success. In 2003, they decided to carry out only the profitable treatment they enjoy. "There are many treatments we say no to because it does not cover our hourly overhead, let alone make a profit."

Their Team is motivated by "a successful bonus system, praise and appreciation for work well done, a challenge to be a World Class Team, being respected, as well as a fair and positive approach. Our 'A' Game days feel like we are on top of the world."

The partners are a long ways from retirement so they see themselves "reducing" our work hours to half but never retiring completely, so as to continue to enjoy the profession we love, to keep ourselves mentally fit and to make a difference to the world." They currently enjoy eight weeks of vacation a year and do not work on Fridays or weekends.

Drs. Doshi and Parmar love their teaching at the Perfect Smile Academy and sharing knowledge in the profession and helping other dentists have a balance between work and play by elevating their practice to another level.

Internally for marketing, they have:
- Before and After albums of smile designs

- Testimonials from patients
- Smile questionnaires
- Smile Makeovers
- Verbal proof stories of how we have changed patient's lives
- Personalized DVD
- Practice brochures

Externally, they have been successful with external décor of their offices, networking, Extreme Makeover UK, newspaper editorial, articles in weekly and monthly magazines and yellow pages. Opening in the evening for new clients did not work well, radio worked at first and less there after, newspaper ads worked sometimes.

"What has really helped is coaching from Bill and helping us design our personal lives to take more time off while increasing our income. We learned the art of dealing with people and selling in a truly non-pressurized and highly effective way. We also understand the importance of a balanced lifestyle with respect to work, play and family as well as higher values in spiritual development. Detailed goal setting at the start of our coaching program was perhaps one of the most profound ways that Bill influenced us...for this, we are truly grateful."

www.theperfectsmile.com

*To exit our town in Hertford every car has to pass our practice. We wanted our building and sign to make a statement.*

*L to R:*
*Dr. Ashish Parmar*
*Dr. Bhavna Doshi*
*Dr. Rahul Doshi*

**The Multi-Colored Reception area:** *Our reception is visible from the street as soon as you enter the Studios. We also know that patients can make a decision about people and places within three seconds. We wanted to produce a unique identity which was different in fabric and colours that made an instant impact. We wanted that instant impact to state that this is a modern, unique practice, making nervous patients feel that they are in the relaxing lounge of a restaurant or bar that they would like to frequent. We wanted to say that we have put a lot of thought into designing this area, in a similar way we will put a lot of thought into your new smile.*

**The Lecture Area:** *This area is our more tranquil relaxation lounge, a great place for our patients to relax in privacy. We have used a colour scheme that allows us to change this lounge into our lecture area. Our lecture area can be used for lecturing presentations during open evenings and also during team training sessions.*

**Other Areas:** *We have had our smiles captured as makeovers, photographed at lovely manor. We love to show off the qualities of our smiles but also the changes in the lives of our patients. Our gallery of photos creates a great talking point to our new patients of how their lives could change as well.*

# Blatchford Game Plan:
# "Spot On" Behavior Checklist

Drs. Doshi and Parmar are pioneers in developing English practices with cosmetic options. They market heavily and work with their teams to develop behavior consistent with the best choices. The Perfect Smile Studio teams do know how to serve well. They see the bigger picture and are branding themselves as different.

Positive thoughts, goals and talk make a real difference in the success of your practice. However, the only concrete evidence of positivity is demonstrated by Doctor and staff action, behavior and results. Putting words into action is a choice. Walking your talk is a choice. Our behavior and results are a choice. Turning goals and lofty dreams into reality is a choice, a choice every minute of our day.

Our London clients, Drs. Doshi and Parmar, call it "spot on" behavior. It is a moment to moment choice to play the game and play it well. In _Maximum Achievement_, Brian Tracy says "Everything counts, everything counts, everything counts." Knowing our behavior is a choice, how well do we choose every minute? What systems are in place in ensure our goals are met and exceeded? "Spot on" behavior is reaching down deep to accomplish your own maximum achievement.

"Spot on" behavior is avoiding sending in the mail an extensive health history to a new guest who will be entering our practice with a prophy. Rather, sit with the guest and complete a shorter health history together. It is time and commitment to make a new guest comfortable.

"Spot on" is having meaningful conversations with guests about their dental dreams. Rather than waiting until the appointment end, a choice in behavior is to ask questions, listen with intention and helping your guest build their picture of a smile. The other choice in behavior is to be "too busy" and avoid the conversation completely.

"Spot on" behavior is utilizing a state sanctioned opportunity for hygienists to administer anesthesia. When a recare patient has a single filling diagnosed, scheduling a separate appointment is a time challenge for patient and practice. Instead, at the next hygiene cleaning, the hygienist can deliver the anesthesia and the Doctor can complete the filling in the hygiene chair.

"Spot on" is discovering your guest's personal preferences for coffee, music, temperature or movies and delivering upon their arrival. Anticipation turns words into action and this earns loyalty from your patients.

"Spot on" behavior is the doctor answering and asking more questions, ultimately giving an estimate to the patient. Trust and loyalty is developed when the doctor completes the diagnosis and gives a fee. More cases are still pending or lost when a transfer of responsibilities occurs in midstream. Completing the job is a choice in behavior. When there is a definite "yes" to treatment and the fee is given, the financial expert in your practice can do the logistics of money.

"Spot on" is an assistant leading his/her room by being totally prepared and orally completing a laminated checklist. It is an assistant running the room on time. In a diagnosis of crowns and fillings, it is an assistant who has the doctor complete the fillings first, knowing the doctor will always complete the crown. It is an assistant who is conscious of patient's time and practice profitability to complete the scheduled work on time.

"Spot on" behavior is seeing the big picture of scheduling in blocks so the doctor has minimal interruptions. It is scheduling hygiene with periodontal patients during the doctor's production blocks. It is communicating with team to meet goal as one.

"Spot on" is seeing every guest as a person and not as a set of teeth dropped off at your office. If you have a picture in your mind of what you would like this person to look like, your own agenda will trip you every time. "Spot on" is acknowledging your guest as a full person with likes and dislikes. Developing their dreams not yours will give you the results at which you are goaling.

"Spot on" is seeing yourself as an innovator, working and thinking about the patient's impressions. Malcolm Gladwell, in his book *blink*, confirms people make up their mind about something in seconds. Therefore, "spot on" is thinking on your feet as well as having systems in place to demonstrate you are worth it.

"Spot on" behavior results from systems of communication, skill building, scheduling and most of all a leader who sets the direction which motivates a team of people who see the doctor's vision as their own.

Bill Blatchford, DDS

## From Blatchford Play Book: Extra Effort

Drs. Doshi and Parmar have led the paradigm shift in creating options for UK smiles. They are essentially salmon swimming upstream against the current as Britain has had basic dental entitlement for 50 years. In doing so, they needed to dig deep and make that extra effort, especially when things do not go their way easily.

>> Reach down deep for that something extra

>> Want it bad enough

>> Learn to play with a relaxed concentration

>> I want my team and I to make that second effort

>> We have more potential than we realize. Use it.

>> A winning team has dedication, they will not accept defeat; they will make that extra effort

>> You need to have a motive which has extraordinary appeal

>> Set a goal to be the very best and then work every waking hour of each day trying to achieve that goal

>> Condition yourself to master case presentation by reading a book on sales or marketing every week.

>> Practice with a video camera. Watch it yourself and eliminate movements or expressions you do not like or are distracting

>> Avoid the word NEED in conversations with your guests

>> Connect on some level with everyone

>> Don't be overly concerned about what other dentists think

>> Always dress the part

# 10

## THE DYNAMIC DUO

### Dr. Lori Kemmet

Dr. Kemmet of Boulder, Colorado is one of the country's leading female dentists. We relish in professional women's success as they are pioneers, blazing new trails for others to follow. Successful and balanced female professional role models are a gift and Lori is that gift. Thank you Lori for being bold, staying the course and taking the higher road.

Dr. Kemmet is listed as a duo. Part of her success is selecting a husband, Jeff Bailey, who has a keen ear for listening, applying action as well as supporting Lori's leadership. They are quite a team and have unknowingly created a fan club of "wanna be's". It is a magical combination of skills creating a unique aesthetic practice like no other. We give them both great credit.

Lori's college interest started in accounting and after her first "B," was encouraged to try Bio 101. When Prof. Eleanor Toersveit shuffled in, Lori thought this would be a very long semester. Out of Dr. Toersveit's lab coat came two boa constrictors. Lori was hooked by Eleanor's passion and chose Biology with a pre-dent focus. Lori's mom is in her 36th year of working with the same wonderful dentist, an important impression for then six-year-old Lori.

How does the duo work? Jeff Bailey's training is eclectic and perfect for his "Manager of Guest Services." He has worked in outdoor education, taught yoga and is a certified massage therapist. He brings all those skills to the table and is a very right brained thinker, a perfect compliment to the talented Dr. Kemmet. Obviously an accomplished clinician, Lori holds Dr. Bill Dickerson of LVI as an inspiring mentor.

Her other mentor is Dr. Bill Blatchford, her coach in the business of dentistry. Lori and Jeff feel the Blatchford bonus program allows the team to feel and think like owners. The team is invested in the success of the practice. Lori and Jeff have proudly written $4500 bonus checks (for a fifteen day bonus cycle) to each team member of five in addition to their regular salary. That must be fun!

Now, about Jeff—originally not involved in the practice, Jeff welcomes new guests and long term guests; schedules an hour to discover their dreams, wants and desires. Fortunately for the practice, Jeff does not discuss technical dentistry or use clinical education to motivate their guests as Jeff purposely does not read x-rays, identify tooth numbers or names. He keeps the right-brained conversation emotional and filled with his listening. He creates trust in that hour and touts the skills of Dr. Kemmet and their team. Money is appropriately discussed with the guest early in the conversation, not at the close. The whole team is proud of their fees and feels deserving.

The importance of these successful conversations cannot be underestimated for this allows the team to deliver ideal dentistry. Can anyone do this? With dedication, study, a real willingness to think on an emotional level and enjoy people, it is possible. It is important to note, Jeff is not the office manager. He is a team member who is talented in his position. Lori feels the very best business decision she ever made was to bring Jeff into the practice. Jeff said, "the number one thing is to find out what the guest wants to accomplish and to make sure they are clear and why." Some smile enhancement verbage Jeff sincerely uses might be, "to do that, it takes a high level of technical expertise, an artistic eye for detail and knowing what kind of enhancement is going to look good on someone. Lori has the passion to do that." That is a non-technical and emotion based endorsement!

Dr. Kemmet is definitely the leader carrying the vision which is very clear in her mind and communicated well with the team. One of her earlier leadership pitfalls was holding onto team members too long who did not share her vision. Another mistake was talking with staff about other staff in trying to gain consensus. Earlier, she feared staff evaluations and now praises in public and private. Separate quarterly lunches with team members allows for constructive feedback, reviewing of strengths and becoming accountable for their future. The team is also given the opportunity to ask Dr. Kemmet for ways that she can help improve all aspects of the office.

Communication issues between team members are expected to be handled by the team members themselves. Dr. Kemmet encourages curious team members and likes doers. She wants people to think for themselves and come to her with solutions. Jeff and Lori both work daily at verbal praise as their team has indicated recognition means more than the bonus check (and they love their bonus checks, too).

Mastering sales skills based on wants, not needs is a continual learning process for Dr. Kemmet, Jeff and their team. She realizes successful sales are a dynamic and the marketplace is continually changing. In sales, one is never finished.

Dr. Kemmet and Jeff have invested heavily into marketing. It is important to note she had a well-oiled machine with systems in place before marketing. All practices need new patients yet, if the skills and systems are not in place to take advantage of new patients arriving at your office, it is what they call in professionals sales, "burning leads." Marketing money is wasted in practices without the internal structure to create a "yes."

To that end, Jeff and Lori have committed a marketing budget of 10% of prior year's collection. They have tried many marketing strategies however, the message and look are consistent. Her website at www.incrediblesmiles.com is solidly complete and timely. They have tried television and newspapers in the greater Denver area. They have a marketing campaign with the Denver Bronco Cheerleaders, extreme makeover campaigns and they judge beauty pageants in Colorado. Lori is the official dentist for three beauty pageants in Colorado. They currently are in five magazines to attract their unique customer. Their main referral source is a personally endorsed spot with Tom Martino, a national consumer advocate. Jeff and Lori researched his audience to see if it matched their target market and vision before committing. The result is about 80% of their consultations arrive from AM radio advertising. Again, a word of caution—Jeff and Lori did their research and this works for them in Boulder and Denver right now. Do not copy someone else's marketing success and expect it to work for you today in your area.

In the past they have found generating internal referrals was excellent for general dentistry. Their cosmetic and neuromuscular guests come from external and media marketing. Currently, they are screening their calls to bring in people looking for aesthetic and comprehensive restorative dentistry.

In Lori's thirteen years of practice, her numbers are interesting to compare. Much effort, focus and thought has occurred since 1992.

|      | Production | Collection | OH%   | New Pts/mo. | Staff | Days |
|------|-----------|-----------|-------|-------------|-------|------|
| 1992 | $105K     | $90K      | Assoc | 16-20       | 0     | 200  |
| 2004 | $2.4M     | $2.3M     | 53%   | 16          | 4,1/2 | 142  |

Currently, Dr. Kemmet reserves one three- hour appointment each day for veneers and averages one full mouth case a month. She and Jeff are in the office Monday through Wednesday and the team is present on Thursday with a full day of hygiene guests. The rest of the team prepares for the next week.

Dr. Kemmet agrees that a great staff is essential to deliver genuine service to guests. She feels the Blatchford bonus system "creates accountability from the best ones and weeds out the turkeys." To earn and maintain staff respect, she has strong standards:

- Remember who owns the business and took the risks to achieve
- Show no favoritism and avoid subgrouping with or about them (absolutely)
- The team wants leadership from the boss
- Love each other, hug each other, respect each other
- Letting a team member go is actually a gift for their growth and preserves your team

Lori has high expectations for her team. She looks for curiosity, passion, potential and honesty. She loves to open doors and be a part of their growth. She gives verbal praise often.

One of her hardest decisions was to fire three staff after an LVI cruise. When the team did not show for seminars, Bill Blatchford said, "you are planning to let some staff go when you return, aren't you?"

Dr. Kemmet is definitely a goal achiever. In 2002, her desire was to work three days a week doing strictly cosmetics and spend more time with their pre-school daughter. We coached her to find a contracted associate with specific treatments and days and no opportunity to buy in. Currently she is finding an implant trained oral surgeon to complement her treatment and is referring her general dentistry to a Boulder group. She also added a dedicated and talented exclusive ceramist and is looking at a second office opportunity in Denver, 40 miles south.

As a Minnesota college student, Lori and friends skied in Vail and she recalls crying down I-70 to the airport. After service in the Air Force, Lori sought Colorado. Boulder is indeed a magical place where early pioneers established green spaces and limited the growth. Bike paths abound and UC-Boulder is the main "industry." Surrounded by skiing, hiking the Flat Irons and mountain beauty, Lori chose Boulder because she saw many VW vans, dogs with bandanas and healthy people. Thanks to Dr. Bob Murphy for saying "There is always room for another good dentist."

Her initial goal as an associate was to make enough money to learn to ski well and make her payment of 55% production by the 10th of the following month. This was a challenge with slow insurance payments. Enter a great man with a savings account, her future husband Jeff. After a year's associateship which allowed for all established patients to follow her, Lori started on her own. One banker, seeing her organization and passion, loaned her $35K to start in her own location in 1993.

Highlights in Dr. Kemmet's practice life have included:

- Being included in LVI book, "Aesthetic Dentistry by Drs. Dickerson and Booth
- Collecting $1M and then $2M the next year
- Obtaining a negative accounts receivable with Blatchford Coaching
- Receiving her LVI Mastership accreditation in 2004, the second dentist to do so.
- Instructing at LVI since 1998 and having Bill Dickerson as a mentor
- Starting their four person ceramic studio in January 2005 and keeping them busy exclusively with Lori's dentistry
- Having a patient ask a life altering question "How would you like to adopt a baby girl who will be born in four weeks?" What a blessing!
- Having Bill Blatchford encourage Lori to reduce her work week from four days to three and actually increase production

Lori and Jeff are loving people who first love themselves so they can share it with all. "Love will make you profitable in life," Lori shares. Success is staying the course and keeping those values as a priority which are important to our happiness. "We refuse to let thoughts of fear take over. We replace them with loving thoughts ASAP." Lori says she asked little Georgia "You have a choice to be happy or sad—which one would you like to choose?" Only you can make you successful. Be committed to your success.

Lori and Jeff are drawn to those with a positive entrepreneurial spirit and see the good in people. They have dedicated themselves to surrounding themselves with people who "feed us," that is people who stimulate them both professionally and emotionally. They think outside the box in problem solving. Lori was one of the first to advertise on television in 1998. There is a risk in being the first in newspapers, magazines, radio and Internet. Reward usually comes with some risk. It has taken money, time and courage to position themselves as the brand for cosmetic and neuromuscular dentistry in Colorado and larger.

Jeff and Lori look for opportunities to give back. As a child of divorce at five years, Lori was put in a position of being more independent and mature than most. She was always drawn to entrepreneurial visionaries. Three health care professionals, an optometrist, a pharmacist and an ophthalmologist "all had a silently huge influence on me. They were fun, optimistic, focused for success and encouraging. People who make a difference in a young person's life are perhaps the biggest gift givers of all."

www.incrediblesmiles.com

*Photo of Dr. Lori Kemmet taken by her husband, Jeff who is equally talented at photography and selling cosmetic dentistry.*

*The Kemmet-Bailey family in Boulder, Colorado. The backdrop is the amazing view from their home.*

## Blatchford Game Plan: The Legacy of Sgt. Schultz

In Dr. Kemmet's office, Jeff Bailey is the initial contact and he spends up to an hour with a new guest, helping them discover and uncover their dreams, fears, desires and ideas. Jeff allows the guest to start with a blank canvas; with Jeff's questions, the guest paints his own smile picture using his words. Jeff is not dentally trained so he doesn't let tech talk get in the guest's way.

In these changing times, people are looking for solid relationships and comfort close to home. Especially, in dentistry, your patients need to feel they know you and can trust you. In dental sales, we have long held the idea that building patient trust is explaining and educating the patient on the technical aspects of treatment. Great acceptance does not result.

Sergeant Schultz on the old comedy, "Hogan's Heroes" had the real attitude for successful dental sales in these changing times. His most often response in a fabulous German accent, was, "I know nothing."

In successful dental sales, we need to have our minds be like a blank canvas ready for the patient to paint the picture. We must assume the attitude that "I know nothing" about this person. I am here to learn.

If you begin the sales process (the time before the patient says "yes") with your answer for them without involving the patient's desires, we miss the whole point of sales. The sales process is the emotional right-brained portion where we ASK about dreams, desires, benefits, results, not how fabulous our preconceived answer will be for them.

A dentist is so technically trained, we inhibit the sale process. Our mind is constantly designing our idea for a perfect smile for the new patient, the grocery clerk, the waiter or our karate instructor. However, in the sales process, we trip over our own feet when we already have a picture in mind for our patient.

Lou Holtz said, "I never learn anything talking. I only learn when I ask questions." Imagine if another football great, Vince Lombardi was a new guest in your office. Immediately you see your ideas of how to change the dyastima, the spacing and flat yellow teeth. Without finding what Mr. Lombardi wants, you begin describing what you would do for him. In telling him about your plan for his spacing and dyastima, he replies (with some indignation) "What do you mean, change my smile? My smile is a Lombardi smile. It is the same as my father and grandfather. No way." On a scale of one to ten, how are you doing on building relationship and trust?

The Boat Sales Person of the Year explained his success by saying, "When I see an inquiring couple, I never begin with a boat in mind." Imagine a dentist as a realtor showing homes before finding the dreams and desires of the client. The dentist would point to the features the dentist sees, like the lovely flowering cherry tree or the beautiful outdoor patio for summer dining. By asking more questions, deeper questions, the dental-realtor could have discovered the potential home buyer has severe allergies to trees and bees. The sale is blown.

For a successful sale, the technically trained must clear their mind. "I know nothing" becomes your mantra. Our job is to help the patient uncover THEIR agenda. Develop a trusting relationship by staying out of the "tooth talk" while you develop a friend.

If you keep asking questions, the patient will paint a picture for you. Their answers will sound like looking good, younger, whiter, straighter, more even smile, looking better, lasting a long time and feeling better about their smile. Ask them to expand on these thoughts. Have them select an after picture to help them visualize their dream smile. Have them describe it, sharing advantages if they owned that smile.

Because you began the conversation with the Sgt. Schultz's attitude of "I know nothing," you allow the patient to paint their own picture. They can see it, it is their idea and they will defend their idea. They will resist your agenda. You put unwanted pressure on them to accept what you had in mind.

Create the opportunity for your new friend to dream into the future about their smile. Start with "I know nothing" and your patient will fill your brain with more and better ideas then you ever thought.

By beginning with "I know nothing," you can avoid the Ricky Recardo line of "you have a lot of 'splaining to do."

Bill Blatchford, DDS

## From the Blatchford Play Book: Keeping Score

Dr. Kemmet and team are very conscious of numbers, time and efficiency. Lori and Jeff are proud parents to Georgia and time with her is the prized commodity. To achieve a balance, knowing the score is essential.

>> Know your numbers and what they mean

>> Know which numbers can change and how to change them

>> Reward your team monthly with an easy to figure and understand bonus

>> Let your team understand the bonus math so they can increase their "ownership"

>> Hire "10's" on your team and be a "10" yourself

>> Use Pareto's 80/20 Rule—the top 20% of your guests deliver 80% of your profits. Who are they? Find out and nurture them.

>> 20% of America moves each year. In a practice with 1000 patients, 200 will probably move. In order to grow 10%, you will need to attract 300 new patients or 25 a month. Who is in charge?

>> Have a daily goal for Doctor and hygiene.

>> Diagnose three times your daily goal

>> Know your overhead per hour and schedule to exceed it every hour

>> Create a game plan when numbers are not met. Who is the source, what is the plan?

>> Know your percentage of lab. National average is 8%. Are you above or below? What does that mean?

>> Create a system to celebrate when numbers are met

>> Team members know the score at all times

>> "I do not know" is unacceptable. Be curious about the score.

>> If you are not asking questions, it could seem you do not care about the score.

# 11

## IT'S THE TEAM

All Doctors have strongly indicated excellent team players are a must. Doctors have shared their agonizing over staff who appear to be on a different path.

- Should I train them better?
- What if I lose the best team member I have?

Doctors rely on great staff to form a team and get the job done. Several team members volunteered their ideas of how they "Play Their 'A' Game.

### Dr. Kim Okamura
Lee Roll, dental hygienist

"Dr. Okamura has a vision of what she wants her practice to be now and in the future. She loves teaching the principles she believes in and empowers her staff to act independently. When mistakes are made, it is used as a learning opportunity. She has the unique ability to encourage all to be a partner in the practice, that it is not solely her practice. But make no mistake, if you don't get the vision, cannot work within the framework, or have a separate agenda, you won't be here long. She acknowledges and rewards your successes and contributions."

The Team Okamura 'A' game is "light, fun and free. You are probably working harder than you ever had, since you are using all your skills. End of day you know you are closer to a goal, you are part of a team and you are a winner. You have been acknowledged by patients, team, Doctor and yourself as a professional. How did we get there? Same way you get to play at Carnegie Hall, PRACTICE, PRACTICE, PRACTICE. Being self-critical, what could I or we have done better? It is a continual ongoing project and that is the fun part."

What is Dr. Okamura's coaching?
- Attention to detail
- Commitment of time in helping all staff learn the elements of philosophy.
- Role play and practice
- Daily question of new staff, "What did you learn today?"
- Reliance and trust in seasoned personnel to be part of the teaching staff.
- Belief in including all staff in the learning process, i.e. seminars, continuing education, conferences
- Belief in the person's ability to achieve all she expects
- Belief in the ability of team member to excel personally.

A perfect day at the Okamura office is "everyone on the same page, knows the goals and using all their abilities to help achieve it. You don't have to carry anyone. Goals are met and it was fun. All acknowledge each other's contributions and BAM is exceeded. Patients are happy as you gave them ultimate care and there is eagerness for the next day. You are proud to be part of this professional team. I often ask, "What did we do right today or this month? How can we do this again? Why did it work?"

"As a dental hygienist, I am fortunate to belong to a great profession. Preventive dental care has evolved to being a gateway to patient's health. I am fortunate to work with teams that acknowledge this important role of dental hygiene, allow me to use all my knowledge, abilities and skills to further the health of the patients and to expand the profitability of the practice. I love contributing and being a part of a growing, successful practice. "

"I set a goal each year to clinically improve myself in some area of dental hygiene. I love the business aspect of dentistry and many team courses and individual reading reflect this. My husband owns his own marine service business and this can and does benefit his business as well. Since learning the power of open-ended questions, I am a much better party animal."

"Keeping her leader focused on the vision and less concerned about being a 'gal pal' to the staff is the only thing I would change. I understand the emotional need for this, but it is why _Leaders Can't Lead_ by Warren Bennis."

More from Lee, "Keep focused on the vision, achieve the daily goals, be consistent and give the gift of a good time and a fulfilling laugh to each patient. Dentistry is fun! Also to ask with each new business diversion and decision, 'How does this fit with the vision and mission of the practice?' If it fits, design the steps to achieve it."

## Team DeCarlo

Dr. Paul DeCarlo's team wanted to share their responses as a group. "I have worked with Dr. DeCarlo for 31 years. He was at a cross roads when we took Blatchford Coaching. He was looking for a different direction to take in dentistry and just having had cancer surgery, he thought maybe he did not want to practice dentistry anymore. I was very scared for what would I do without him? Who knows what would have happened had we not decided to get on board with Dr. Blatchford. Another said, "the Blatchford program gave him the 'permission' he needed to present large, full restorative cases without hesitation. His confidence level has soared."

The DeCarlo 'A' Game is "peaceful days practicing the kind of dentistry that brings us top notch patients who appreciate beautiful cosmetic dentistry. Also having grown enough in our practice to realize not all people can afford dentistry as we see it, but humble enough to float a patient along in good dental health until his or her dreams of a beautiful smile can be within their reach." Another said, "the schedule runs smoothly and all problems are solved with no big event. Good office communication is a must—Team work is an absolute necessity and a good plan of action early on to avoid trouble spots helps. Also, it is good to make bonus." Another team member added, "the perfect day is a delicate balance. It involves crown/bridge/veneers from 8 AM to 1 PM with a production goal of $5K. We have two productive consults a day, emergency time and seating in the afternoon. All is accomplished by 5 PM. We do the perfect day in writing and we strive for it every day."

What keeps them in the game? "Oh, the love of dentistry, which combines my artistic as well as mechanical skills and all delivered in a structured environment. I like the new techniques, the world of cosmetics and the happiness it brings to so many. We have been a part of turning lives around through a beautiful smile. That alone keeps me coming back." Another 26 year team member said, "Love of people" keeps me in the game. My contribution would be to put everyone at ease with that warm, fuzzy welcome feeling."

Another said, "Our Doctor died of a heart attack. Dr. DeCarlo bought the practice and I had been asked to 'stay on a while.' I introduced myself to Dr. DeCarlo in June of 1974 and said "I will stay a while. So, what is 'awhile'?"

Coaching from Dr. DeCarlo looks like excellent communication and everyone is allowed to have an input. He always encourages us to come up with new ideas and to reach for our goals. Another said, "Love Dr. DeCarlo's leadership style! He involves the entire staff. We have key employees in their best job locations, which is a must! We discuss goals, plans for the future and the road ways to obtaining is reviewed. Then each of us is allowed the freedom to reach for the stars without constant supervision. Another said, "Dr. DeCarlo is not a micro-manager. He is always encouraging us to do our best. He trusts us." Another said, "Dr. DeCarlo trusts our decision making, we discuss many things and continually keep contact on the office pulse. He is a leader with definite ideas but he always listens to us.

"We are reaching our goals, receiving larger bonuses, doing more cases and having more time off with pay. Our goals? "Taking our practice into the next 10 plus years and improve." Opportunities? "I see a lot of people for bleaching—many times they end up doing veneers and ask a lot of questions, using the right approach, they will do a lot of work." Another said, "I like to keep informed even though I am in hygiene. I need to know where we are in the current working numbers—all of us are involved in the office goals! I can always contribute the numbers by my relationship with the patients. I am always working toward providing our patients the best information on their dental futures, keeping them involved in what we do and how well we do it!"

## Team Ziegele
Helen, hygiene—Jen, assistant—Anne, coodinator

Describing the Ziegele practice, Helen said, "I feel like I have a stake in this practice, it isn't all about making money for the doctor. It makes it more fun and certainly more interesting for me." Jen said, "I understand how the bills get paid and how things get done, so I'm more willing to do things at the end of the day—Dr. Ziegele is also willing to see our side, won't abuse our time and gets us out on time."

Helen noticed in taking the Blatchford program, "April is more focused and very determined to be the best. We have goals so we aren't coming in every day and just hoping things work out." Anne said, "I think she is more focused. I think she's more willing to take risks—marketing, trimming staff, etc. The vision is clear enough to take risks within the parameters."

Playing their 'A' Game "feels great because of emphasis on cross-working. Everyone picks up the slack and looks for the slack without being asked. This includes Dr. Ziegele—she'll clean our rooms or run instruments, too," says Helen. Jen and Anne agree. "There is high energy and enthusiasm with lots of laughs. Our schedule is full, everyone is busy and having fun."

The team thinks Dr. Ziegele's coaching is "very clear in what she wants, and then she trusts us to do it. It doesn't have to be her words or Blatchford words but gives us the freedom to make it work for us. I feel comfortable being able to do what I know she wants me to do. I do not have someone looking over my shoulder and criticizing me," said Helen. Anne importantly said, "she does not micro-manage us." "I feel like she keeps us all on the same page, we are all thinking towards the same goal. She makes sure she is always 'up' so we are pulled 'up,' too. That's the hard part about being a leader," said Jen.

Anne said "everyone is treated equally, regardless of first impressions. We are all trained in all aspects of office and cross-trained. We all take a lot of advanced education too so we're ready for anything that comes our way. We absolutely review our great days and go over how to make them even better. We have also learned not every day is perfect and that's OK, too. Block Booking has taught me I would rather not have her busy with a lot of junk which may be hard to collect. Instead, we work on our skills. That way, I've got a spot for big work I can soon utilize. It's not as scary anymore because I know there's something right around the corner." Helen said, "We role-play to keep our communication skills sharp. We do this every week and even videotape a lot. In our evening meeting, we acknowledge what each other did right—give high fives to each other in evening and morning after huddle like—Way to go, Team. Let's go!" Jen said, "We practice our patient interaction skills to make sure we're ready for every patient who walks in the door."

Their biggest challenge for Anne is, "learning how to shut off the outside world and just be here, to be present, in the moment." Jen said her challenge is "reading the required sales/marketing books for every week book club. Know that people called us for a reason—it's OK to talk to them about what they want and to follow up with them."

Anne said, "I check and monitor numbers every day—that's basically my job! I make sure our schedule is maximized our collections are doing well. We all know our numbers and how we can change them, what we have to do for the bonuses we want, where we are on the bonus at any given time."

## Dr. Lori Kemmet
JaneAnn Engel

I was 14 years old when I started in dentistry. I had the glamorous job of cleaning the office of our family dentist. That was back in the days of spit bowls and motor driven drills; when dentistry was all about the dentist and not the patient.

Throughout my high school years, I progressed to file clerk and receptionist, and eventually trained as a chairside assistant.

After majoring in Fine Arts and living in Oregon, a state that was hard hit by the recession, I moved to Colorado. I found it easy to fall back on my dental skills and soon became employed by a periodontist and later a pedodontist. While I enjoyed these occupations, I found I needed to satisfy my creative and artistic urges and embarked on my graphic design career for the better part of 14 years.

Life has a funny way of being cyclical and I found myself relocating again, this time as a single parent. After being away from dentistry for over 14 years, I answered a calling to return to dentistry. At this point in my life (I was now in my early 40's) my wisdom and maturity led me to seek out a dentist who I shared a common vision with— someone who was progressive, a master at what they did and saw the future of dentistry as an amazing journey of growth. That someone was Dr. Lori Ann Kemmet.

Dentistry in the past was all about the dentist. There was no room for career growth, no room for new ideas, and no room for a future. In other words, no leadership. Today, dentistry is all about the guest in the practice.

At Incredible Smiles™, the office of Dr. Lori Kemmet, I have an exciting future in dentistry. Dr. Kemmet has shared her vision and goals for the future with her team, empowering them to think bigger, think outside of the box, and to help shape the future of dentistry.

At the time I began working with Dr. Kemmet, she was beginning her coaching program with Blatchford. As a team, we witnessed firsthand the growth and potential for change that existed within the practice. Dr. Kemmet was bold in striving toward her goal of becoming the very best dental practice. She has shared that ride with her team, learning and implementing the sound strategies of the Blatchford program.

Our teams 'A' game is awesome! We have an incredible staff that shares a common vision and we try to make each day better than the day before. We communicate often by beginning and ending each day with a 20 minute "huddle," meet as a staff for one hour at lunch once each week and again for three hours every other month. We share in a bonus system based on production and collection. It encourages each team member to have an active role in the production and growth of the practice. We are all compensated like part-owners. We strive to exceed the expectation of each and every guest and deliver five-star customer service at all times. We are currently working together on developing systems for all areas of our office to better exceed the needs of our guests, to increase production, decrease time spent in the office, which creates more time spent with our families, and improve the flow of the day.

We review each day by discussing what worked, what didn't work, areas of concern and what did we implement today that can be carried over to tomorrow.

What keeps me in the game is the challenge and satisfaction of striving to be the very best. I look forward one day to coaching other offices in the Incredible Smiles™ way.

I am a lifetime student and have completed many courses and seminars in an effort to grow, change and remain open to new possibilities.

The most important thing I do every day is provide outstanding customer service to each and every guest. As Howard Schultz, CEO of Starbucks said, "The key is heart. If you pour your heart into your work, or into any worthy enterprise, you can achieve dreams others may think impossible.

## Dr. Michael Reece
Sherran Strong Bard

"Several stories can be told by all of us about patients that will always be remembered. We had a young lady come in for a consultation about 11:30 one morning. She was so petite, she looked about 13 years old. In the interview, she revealed she was a senior at Texas A & M University, about to graduate. Her enamel was completely gone from the linguals of her teeth. She, however had noticed her incisal edges were not as straight as they were in high school. About to have senior photos made, what could be done?

It was rapidly approaching lunchtime and we all know how important that is. There was just something about this young lady. I told Dr. Reece to go ahead to lunch while I finished the financials and scheduling. Alone together, when I asked her if she had an eating disorder. She started crying and so did I. "How did you know?" she asked. I explained her teeth told on her. She admitted she knew and was in treatment.

I told the young lady the fee to restore her teeth was approximately $20,000. She did the obvious, cried again and so did I. She only had $3,000 in her education account and was hoping to restore her smile with that. So, I told her to go home and pray about it and I would be in touch. I called a patient who is also a child therapist to discuss this condition and treatment. The therapist said, "Ask her to see me. I'll do this at no charge and let you know if she is or isn't in treatment and how she is doing."

I called the young lady and she agreed. She was doing fine and had experienced a terribly abusive childhood. She had decided to be a lab tech and was about to apply to Baylor to start the process. I talked to Dr. Reece; he volunteered his time to do this case and I volunteered my time. We worked on our day off. I called the lab and they donated the case at no charge. We did her veneers and placed them for $3,000. She wanted to contribute to the case. The day we finished her case, she left to go eat ice cream. She had such sensitive teeth, she hadn't eaten it in so long.

The young lady was so inspired by the result and the fact we used our resources to help her, she applied to medical school and was accepted. Baylor, no doubt. She still comes here to visit when she speaks to graduate students. Her life was restored, her confidence in humanity restored and her faith that there are still good people in this world was the real story.

This is a life-changing thing we do, not just fix teeth.

## Strong Doctor, strong staff
Keri Weron, patient coordinator with Dr. Bob Knupp

"I was working endless hours in retail with Loreen Knupp. After much of my complaining, she suggested her father needed a receptionist working normal hours. Now, he and I are a real team. He leads by example. We motivate each other and are the driving force in the office.

We are still working on finding the right team composition. We have some staff changes which will help us get there. We want to work with people who all want the same thing. We want to BE PRESENT and remember who is the most important thing happening right now. We have discovered many dental staffs do not want to learn to sell a better way. They want to stay stuck in talking about NEED and pathology rather than wants. It won't get the job done. To develop relationship and trust with our guests, it takes every team member participating full out. We are still working on this.

Our focus is to help people get what they want, make them feel comfortable; ask questions to discover what they truly want. "I've had great responses when I tell people, 'this is not about us; this is about you and what you want.' Most people are not prepared for this in dentistry."

Keri's perfect sequence in the Knupp practice? Receiving a phone call connect from the Internet where they selected us over other Northshore websites. We ask questions. We tell him that this is about him, we will help him get there but he has to give us directions, just like a car. We tell him to look at other people's smiles, find out what he likes and dislikes.

When he arrives, we talk and find out he hates his teeth, won't smile, is getting married in August and his mother wants him to have a new smile as a wedding gift. He feels he could sell anything if he just felt comfortable about his smile.

The office is quiet with just three staff. Start at 8:00 and complete at 1:00 PM. Everyone is excited, including our patient. We let him look and he is STUNNED. He cannot contain a laugh as he can't believe this is his mouth. His eyes get red and watery (he is not alone) and he just laughs. He stumbles over 'thank you' and we respond, 'thank you for letting us be a part of this.' We walk out on a high. It is the greatest. Days like this keep me going.

Blatchford Coaching has added much to our office and my personal life. You have made me realize everything in life is a choice; my choice. In the past, I have allowed others to make me angry (again, my choice).

Dr. Knupp is an accomplished wildlife photographer. He is now applying his skills to patient glamour shots after a photography course with Dr. Rhys Spoor.

## Dr. Mike Kellner's team

Dr. Kellner's leadership is described as, "respect, enthusiasm, accepting of constructive criticism and delegating. Their 'A' Game is "total booking with one procedure in the morning, a new patient consult in the afternoon along with several smaller procedures.

Communication in our morning meeting, the previous day is reviewed (good or bad). We always give 150%. That's our motto. What keeps us in the game is relationship in the office. We are there for each other and willing to accept mistakes made. There is no one who is perfect in the world and encouragement is the key! The biggest challenge is mimicking a perfect block booking day.

Being the office manager, on a daily basis, I calculate the bonus structure for the team and throughout the day, letting everyone know the numbers. What a movitator!!! We all affect the numbers as a consultation is a team effort, from initial greeting to reviewing financial arrangements and discussing their dreams. Everyone in the office is involved and willing to do whatever it takes to make our guests happy."

## Dr. John Kelly
Kat Ganshirt, hygiene

"I chose to work with Dr. Kelly because it was a small office; I felt was on the verge of exciting changes. My first day, I participated in a Blatchford seminar which was very different from any other management seminar I had attended. It has helped our office in many ways but I feel it personally helped me with the way I listen and speak with patients. I have become a better communicator. I think the most important thing I do is to help people realize their desires for their health and smiles.

Our team has found having goals keeps us motivated and we can all affect change in those numbers. We are able to measure how well we are performing by monitoring closely our production, collection and acceptance rate."

## Dr. Rhys Spoor
Jamie Purnell, RDA

"I've been in dentistry for almost 20 years; it was strictly by accident that I found dentistry. In my junior year of high school, I signed up to take a Health Occupations class for my senior year and over the summer my instructor for the class called me and wanted to know if I was interested in a summer job, hence my very first Dental Office. I was the sterilization assistant and only worked part time. It's really a wonder I stayed in dentistry for so long because the very first thing I was shown how to do was clean the traps. But I survived that and came to really enjoy my work, especially once I started working with patients. I was very fortunate over my years in dentistry and (most of the time) worked with great doctors who took great pride in their careers. I changed offices only through relocating with my family and after each of my children were born.

I came to truly appreciate and enjoy the esthetic side of dentistry and was drawn to those practices. In 1995, I was working for a doctor with a desire to take his practice to the next level and we signed up for coaching with Dr. Bill Blatchford... little did I realize this would be an opportunity where I would change how I myself viewed dentistry and my own place in it. I became refreshed and discovered a new passion for my career.

I feel so fortunate to be a part of my current practice. I chose my doctor based on his reputation for excellence and his passion for esthetics. I share his passion and knew we would be a good match.

After so many years in dentistry, you can really tell the difference between the doctors who are driven and strive for excellence, who enjoy challenging themselves and those who just are happy to go from day to day the same way they have always done. I have seen many different leadership styles and can tell you from a team member standpoint, there are is a night and day difference between the doctors who have a clear vision for their practice and can empower their team to the point where they become the practice's biggest advocate. Others resent having to pay your salary, let alone offering any kind of incentive or bonus and who really never get the big picture.

What I have seen in practices being coached by Dr. Blatchford is there is a strong feeling of team and a new found sense of purpose with which business is operated on a daily basis. Creating a clear practice vision and creating an environment where each team member is valued for their contributions is key.

As with any kind of transition it's not without its growing pains, but it is through these growing pains that the true team spirit is created; you grow together. That's how you find out who on the team is committed and who is a weak link. I've seen doctors struggle with a single team member they really like but who just doesn't share the vision, or have any desire to change the way they do their job. It's these people who create tension and negative energy and can ultimately doom the success of the practice. My advice to any employer is to find people with the right can-do attitude, everything else can be taught.

Once you have the right team... Now is the time to rock & roll. What works to motivate people? In my opinion when everyone feels they are valued and appreciated, that's when you can create synergy. It all starts with small compliments whenever possible then empowering team members to make decisions on their own that contribute to the practice vision. These are the leadership skills that get results.

When everyone knows the goal and is motivated to reach it... look out! Great things can happen. It becomes like a dance, each team member knows their role and knows the roles of the others on the team so they can support one another. In my current practice, we are always on the lookout for what the other person is doing so we can contribute to their success. It's the most important thing we do every day. Also we can rely on the fact that each person knows their role well and whenever possible, we share our enthusiasm with the skill of our co-workers and our patients. This serves two purposes...

1. It makes your team members feel good to hear you complimenting them in front of patients.

2. It shows the patient how much respect and admiration we have for each other as well as the doctor. This creates trust with the patient and a feel good environment for everyone.

Example: Maria who greets all our patients both on the phone and when they first come in the office is always saying to patients about me, "Wait until you meet Jamie, she is the best! She is the doctor's assistant and she is going to take such good care of you!"

Example: We keep a very full schedule, (accommodating everyone is our biggest challenge in the office) and there are often times when we will slip in a consult and if they are ready to go, we don't wait and reschedule them for records, we do it right then... It's not at all convenient and it's more work, but I do it happily because I know it is key in the success of the practice, (this is an example of where my ability to effect change in the profitability of the office comes in. If Maria did not feel like she was supported in trying to get people going when they were hot and ready to go, it would surely effect our teamwork and profitability)

Each of us on the team have our areas of specialization, strengths and weaknesses but we all pitch in wherever we are needed. Recognizing the strengths of each person and using them to their fullest is a must.

Personally I'm motivated by knowing I'm part of an exceptional team; I appreciate the caliber and excellence of my doctor and co-workers. While that is a true statement and from the heart, I have to be honest and say that where my heart is really is with my family, especially my two young boys. What I am motivated by most is my time off and having flexibility to choose my vacation times around them. Let's face it, what we all crave most is balance in our lives between work and family. Knowing I have a career that values my contributions, pays me well with opportunity for growth in that department and also allows me vacation time to be there for my family is absolutely priceless. For this, you will get the very best I have to offer. I will be on time, dependable and committed!"

Sincerely, Jamie Purnell

www.yourcomfortsolutions.com

## Blatchford Game Plan: No Telling In Selling

The winning teams are skilled in people conversations. They know the bigger picture and build trust with guests by asking questions and really listening. They know the 80/20 rule applies to successful sales in that you want your guest talking about their dreams and ideas 80% of the time.

Even quiet dentists and their staffs seem to talk too much during the sales process. Our four years of dental school and many continuing education courses have given us enough technical fuel to share your excitement and your plans for their mouth. You bore your patients and it is a fluke if someone says 'yes' to more than a broken tooth.

The sales portion of dentistry is when trust is built and relationships are formed. L.D. Pankey said "Know yourself, know your patient." Too often this is interpreted as know their 28 teeth. Become acquainted with your established patients and especially new guests in a different manner. Because you know nothing about the standards, values and dreams of this new guest, create different systems so you can develop their important trust.

When we talk technical dentistry during the sales process, you have not shown them any effort on your part to be interested in them and their dreams. Because we make decisions permanently, instantly and emotionally, when you start talking about your ideas for their smile without even knowing them, this is an affront to people and generally, they decide to turn you off. You can physically see these signs when they cross their arms, eyes looking for an escape and nod their head like they understand or care of what you are speaking.

Consider the value of trust and relationships. How do you develop and maintain personal friendships? The same factors are important to have a successful business. Time or the perception of time is an important factor. Caring is the other.

Creating time in a busy dental office is a matter of perception.  If a new patient enters your office during a triple booked procedure with double hygiene going, where is the relaxed atmosphere we so desperately want?  Always schedule new guests in the morning when you are block booked and the office really is relaxed and elegant. Be a great host to offer coffee, teas, juice in a real cup with a real napkin. Attractively framed after pictures adorn your walls and reading material is hardback books on area history, industry, humor or foods.

Show time and caring are important by inviting your new friend into a separate consult room to share their thoughts and information. Avoid handing them a clipboard, sitting alone and completing boring material.  Make your forms short and do it with them.  Make it interesting.  A consult room should be a neutral site, one without an x-ray viewer, sample bridges which come apart or sharp instruments.  If it was once the Doctor's office, unload all the old magazines and dental items.

Your attitude and skill during these first ten minutes is to discover a new friend.  Your job is to connect with them at some level. Interestingly, they do not care a lot about your family, experiences or thoughts.  Focus on them.  People think you are a terrific friend when you ask questions about them, their thoughts and ideas.  Show you care by asking them questions and more questions.  Do not come up with solutions at this time as it is too early.  If they say, "I would like my teeth to look younger, my smile whiter"—a unfocused staff might say, "We could bleach them here or you could take it home."  That is a solution too quick.  Instead ask, "When did you first notice this?" "Tell me more about that?" "What have you tried so far?"

What you will find when you ask questions and show your caring, many people will warm to you and share much more then they had thought of initially.  Someone who initially inquiries about whitening could have thoughts of never liking their smile, being laughed at in junior high, not having a lot of teen age fun all based on their perception their teeth didn't look so great. All this still influences how they react to others. You will discover much about your new friend because they trust you.

The unskilled staff member above will possibly sell a bleach kit. The focused staff member who asked more and more questions with little or no dental tech talk may sell an unknown quantity of resulting satisfaction. Cut out the tech talk and ask THEM questions. It is a win/win.

Bill Blatchford, DDS

## From the Blatchford Play Book: Team Rules

>> Coach calls the game

>> Be on time. Lombardi time is 15 minutes ahead of regular time

>> Wear your uniform. Be proud, look your best and make your team look good

>> Prepare yourself mentally to play the game

>> Wear your game face proudly

>> Play full out as you never know which play will make the difference

>> Start your day with an effective morning huddle 15 minutes before your first play

>> Be accountable for your actions. If the ball comes to you and you miss it, create a plan for that not to occur again. Accept responsibility and move on

>> Do not hog the limelight. There are no stars on a winning team

>> Make your teammates look good. Give them credit all the time

>> Do not start derogatory or gossipy conversations about your coach, your team or the fans and do not listen to any team member who is the gossip. Instead, take them by the arm to share their "story" which the person who is the subject of their wrath. Bottom line, no trash-talking on the winning team.

>> Treat other staff how you want to be treated

>> Do not make anyone smaller than you

>> If there is a problem, go to the source

>> No whining. Instead, contribute positively and constructively. If you do not agree with something, think of a different plan and present it. Whining is a losing skill.

>> Never admit to anyone you are tired, angry or bored

>> Never carry a grudge. It is a waste of everyone's time

>> Include everyone on your team in communication and training

>> Holding "secrets" will destroy a team

>> Learn something new everyday. Read a sales or marketing book and apply it to your game.

>> As a team, donate skills and time once a month to community service—walking dogs at the animal shelter, serving homeless meals, adopting a single-parent family, etc.

>> Do volunteer dentistry in your community once a quarter. The whole team participates.

>> Either you have your reasons or your results

>> Be a team player 100%. During the game, you are focused. Home or relationship concerns are not part of your work conversations.

>> Do not consume food in the work areas

>> The winning players are those who think and know they can win.

>> Learn the most important skill in sales—listening.

# 12

## MANHATTAN PRACTICE

## Dr. Jay Neuhaus

Dr. Neuhaus grew up in the Lower East side of Manhattan, the grandson of Eastern European immigrants, the kind who worked hard, had high ideals and wanted to provide freedom for their children and grandchildren. As a child, Jay often saw the beautiful and quiet streets surrounding the only private and gated park in Manhattan. Gramercy Park is a neighborhood surrounded by stately brownstones, the National Arts Club, the Player's Club and the largest dwelling in Manhattan, the Sonnenberg Mansion.

This is where Jay practices and to him, it feels like a small town. "I have a small town practice in the middle of Manhattan." He knows his patients well and has generations of families and offers dentistry just like other areas. It is just located in the heart of one of the largest cities in the world. After grade school, high school, college and NYU Dental School in Manhattan, Jay spread his wings to do a GPR at Albert Einstein Medical College in the Bronx. Further, he worked in a general practice on Staten Island, yet he always remembered the quiet beauty of Gramercy Park.

Three years after dental school, at age 27, he found a practice through a brokering agency of NYU. A 65-year-old part-time pedo prof at NYU and full time general practitioner, Dr. Isadore Samuels was interested in selling his 35-year-old practice after a near-death experience in a car accident. Though told he would never walk again, he fully recovered and continued swimming a mile a day during his lunch hour. Dr. Samuels, "Iggy" as he is affectionately known, "was like a father to me. I had worked three months with him before purchasing and he continued to work with me for the next ten years."

The office is in the lobby of a six story residential apartment building and had three ops, a private office, reception area, two bathrooms and a lab in 1000 sq. ft. He was a solo practitioner with a full time hygienist and a full time assistant/receptionist "who actually smoked cigarettes while working! Boy, have times changed."

"What I liked best was he only practiced four days a week and had 1.5 hours for lunch to swim AND HE HAD NEVER EVEN HEARD OF BLATCHFORD! He took the summers off to pursue his photographic hobby and his hygienist and assistant kept the practice open and income coming in ('I'm not sure how kosher that was'). He was grossing $150K, paid $285 monthly rent, and was netting 60%. Dr. Samuels carried the note for my $75K purchase. Not a single patient was lost during the transition. Iggy also had a 'pied a tier' in the same building and I was able to take over that lease. I was on top of the world."

"When I first started practicing, I had no financial goals—BIG MISTAKE! I went wherever the practice led me. I did minor renovations and then remodeled to have four operatories and things moved along well for me but then I stagnated. Costs kept rising with rent presently $4K, increased staff to two assistants and 1.5 hygienists plus a receptionists and a part-time associate dentist, all in 1000 sq. ft. I couldn't seem to break out of $600K gross." He married a special gal, April, at age 31, bought his dream home in Scarsdale, had three wonderful children and expenses were increasing at a much greater pace then his practice. " I wanted to move to the next level, not quite sure what that next level was."

Lynda Miles said I had a $1M practice hidden in there but I still couldn't reach it. Then all hell broke loose. I had a receptionist who had worked for me for 15 years and I trusted her with my life. I would have done anything for her because of her seeming devotion to the practice. You guessed it—embezzlement. It was a kiting scheme whereby she would steal cash and then make up for it by fraudulently charging various dental patients' credit cards. When a patient noticed their erroneous credit card statement and would question it with my receptionist, she would make up some lame excuse to them, credit their account and charge someone else's card. After many long days and sleepless nights, I was able to figure out her scheme, had her arrested and charged with a felony and forced to make partial restitution. Believe it or not, today she is working for another dentist not too far away who knows the whole story. Will we ever learn?"

"This was the lowest point in my professional life. I was ready to throw it all in. I went to an evening at the Westchester Country Club to hear Bill Blatchford and really liked what he had to say. When I heard the price of the program—NO WAY! My wife April insisted it was worth it if it would restore my faith and happiness in dentistry. Not only did it accomplish that, it got me to that next level and beyond. It also brought me to another highlight which was getting involved with LVI and making photography a part of my practice. Dr. James Klim helped me put together a photo studio complete with studio lights, umbrellas and posing tables.

When we are playing our 'A' game, WATCH OUT! Everyone knows it. The patients become alive as well and they enjoy the experience even more. There's no stopping us. We believe in ourselves. We're performing at our peaks. We're selling ourselves, our skills and having patients think about what they can get and what they want through our skills. We're 'bragging' about how much we love what we do, how we love to refine and advance our skills through continuing education courses. We're all on a "high."

I started out knowing I would be successful; I had lots of self confidence. I started out as an electrical engineering major because I like to tinker and build things. I then switched to computers and when I knew I wanted dentistry, I graduated with a psychology degree (has that been helpful in understanding patients, staff, family, friends and myself) with a 3.9999 index (B in gym).

I am profitable because I was able to combine a tremendous increase in my net profit with a reduction of my hours and days at work, leaving me more quality time to spend living and sharing with my family. I was able to reduce my staff to three as well as eliminating all evening hours, and increasing everyone's time off with pay to nine weeks per year. We work 8 AM to 3 two days and 10 AM to 5 two days. Anyone can become profitable if they set their goals and have the coaching necessary to reach them. You don't have to reinvent the wheel. If it has worked for others, what makes you think it can't work for you?

I have built my practice through word of mouth and internal marketing. I am fair and respectful with my team and therefore several have been with me for twenty years. I speak to my patients on their level. I am not high and mighty but try to be trustworthy.

Pitfalls in my practice happen when I let my practice lead me rather then me lead it. I was too busy being a technician to realize the embezzlement was occurring. I always used to hire only experienced dental personnel, overlooking their communication and people skills. My latest team member is former flight attendant. I always thought somehow my staff could read my mind and realize what I wanted. How could they when I wasn't even sure where I was heading?

Starting Bill's program, my gross grew from $700K to $1.2M.

Collections went from 90% to over 100%. We do no billing. Everyone pays at least two days in advance of treatment. My overhead went from 70 to 60%. My staff went from five to three. I currently see 15-20 new patients a month.

I used to do one or two crowns at a time and many amalgam restorations. I thought I was flying to do a quadrant of amalgams and reached heaven when I could do a quadrant of indirects. I avoided posterior composite directs because I never believed they were strong enough. I was better at talking patients out of work then finding out what they really wanted.

I do ideal treatment plans ONLY and then will only do the ideal at whatever 'profitable' pace the patient wants. I no longer compromise on quality for bargain hunters. I have in progress right now five full mouth cases in patients that pay $60-$75K two days in advance before I even lift a hand piece. I am no longer afraid to lose patients who do not see my vision. I used to feel rejected but now I'm happy the non-profitable people are leaving on their own. Most of our patients stick with us and eventually do ideal work when the time is right for them, NOT FOR ME!

Since taking Blatchford, I have read many books on leadership and we have daily huddles at the beginning and end of the day. We have weekly one hour staff meetings and monthly four hour skill building sessions. I am constantly honing my leadership and communication skills. I used to be terrified to speak in front of a group. Now, I actually feel comfortable presenting a Power Point talk to groups of specialists.

My staff is motivated because they realize our goals cannot be met without their input. They feel needed. They see a direction. When they see me excited, they get excited. They are motivated by leadership.

I struggled with reducing my staff. They were loyal and had stuck it out with me for a long time. When I realized that one was not on the same vision bus as me, I had a very difficult time letting her know she needed to get on or off the bus. I toiled with the decision for a year—BIG MISTAKE! She finally got off the bus and six years later, we are still friends. Another major struggle for me was looking at our numbers rather then just going with the flow. Even when things were stagnant, I felt I could make a very good living. Bill coached me to make my practice flow in the direction I chose. I had to lead rather than follow. This was a rude awakening. There are actually choices out there. You can decide exactly how profitable you want to be. Becoming a leader rather than a technician was difficult for me.

Another struggle was financial arrangements and sending hundreds of statements monthly. We were bogged chasing insurance claims. Now we collect all fees at time of service (under $500). We have no accounts receivables and actually had two patients pay $60K in advance for treatment with us and yet, first had to see several specialists before I even touched a hand piece.

The other difficult decision I made which has paid off handsomely was to present ONLY what I considered the best cosmetic dentistry out there for our patients and then stuck to my guns and refused to compromise. Our profit margin shot up!!

I will be in semi-retirement in five years, still working two days a week. I want to be starting a full mouth case each week. I will be spending time producing a very successful television program called "Extreme Makeover—Oral Edition" which an individual's life is portrayed and how it changed dramatically with a makeover. I will have guest specialists. I will have the same team composite I have now but will be living in Florida commuting to New York on Tuesday AM and returning Wed night. I will be 3-4 times more profitable and working half the time. My staff will be earning over $100K each. I feel I met Bill too late in my career. If I had only known these things at the beginning of my career, the above would have happened at a much younger age. I do want to spend some good chair time as long as I can still convey my love of what I do best to my team and patients. I still want to get that satisfaction from giving my patients what they've always dreamt of.

Internally, we have brochures, welcome and thank you cards, newsletters, gifts for referring patients, birthday cards, Thanksgiving cards, freshly baked cookies, fresh juices, coffee, tea and water, aromatherapy, hot and cold refreshing facial towels, reflexology, limo pick-up and return for full day patients, boxes of 'Neuhaus' chocolates sent to work, wireless headphones and overhead video, paraffin wax hand treatments and making patients feel as welcome as a guest in our home.

Externally, we have never done anything except a website. One day a salesperson came to our office and, uncharacteristically, I listened. It was a coffee cup campaign in which my personalized cups would be used in local coffee shops, and coffee and donut carts in the neighborhood. I agreed with one condition—I wanted a free editorial written about my unique practice. The editor came to us for a cleaning and experienced all the spa treatments. He wrote a nice editorial in a local free newspaper. The spiral begins. A few months later, a freelance writer from the NY Times called and was doing an article on spa services in dental offices and how that was aiding in profitability. She read about me in the free local paper. The article appeared in the Sunday NY Times. I received a call from ABC Eyewitness News doing a segment on spa dentistry. Cameras were in my office and I got my first taste of television. Then a Korean television station jumped on the bandwagon and filmed a segment in my office. The initial cup campaign wasn't that great but it sure lead to other things.

No more going with the flow. I have just hired a PR firm for new logo, updating my website and new image. If I want to reach my five year plan, I will have to lead the way.

www.gramercydentalarts.com

*Dr. Jay Neuhaus*
*"Work smart and*
*relax hard."*

*On top of the world*
*with April.*

*PROFILE*

## Blatchford Game Plan: Cosmetics Anywhere?

Dr. Neuhaus has evolved into an elective practice. To achieve his dream, he relied on his general practice to brand himself, create trust and relationships and financial support. This put him in a better position to be more selective.

Many dentists live for cosmetics and reconstruction—the cosmetic home run which will make a huge monetary difference in their monthly bottom line. How tightly niched can you be in cosmetics and still make a living? Can it work in every area, as touted by some?

Consider cosmetic work is not covered by insurance. Good because it then becomes your patient's choice. Because cosmetics are not insurance driven, a certain sophistication of skills and mastery in psychology in sales is necessary to have a general dentistry patient say "yes" to treatment not covered by their insurance. If your practice is insurance driven; mentally you and your staff are tied to insurance fees and maximums, it is a real challenge for optional cosmetics to have a great impact in your practice. If your staff knows each patient's insurance coverage by heart, it is an indicator insurance is the air in your office. It would be rare for a ten veneer case to happen in this practice, even if the Doctor and team are highly clinically trained.

Because cosmetic and largely reconstructive work is non-insurance (in a $40,000 estimate, how much will be covered by their insurance?), mastering sales skills by each staff member, not just the Doctor, will make or break your cosmetic acceptance. Unless sales are studied, mastered and applied with excellent open-ended questions asked with your patients dreaming into their future, the conversation will likely go the deep hole "technical route" of NEED and the patient will ask, "Why should I do this?" "Will my insurance cover this?" "Oh, no, I don't think so." "I am not interested." The cosmetically trained dentist thinks, "no one in my town is interested in cosmetics but I love learning."

Learning just the clinical techniques of cosmetics will not result in cases accepted. Study relationships, build trust, psychology and discover why sales is a never ending process with every team member involved. Cosmetic success takes a paradigm shift for each team member.

Study the composition of your drawing area. Though we want to democratically make cosmetics available to everyone, there are some sets of people who are much more interested and can dream their dreams more easily with some "wiggle room" money. If your small area is the home to trust funders and wealthy transients, it may work for a tightly niched cosmetic and reconstructive dentist without general dentistry or even a hygiene program.

If, on the other hand, your smaller area is composed of solid blue collar citizens depending upon an annual harvest or the shaky continuation of the foundry for their living, your approach to cosmetics may come from their dream of saving their own teeth, not having teeth that come out at night and having teeth that work. To market strictly "cosmetics" may not work well. There is no "wiggle room" for these folks and they believe in longevity and value for their dollar. This practice will be successful with a solid general dentistry base and skills that offer value and longevity. An occasional home run will occur.

Dr. Brian Saby of Red Deer, Alberta, concurs. An accredited member of AACD, Brian had externally marketed, focusing on cosmetics. He discovered potential patients perceived cosmetics was all he did. Since the majority of his cosmetic work comes from regular patients who have been shown the possibilities, he changed the focus in his ads to attract the average patient.

What may work well is for the dentist to learn technical skills others may not be offering in the area, like automated endo, implant dentistry or cosmetic dentures.

Numbers and skill come into play. Cosmetic acceptance usually has a longer acceptance time. Thus there are huge oscillations in the income stream from month to month. Dr. Rhys Spoor of Seattle advises, "Cosmetics will naturally occur in a happy general practice. Pick the easy ones and feel great, referrals will come. Leave the hard ones for the dentists equipped to handle this and all the headaches which can result." Can you do cosmetics anywhere? Yes, but if that is exclusive, you may only work two days a month! Cosmetics anywhere? Yes and usually with a solid general dentistry base. Study your demographics before you niche your practice too tight. Make cosmetics a part of what you offer mixed with other services.

Bill Blatchford, DDS

## From the Blatchford Play Book

Leaders work with the team to discover why there was success or if we failed, how can we create systems or conversations to not repeat that mistake. Dr. Neuhaus in Manhattan feels he has a community practice. He is not anonymous in a big city and learning from successes and failures keeps a winning team moving forward.

### Post Game

>> Create phone skills, a tag line and message that set you apart. It is your first opportunity to impress. Be bold, be different

>> Cross train each team member including the Doctor. Learn to answer the phone, make firm financial arrangements, have meaningful conversations about patient dreams, clean a room, run a day sheet, sharpen instruments, make appointments and operate the computer.

>> Practice introducing guests to staff members, sharing what you have learned and making your guests feel special.

>> Analyze plays which have not worked in your office. Make changes, build skills and reconstruct confidence to move forward

>> When you have had a great game, replay it. What worked? Why did it work? How can we do it again?

>> Analyze the time factor of how long a guest takes to build a relationship of trust, moving to acceptance

# 13

## REINVENTION

## Dr. Zach Hodgins

A bright, people-person, young Zach Hodgins has experienced much in his short dental life. He has associated with a great dentist, worked the PPO/HMO route then purchased a run-down insurance driven practice and completely transformed it. All this has made him a better person and a better dentist. He feels his greatest successes have been his interaction with guests and the lives he has been able to touch. Does Zach have all the right stuff, or what?

Originally, he thought he would be a biochemist and design drugs to fight disease, cure cancer or even male pattern baldness. Earning a biochemical degree at U. of Virginia, Zach did some research projects involving the interaction between zinc, DNA and RNA. Though interesting, Zach felt he would be laboring long and hard with little interaction from anyone "on the outside." He could not see himself surrounded by people who knew a whole bunch about very little. He knew he needed something different.

Visiting several dental offices, he could see dentistry fulfilled his entrepreneurial spirit, his love of science and his desire to create and maintain relationships. A minor blip was a mistake made by the Florida State Board of Dental Examiners which caused him to "fail" the State Board by .007. Later, after examinations by an expert witness, several of his grades were inadvertently omitted thus causing the "failure." Four months later, the license was reinstated. Money wise, Zach had a partial scholarship to U. of Virginia and worked as well. In dental school at U. of Florida, Zach worked in research in oral biology and graduated with about $100K in student loans.

His one year associateship with Dr. Charles Martin of Tampa was a highlight. Dr. Martin initially was looking for a partner. He shared his dental experiences in Las Vegas and even coached Zach through his first veneer case. "He turned me on to LVI and for that I will be forever grateful."

Then, for six months, Zach saw 30-40 patients a day working in an HMO/PPO dental clinic with a take-home of about $175K. He found a practice ten minutes from his home which had grossed $320K in 2002.

The purchase was an emotional decision, as all decisions are. It was in Winter Park, close to his parents in Orlando. Winter Park has 100 year-old oak trees lining the streets, is quaint with beautiful parks and lakes which is completely different than the rest of Central Florida. And best of all, Winter Park is a very affluent suburb of Orlando where people want the best and can afford it. Golden Proportions Marketing confirmed to Zach that Winter Park would be a great place to practice. And Zach did not want to continue to be an HMO/PPO dentist.

The practice was on a busy intersection, second floor. Zach even visited several days and "the schedule was jammed with good stuff." Emotionally, he was ready and for $229K, the practice was his.

When Zach actually took the practice over, he realized it was an old, rundown family practice. Equipment was ancient, facility was dingy and "the dentistry was less than stellar." To say the practice took insurance was an understatement. "If there was a discount fee plan/PPO out there, they took it and so did I because I wanted to keep as many patients as possible."

He discovered the gross of $320K was using fees they would like to have collected, not the PPO fees of actual collection. The practice actually belonged to 25 different plans and 85-90% of collections came from PPO's, plus discounts to friends and colleagues of the former dentist.

During this transition, Zach was referred to Blatchford by Dr. Rhys Spoor, an instructor at LVI. Zach had confidence he could turn it around and produce more income than the seller. Dr. Hodgins has done well in building a general practice, attracting larger cosmetic cases and learning sales skills in thinking on the emotional side of the brain. At this time, he is down to three PPO's which represent about 35% of his collections. He does all this with one full time assistant, a reduced-hours receptionist and two hygienists two days a week.

Dr. Hodgins feels Blatchford Coaching has helped in instilling leadership, better communication with team, case presentation skills, books to read, encouragement to "stay the course," and the whole encompassing effect.

In 2004, his collections had grown from $320K to $785K. His lab expense is 11% which means he is selling a healthy amount of crown and bridge. He is spending between 10-12% for marketing and it was this marketing which caused notice for a known facial plastic surgeon to ask Zach to join him in a spa complex in a more upscale area of Winter Park. He is thinking seriously of this half-hour move, taking his existing patients with him.

A downer for Zach during his growth was discovering his very reliable, always able receptionist had committed insurance fraud by submitting claims for work on her family members who were never seen by Dr. Hodgins. Zach checks numbers carefully and found credit balances in A/R; this was the tipoff. He called to confront, changed the locks, excused her from the team, police investigated, she repaid money to insurance companies and no charges were pressed.

Zach's marketing includes an endorsed radio spot of two radio personalities who had their teeth whitened.  They speak highly of their experience, how others react to their smile and invite listeners to do the same.  Cost is $325 per spot or about $3K a month.  Zach wanted to showcase his veneers but whitening was the choice and the radio continues to do well for him.

Many areas of Florida experience "the season" when snowbirds live from November through May with the heaviest months being January through April.  Zach is building a larger general dentistry base to count on during the lean summer months.  He is attracting, through external marketing, a fair number of cosmetic and reconstructive cases who then ask, "can I send my family to you?  Do you do general dentistry, too?"

He is rethinking his ads and website of www.dentiststudio.com.  He sees he could be too tightly niched into cosmetics.  He has added implants through the Misch Institute and will have his IV sedation license in December. He enjoys dentures and does two to four a month at his current fee of $6K.  His goal is to be a "one stop shop."

www.dentiststudio.com

*Newlyweds Zach and Brittany Hodgins are pictured during dinner at Four Seasons Resort on Peninsula Papagayo in Costa Rica. They are about to enjoy fresh tuna and wahoo caught earlier in the day while deep sea fishing.*

## Blatchford Game Plan:
## Reinventing Your Practice with Double the Results

When Dr. Hodgins purchased his practice in a dream location and discovered the true nature of his purchase, he had the opportunity to reinvent the practice. What does he want it to be in 20 years? Who does he want to be attracting? With Dr. Blatchford's help, he moved from Point A to Point B and is doing very well, thank you.

What if your business burned down and you had the opportunity to reinvent it? Knowing what you know now, is there anything you're doing now that you wouldn't get into? Are there any relationships you would avoid?

Answers change but questions don't change. Therefore today, 70% of our past decisions have been wrong or below standard. There is a story of Albert Einstein, while teaching physics at Princeton, a student noticed the questions on the physics test were the same as last year. When confronted with this, Einstein said, "Yes, the questions are the same, but the answers are different."

We must be masters of change, demonstrating great flexibility. What it takes to successfully reinvent your business is intense future orientation. You must develop clarity for a five-year fantasy. With clarity, you increase the likelihood it will come true. Make a dream list. We must be strong in where we are going and flexible in the how. The future only matters, not the past. "You cannot jump across a canyon in two jumps." In other words, it is not possible to hang onto the past while looking to the future.

Any investment takes time, money and emotion. To achieve the fantasy, we must differentiate between facts and problems. Facts cannot change but problems can be solved. Focus on which are the most important solvable problems. How will you solve them to reinvent your practice?

Most major changes should have been made sooner. In other

words, we have known of the problems in our practice for a while but failed to focus and make the appropriate decisions to create a different result. Andrew Grove, former President of Intel Corporation, said change should be done about a year before it is. To reinvent your practice in the next five years, decisions need to be made now.

Tracy had been selected to speak with over 100 graduates of Blatchford Coaching. We requested Mr. Tracy orient his remarks specifically to dentistry and presenting larger, optional treatment. Tracy created an electric presence, as his talk was so meaningful.

He said the three functions of an executive (you, the dentist) are to innovate and market, set and achieve goals, perform and get results. Results are everything. Set a goal to double your net income next year. You must be clear about the goal and flexible in the process.

To be the best, you must want to be the best. You must first have the desire to be the best. Average will no longer do. To achieve your goals of doubling your net income, ask yourself, the following:

- What business am I in? What business should I be in? What business could I be in?
- Who is my client? Today, tomorrow, who should be my client? Who could be my client?
- What does my client consider valuable? To feel better, to be happy?
- What do I do especially well? Today? Could? What should I be doing well?
- What are the constraints on doubling my income?

Tracy oriented his remarks to dentists who want to be in the top tier of dentistry. These dentists not only want to be the best, they want to be recognized as the best. The perception of quality is directly related to profitability. Everything counts and in creating the perception of quality, 20% is service and 80% is in the way that service is delivered. In other words, dentists can be excellent clinicians but the patient's perception of your clinical quality is based more on the delivery of that excellent service by you and your staff.

What is stopping you from doubling your net income next year? Obviously, increasing revenue and decreasing expenses is an answer but the focused use of our time makes a greater difference. Everyone believes his or her dance card is full. If we could change 10-20% of what we are doing, it can achieve an increase of 80-90% of profits. What should I discontinue doing? Stop doing things that others could do better.

Most dentists and staffs are on "task overload." We do things because "we've always done them this way." We fail to look outside the box to examine what is most important and how we could do it more efficiently.

Tracy said to fire "clients from hell" and focus on positive people. If a patient's visit doesn't go well, they tell 13 others. If it is good, they tell five people. Since everything counts and nothing is neutral, we must work to position our practice and ourselves in the marketplace. Think of a grid (series of squares) in the mind of your patient or potential patient. One of those boxes is you. What is in your box? What they see is what they think of you. What are they thinking and saying about you? What words would you choose to have them thinking or talking about you? How can we do more things to create this impression? Your customer's perception is the only thing that counts and it can be created either by design or by accident.

Everything counts and it takes continual mental preparation of each event. Keep asking yourself, what else? What else? When modest and humble Wayne Gretzky retired, he was asked to share the secret of his success. He said, "Maybe what separated me is that I had passion for the game," he said. "Secondly, I was dedicated to it. I prepared for every game and I always felt like I hadn't done enough. If I had three goals I wanted to get five goals. If I had seven points, I wanted to get eight. I approached each game as if it was a Stanley Cup game."

In sales, think of yourself as a consultant and partner to the patient. Ask good questions and listen. Make recommendations by including the patient, like "What WE should do next is"... "Our next step is...." Working as a partner and including the patient create urgency. Listening builds trust, which constitutes 40% of the sales process. Listen attentively, pause before replying, question for clarification ("how do you mean?") and give feedback by paraphrasing in your own words.

Bill Blatchford, DDS

## From the Blatchford Play Book:
## Keep On Keeping On

When the reality of his purchase hit Zach, he knew he needed to reinvent his practice from PPO's to elective dentistry. He kept on. His persistence paid off emotionally and financially.

>> You do not know which is the winning play of the day so play full out all the time

>> As Winston Churchill said, "Never, never, never give up."

>> Praise, monetary bonus, recognition make a huge difference in moving forward

>> Any change in practice environment improves productivity according to the Hawthorne Study. Reupholster the furniture, paint the walls, new pictures all gain the team's attention.

>> Keep reading a new book, CD, every week

>> Don't quit until you've accomplished your goal

>> Face each problem, solve it and move on.

>> Each roadblock makes you a stronger person

>> Keep knocking on the door of opportunity

>> A man is never beaten until he thinks he is

>> Life is a grindstone. What you're made of determines if it will grind you down or polish you up.

# 14

## MANY LESSONS

## Dr. Brian Saby

Dr. Saby of Red Deer, Alberta at 47 years old, is totally free of debt and has the ability to retire. His only material inheritance was room and board for first year of undergraduate school. Brian loves dentistry and wants to continue to play the game. How did he arrive at the magic juncture of retirement choices? He has tremendous focus, has learned and implemented many valuable lessons and always carries the bigger picture of excellence.

Red Deer is a small blue collar town near the Alberta oil patch. Pickups with gun racks, dogs and cattle are the norm. Yet, Brian is an early accredited member of AACD and has offered cosmetic excellence in Red Deer, an insurance driven community in a country with national health care. Brian feels the four things that made the greatest impact in his career are:

- Hiring Bill Blatchford as my mentor and coach on dental business. With goal setting on financial management, "I set up retirement planning and stuck to the goal. I also knew I wanted to practice independently and as my parents were school teachers, Bill was my mentor as a leader, owner and entrepreneur."

- In the early '80's, taking Pankey Continuums offering

philosophy which changed his life. "I aspired to provide excellent comprehensive treatment. I aspired to perfection."

- Becoming the first accredited member of American Academy of Cosmetic Dentistry in Alberta and becoming an AACD examiner. This experience has "taught me how to self judge my work and set me up to be a leader in the field of cosmetic dentistry."

- Founding member of Alberta Implant Seminars which has met monthly with the leader being my prosthodontic classmate wanting to expand his implant placement service by teaching general dentists to restore dental implants. This has put me on the cutting edge of implant prostho and we have even developed some innovative restorative protocols that are now becoming mainstream.

To totally retire all debt, Brian and his fun wife, Linda, created a practice and home budget and stuck to it. Brian's comment, "A budget is not a penalty. If you find you cannot live within your budget, either reduce your discretionary spending or raise your budget. Often a budget is set that is unrealistic and it becomes a habit to go over budget."

Another quality that makes Brian different is his dogged determination. "Once I set a true goal, I will do whatever to complete the goal. I do not mind being uncomfortable. I will happily wait for the payoff rather then expecting the reward first. In problem solving, I am more willing to try an innovative approach to achieve a result. Failure is OK as long as I learn from it."

At 15 years, Brian observed the lifestyle of the local dentist. Brian graduated high school a semester early (Brian says "a snot-nosed 5'2" 17-year-old") and did physical labor in the summers and Christmas to graduate with a dental degree at 23 and only $30K in debt. After a one year ski area dental associateship, he wanted a more active social life. Near Red Deer, a dentist had a satellite practice in Sylvan Lake.

Brian looks back at how immature he was (he was exactly the kind of guy he cannot stand now). Brian became the owner in 1983 for $180K, just as the wheels fell off the Alberta economy....remember the gas lines in 1982-3?

He was the only dentist in Sylvan Lake, a bedroom community of Red Deer. The shock was, unlike an associateship, Brian was now accountable for his actions and results. He was working five days a week, every other Saturday and some evenings with three weeks vacation a year.

During the Quest* program, Brian decided to:
- Become the best technical dentist in central Alberta
- Have a successful and profitable practice
- Work four days a week, take lots of vacation with no change in bottom line
- Do whatever it took to achieve 1, 2 and 3.

Brian decided to move to Red Deer with 40 dentists and 15 miles away. He learned patients like to 'shop up' and he felt Red Deer was the answer. His Sylvan Lake patients moved with him and he paid the Sylvan Lake rent to keep another dentist from starting.

Shortly, Brian purchased 1000 charts for $6K from a faltering Red Deer practice and about half the patients were able to be converted into some of today's best patients. Several years later, he was able to buy another 1000 patients from another dentist in demise with a great return. Concurrently, Brian was gearing up with good continuing education of Pankey Institute and started the AACD accreditation process.

Brian had a period of 'the staff is the enemy' and learned some valuable lessons. He was running the practice by consensus and thinking the staff were friends and 'sounding boards.' He saw them as 'partners.' A fairly traumatic event of a dental friend's suicide over a sexual harassment issue had Brian rethinking his role as leader. "I

* Started by Bill Blatchford in Canada

know now that my employees are employees. They will do what is best for them. I make the decisions in the office, they perform to the standards I set, or they are gone."

Lessons Brian has learned about staffing is the leader must know what you are looking for in a staff member. Look for your dream employee. Brian wisely has learned, "People do not change much. I have learned I do not have the time or inclination to be a personal growth center. If you find you selected the wrong person, don't waste time or effort in trying to train a duck to be a swan. Sell the duck and buy a new swan."

Another lesson from Brian is to be a successful leader, you need to make decisions. Some decisions may not be popular with your team. "Get over it," Brian advises. The leader must be interested in results and respect. Make decisions consistent with your vision. "Wishy-washy doesn't gain respect."

Though Brian's team has consistently bonused which makes them one of the highest paid in the area, he feels bonus is not about the money but is an affirmation they are doing a great job. Even this is not enough, for a leader needs to hone communication skills, which is a challenge for a man in an all women environment. Brian has learned he needed to:

- Become an excellent listener
- Try to figure out the hidden message sometimes
- Pay attention to little things before they become chasms
- Ask questions to find out the real concerns
- Praise goes a long ways; catch your staff doing things well and compliment them specifically and sincerely.
- Never be in a bad mood as it really is a power play. Either go home or get therapy.

"When the team is playing their 'A' game, there is an immeasurable sense of pride being a team player. There is pure joy when everything works out and the days fly by and it is fun…and I make a pile of money."

Brian's pursuit of cosmetic excellence began when DenMat introduced Cerinate Laminates in Edmonton. "They encouraged you to bring photographs of your work. I received the Harold Chase Award for Cosmetic Dentistry, a photocopied certificate on yellow paper was my first cosmetic award," Brian remembers.

Brian's offerings include cosmetics, implant restorations, high end cosmetic dentures, aesthetic posterior restorations, occlusal treatment and periodontal therapy. Another lesson from Brian, "I got into cosmetic dentures by default. I never set this as a goal. In the Edmonton Implant Study Group, our mentor started us out on denture construction (learn the basics). He is a prosthodontist who was taught by Earl Pound, the granddaddy of denture construction. To help us with learning denture esthetics, we brought Dr. Steven Sawdusky, an Edmonton prosthodontist. Steve is a denture specialist who has an amazing knack for esthetics. We brought patients in and did tooth setups. To top it off, I spent three days with Dr. Turbyfil at his denture course. I realized the dentures we were producing were well above average so I doubled my fees and started marketing esthetic dentures."

Success to Brian is a balanced approach and enjoying the process. Enjoy the journey, not just the end results. He feels anyone can be profitable if they know where they are going, are willing to change as well and act like you want to be.

Brian has moved from $400K to $850K and for the last two years has produced $1M. He projects production/collection at $1.2M for 2005. He is profitable by working four days a week and taking eight weeks of vacation, including a month in the summer. Out on time at the end of the day, Brian produces 80% of his daily goal in the mornings. He is never double booked and rarely runs late. Stress is gone because of excellent scheduling. The practice has been insurance free for 15 years and they do complete the insurance form to give the guest. This staff has reached bonus every month for the last two years and last month, earned $2,000 each in bonus. Brian keeps his overhead at 60%.

Brian feels the biggest struggle on the path to profitability is keeping focused, keeping on track. When things are going well, it is easy to slide into complacency and lose track of where you want to go. If things are not going well, you can become bogged down and lose your dream, your vision. "History is history, the future is up to you."

The Red Deer practice has 15 to 20 consultations a month. Ideal comprehensive treatment is offered to achieve the best result. Not every patient says, "yes" and sometimes the treatment is phased or fit into a budget and occasionally the patient moves on to another dentist. "I sleep comfortably knowing I did not compromise."

For internal marketing, Brian keeps his officer décor current and promoting his product. He has a flat screen monitor with the same frame as his certificates and diplomas. This PowerPoint presentation runs continuously sharing before/after transformations, emotionally markets dentures, implants, confirms to guests they are making the right choice being in Dr. Saby's office.

External marketing has become Brian's forte. Brian has explored different facets and finds currently what is working to target the 40 plus market in Red Deer, is a good website (www.saby.com), a full page yellow page ad, newspaper ads and three thirty-second radio ads a day. He has been involved in external marketing for a number of years and it is paying off. "You establish yourself as the premier dental office by telling people you are just that. Over time and with repetition, you become known as the leader in the dental field. As you fill that niche, there is a decrease in emergency calls and bargain hunters. The number of new patients decrease as the quality of patients increase."

Brian feels his determination and competitiveness attribute to his success. Yet, if he doesn't win, he is OK with that. "As long as you do the best you can under the circumstances and that you honestly gave it your best shot, you won to some degree," Brian feels. He feels strongly, "at all times, you must be honest with yourself and others. On this, there is no compromise."

Brian's last minute thoughts:

- Finding a role model, mentor and coach has been one of the most important things I have done to become successful. We make decisions emotionally and it has been extremely beneficial to have an experienced coach who is not emotionally tied. Find a mentor or mentors, develop a relationship and you will not regret it. Every top player needs a coach.

- Bill has helped me with some of the major decisions in my practice and is batting .1000. On the times I was not an active client, Bill has helped me after I have made some poor choices. I appreciate that he is available and knowledgeable. One of the big benefits are the monthly conference calls led by Bill on a topic and the sharing with other successful dentists information and support.

www.saby.com

*"Striving for new heights even though you may not know what you are doing."*

*Saby family. Brian is the one in back.*

*Dr. Saby, accredited AACD member since 1992.*

## Blatchford Game Plan: Your Agenda Costs You

Dr. Saby and team have worked extensively on their sales skills. They know they cannot talk a patient into treatment. They know if they begin the conversation with their idea of how this person should look, it will ruin the sale. They work very hard to allow the patient's ideas and dreams to be what drives the conversation. Not only is this more successful, the patient feels heard and included.

A dentist is so technically trained that it inhibits the sales process. A dentist is constantly designing in their mind what their idea of a perfect smile would be for a new patient, the grocery clerk, the spinning instructor, and the waiter. You can't help it! And, this is what makes the end result so excellent. However, you trip over your own feet in the sales process when you already have a picture in mind for your patient. Your agenda will cause you to stumble.

The sales process (the time before a patient says "yes") has no opening for your agenda or picture of what you think a person should look like. How can you have any listening when you already have your mind made up? For a successful sale on any item, the value must be present. If the buyer has little idea of what is possible, our job is to ask questions and uncover those hidden values. Our job is to help the buyer deepen their values and give them what they want. If you already have in mind what you want them to want, a successful sale will likely not take place.

In the sales world, they refer to dentists as "non-selling health care professionals." Our technical training creates a natural path of educating our patient into submission. We draw pictures on bracket covers and speak with words not understood on the street. Another paradigm we hold is our patients NEED to have this treatment. Non-selling health professionals thus talk our patients into understanding the treatment we think they need.

The end result is, the patient accepts only what they think they

NEED right now. They are not exposed to dreaming about their idea of a beautiful smile or chewing with comfort. The result is a little treatment is accomplished on many people. The dentist and staff continue to run from chair to chair. The dental zoo endures.

Dentists are not the only carriers of agenda overload. Staffs also subscribe. How can you tell? When you see the picture of Vince Lombardi, what are your immediate thoughts? The Boat Salesman of the Year said he attributes his success to "I never begin with a boat in mind." Do you begin with a smile in mind?

For a successful sale, the technically trained must clear their minds of their own agendas. Our job is to help the patient uncover their agenda. Develop a trusting relationship by staying out of the "tooth talk" while you develop a friend. Ask questions to uncover their hobbies, if they are new in town, what interests them. Dr. Bob Barkley said, "You can never sell anything to a stranger."

By asking questions, you help your patients uncover their own agenda. You must think of your mind like a blank canvas and the patient is painting a picture for you. This is where we have our wires crossed. We think we need to paint the picture for the patient. This is our pitfall in sales as the "non-selling health care professional."

Ask your patient a future focus question rather than the usual, "do you have any concerns today?" Ask what they would like their smile or dental health to be like in twenty years? Now, you are making them think with the right side of their brain, the dream side, and the decision side. Their predictable answer is the desire to keep their own teeth. Ask why. Probe deeper. Ask more questions. Keep asking questions like, "What benefits could you see by keeping your own teeth?" "Tell me about your dental heritage." "Is keeping your teeth a family tradition?"

If you keep asking questions, the patient will paint a picture for you. They will tell you what is important to them. Their answers will sound like looking good, younger, better or lasting a long time and/or feeling good.  Ask them to expand on those thoughts. Show your after pictures to help them visualize their dream smile.  Have them describe it and share what advantages they could see by having a smile like that.

If you allow the patient to paint their picture, they will own it.  If you arrive with your agenda in mind for them, they will not see it for themselves.  You will end up putting unwanted pressure on your patient to accept what you had in mind.  Create the opportunity for your new friend to dream out into the future about their smile.  Have them describe it and they will own it.  For greater success, drop your agenda for them.

Bill Blatchford, DDS

# From the Blatchford Play Book: Jump and Shout

External marketing is branding yourself as different which has been the very antithesis of established dental circles. You may be the first. It takes courage, boldness and a real sense of self. As Dr. Brian Saby started marketing early on and in Alberta, it was against the establishment. He utilized ingenuity in becoming known. He called the local paper to write an article about his new recumbent bike with the "hook" as a dentist, he needed to keep the circulation going in his hands on his ten mile daily ride to his office. He then started an informational column in his local paper. And the beat goes on. Now Alberta's dental advertising laws are more liberal than the US.

>> Be a participant in your community, not an observer

>> Have a great website and host

>> Be enthusiastic about life

>> Think of marketing as helping your community be stronger

>> Everyday think of small ways to improve your practice

>> Get excited about dentistry. Be thrilled you chose to improve people's lives

>> Use the radio for getting the word out

>> Take part in festivals, fairs, art shows, etc

>> Place media ads in well-read publications

>> Get professional help with the design

>> Have a visable location with excellent signage

>> How about "community service" digital clock, temperature sign at your office?

>> Wave the flag

>> Sponsor a ball team

>> Become the local dental expert by giving talks on dentistry

>> Join a service club and be active

>> Look for ways to do business locally

# 15

## THE TEACHER

## Dr. Kim Okamura –"Pound for Pound"

Dr. Okamura is the energizer bunny. She is five feet tall and all of 98 pounds with her favorite sport being basketball. We feel, pound for pound, Dr. Okamura is a most profitable dentist with an overhead of 49.1%.

Practicing in the north Seattle area, Kim has purchased and combined three practices in her 18 years of practice. Her goal has been to create a $1M practice. She was $24K short when 9/11 happened. This horrific event greatly affected people's priorities and her highly niched cosmetic practice. With media marketing, she produced $738K in 2004, working three days a week. One million is still the goal.

Clearly, one of Kim's outstanding qualities is her clarity of vision and her ability to communicate her vision with passion and enthusiasm. She sees the bigger picture, knows where she is going, has specific number goals and, consequently, great team that is attracted to the challenge. Dr. Okamura tends to have long-term staff that share her pace, vision and demand excellence of themselves. She is the coach.

As a female professional, we feel she has worked through the leadership challenges. Her team knows this is a business. Dr. Okamura hires staff for strengths and she believes in their abilities. She lets her staff know it is OK to make mistakes. In fact, she encourages them to step out and be uncomfortable. When a task or conversation is not up to par, she communicates with the question, "what did you learn from this?" She expects and receives 200%. She is fiercely loyal to her team and really believes in them.

That said Dr. Okamura feels she is so loyal, she hangs on too long. One of her pitfalls as a leader has been becoming emotionally attached to people vs. a business-like attachment to the practice. As a leader, she feels she could make those tough staff decisions earlier. She has a timetable for new staff to learn skills, read books, be accountable and apply themselves for results. Kim pushes herself and expects the same from team. They read sales and marketing books, practice sales conversations, tape themselves and improve. It is all about practice, practice, practice. In practicing the sales skills, she likes to play the "what if" game, creating scenarios of possibilities. What if a guest said..., how would you respond? Her staff always participates in the monthly Blatchford staff conference call, sharing and learning from others. Kim uses "fireside chats" and learning is a big part of being a team member.

Kim's goal is to practice three days a week so she can balance her life with family and fun. This has been a real challenge for Kim as she loves being a good mother, great wife and taking time for herself. She works at the balance. Her husband, Tim has owned and operated three 7/11 stores and now is into commercial real estate investments. The Okamura family lives in Redmond, WA (home of Microsoft) so Kim commutes 30 minutes across Lake Washington to work. She feels this distance has not affected her cosmetic attraction as her practice has 19K cars a day pass her office and her marketing is aimed at greater Seattle market. Currently, she has huge poster size copies of her current ads in her windows. Kim practices four days a week; her goal is to practice three days a week.

Kim's foray into dentistry was circuitous. Dr. Okamura is the oldest of five children of first generation American born Chinese immigrants to Seattle. As the oldest, much was expected of her with the emphasis on education. While being fiercely independent and unfocused in grade school, she eventually buckled down and won an academic scholarship to Seattle Pacific. Her father was very disappointed when she chose not to continue after her first semester. Instead, she took a year long dental assisting course and while working for a year, she was encouraged to take her hygiene prerequisites and was accepted. At the same time, her professors encouraged her to apply to dental school and she was one of five women graduates in the class of 1987 at U. of Washington. Her motivating factor was encouragement from others. Is there a lesson here?

Tim patiently waited for the focused Dr. Okamura to complete dental school before marriage. Kim felt she wanted to practice three years before having children but they came earlier. She took three months off, hired a locum and grandparents insisted "no daycare" so they cared for Timmy while Kim continued to build her practice. A daughter was born several years later with the loving pattern established. Their children are flourishing in academics and sports.

All three practice purchases were within a one mile radius. Initially, she purchased a small family practice on the decline from a retiring dentist for $85K. She worked hard to build it up and after two years was looking for "what else?" A dentist with a good reputation was retiring for health reasons and with $135K practice purchase, she moved into his larger and modern facility with one staff. After seven years in practice, she paid full fee of $225K for a practice with plans to renovate and move to the visible and convenient location. This turned out to be the most uncomfortable purchase as the selling Doctor (unknown to Kim) had not told his staff, his receptionist wife or hygienist daughter about selling. When Kim arrived to meet them, it was announced and there was immediate distrust and upset. Dr. Okamura feels she lost about 20% of the patients as she re-formed her team and found a facility to attract cosmetic possibilities and had it remodeled.

She is five minutes from I-5, the major North/South corridor, close to busy Northgate Mall with Nordstrom as the anchor store and close to the University district. It is a stand alone one-story leased building with parking and so very visible. Kim feels practice purchases are a sure way to add opportunities to a practice. Even today, she is mindful of the possibilities.

Dr. Okamura coaches to meet goals as she is basically supporting the family with Tim in commercial real estate investments. This is a numbers game. They want to gross $1M, netting half. They want to do a full mouth case once a quarter. This means attracting and diagnosing about four a quarter to meet that goal. Her external marketing, website and networking bring in the larger cases. Internal marketing, service, conversations and comfort keep existing guests referring their friends and family to Dr. Okamura. Her current crown fee is $1574 and veneer fee ranges from $1870 to $2200. She uses Northwest Esthetics, an excellent laboratory owned and trained by Dr. David Baird. Unit lab fee averages $345. Hygiene goal is $1200 a day three days a week.

Updating and upgrading is constant. Kim has studied with Dr. David Baird and at Las Vegas Institute. Her mentors include Dr. Bill Blatchford and her father. Her computer software is SoftDent and she wants to replace it with Dentrix or Eaglesoft. She wants to become certified in IV Sedation, take Jim Carlson's cosmetic denture course to add to her repertoire as well as complete the Pacific Implant Institute. Her five year goals are greater practice growth through listening and verbal skills, achieving more closing which means more bonusing for staff and even further niching her practice in cosmetics by eliminating general dentistry procedures.

Since moving to her new space in 1999, Kim has focused on marketing excellence. Her marketing budget is 7.9% of gross. She works with Korey Korfiatis, Wenatchee, WA of Saggezza Marketing to create memorable right-brained print ads in Seattle magazines and her website of www.kimokamuradds.com  Catch the energy in Kim's photo and wonderful words about Lee, her accomplished hygienist.  Kim also has an e-newsletter which is so appropriate for computer based Seattle.  Dr. Okamura has three patients a week enter her practice through her website.  Notice the consistency in marketing and presentation of her logo, name of practice is same as website and same on letterhead and throughout. The message is straight forward and not confusing.

Dr. Okamura coaches to the numbers and profitability is the result.  She feels being profitable is a distinct goal and anyone can do it if they set their mind to it.  Her practice is a distinction because of her different life experiences—each has pushed her to new levels each time.  A struggle for her is taking the time for herself to recharge her batteries and self-renewal.

Dr. Okamura's cosmetic practice has come by vision and careful design.  She feels in converting a general practice to a strictly cosmetic practice, you need:

- An advocate like Bill Blatchford to coach you to success
- Clinically excellent and extensive skills to "walk your talk"
- Confidence, be a risk taker, be creative, like new challenges, understand the culture and psychology of cosmetics and REALLY WANT IT!
- Communication skills to build team and to converse with your guests
- Strong and focused marketing

A practice such as Kim's has high wide fluctuations in monthly income as there is no significant general dentistry base. "You must watch your numbers and carefully plan.  Do not buy the big toy when you have a good month.  I do not worry when some blocks of time are not filled.  Be prepared for the big case by thinking and behaving with readiness." She leads by encouraging her team to "focus on the big picture and the little thing are no big deal."

Dr. Okamura finds it fascinating to observe subtle changes in her practice. Currently, she is seeing more guests arrive who have done their research homework on the internet and with friends. They arrive knowing what they want and they have selected Dr. Okamura to do the work.

www.kimokamuradds.com

*Jumping to new heights is Dr. Kim Okamura. This picture is from her website and patients have said, "I chose you because you look like fun."*

*As a highly niched practice, marketing is the key. View an Okamura ad at the back of the book.*

# Blatchford Game Plan: Ten Year Plan

Dr. Okamura is a goal setter. Purchasing three practices and molding them into one highly niched cosmetic practice didn't just happen. Kim and her team know five years out of their marketing budget, their continuing education courses, equipment purchases as it is all on a schedule. A ten year plan is an excellent map for any aspiring dentist.

Ten years from now, at the beginning of 2015, how well will you have guided and pushed your practice and life towards the goals and principles you have set? Or will 2015 bring another year repeating the same mistakes and small thinking of many other years? The choice is yours: to plan with diligence, develop new skills, commit with a vengence and create outstanding results or to bump along and hope things will change for the better.

Every astute businessperson will share with you the positive energy and great results that occur when you take the time to develop a Ten Year Plan. It is really a map of where you want to go. Start by writing down how old you will be in 2015, the age of your spouse and each child. Just that act alone will shock you into action.

Why Ten Years? By projecting ten years out, the problems and objections of today disappear. What are our objections? Time and money are the two main "reasons" why we don't tackle our main obstacles today. By creating an ideal practice and great life ten years into the future, we eliminate the big barriers of today and can focus on smaller steps we need to take to achieve our ten year goals. Big goals seem more possible when you project ten years out.

The Ten Year Plan stems from a real knowledge about yourself, your philosophy and where you are going in life. We call this your personal vision and it spills over directly into your practice life, also. What are your values? What is passionately important to you? What difference are you trying to make for yourself, your family, your patients?

What are the five most important values in your life? What do you stand for?  What are the organizing principles of your life?  What are your core beliefs?  What virtues do you aspire to?  What will you not stand for?  What would you sacrifice for, suffer for and even die for?

Put them in order of priority.  When you observe your own behavior and actions, they indicate to you what are your real values.  These values will shape your life and practice in achieving your Ten Year Plan.

The Ten Year Plan should start with your personal life as your practice is a portion of your life, not the whole.  Work is a most important focus and there must be a balance so you have a wonderful family and personal life, too.

It is important you write and speak this Ten Year Plan as if January 2015 is now.  If you are now 47 years old, you would say, " I am 57 years old" rather than "I hope" or "I will."  Speak as if you already have accomplished your Ten Year Plan.

In addition to your age, set a goal for your physical life.  What is your weight in 2015?  What is your heart rate, your cholesterol count, your resting pulse?  What have you accomplished  physically by 2015?  Are there some new skills or new levels of accomplishment which you have achieved physically?  Martial arts, climbing, hiking, running, biking?

List your children and what they have accomplished in 2015.  Occupations, college graduations, your grandchildren?  What hobbies do you have or are developing?  Where have you traveled?   What strong friendships have you developed?  Describe your life in 2015.  Are you married and living where?  Describe your home, location and features.  Describe your spiritual life and involvement.

Concentrate now on your practice.  Where is your practice located in 2015?  What does the office look like?  What high tech equipment do you have?  What is the niche in the market you are appealing to?  What is your reputation in the community?  Who do you work with and what have they accomplished?  How long has your staff worked with you?  To whom do you refer?

What are your technical accomplishments in 2015?  Are you an accredited member of a prestigious and rigorous course or organization? Are you a graduate of courses in areas of dentistry for which you have become known? How have you become a leading member of the dental community?

Specifically in your practice, who are your patients? What is your average case size? What attracts patients to you? How many days a year do you practice? What is your percentage of overhead? What does your practice day look and feel like? Are you focused on fewer patients and accomplishing more? What are your accounts receivables? What is your acceptance rate for your suggested treatment? What skills have you learned in the last ten years to be able to accomplish this?

What plans did you make in 2005 for your retirement funding? What will that total and how did you invest that money? By 2015, are you financially free of debt? What are your plans for retirement?

If you are not still practicing in 2015, what is your exit strategy? Did you develop a solid plan for a good transition for your patient care? If you are practicing in 2015, what is your transition plan for your practice? Will you leave your practice completely or will you still have a selective practice seven to ten days a month? What is the arrangement?

A Ten Year Plan needs to be specific and real. When you take the time to write as if it is 2015 and dream about what might be possible, without the constraints and barriers of 2005, your dream can become a reality. The specifics in the Ten Year Plan become the basis for concrete goals. These are then broken down into ten year, five year and one year goals and then, even projects. If you want to have specific things happen in your practice and your life by 2015, what skills and preparation do you need to start now to have mastered that area by 2015?

Be outrageous. Dentists are held back by some constraints that are unnecessary and unwanted. If you could have your life and practice anyway you wanted, how would it be? Plan now for 2015 and you won't be disappointed.

Bill Blatchford, DDS

## From the Blatchford Play Book: Winning Team

Dr. Okamura is a real teacher. Her mission in life is to help others see the possibilities in themselves. For that, she is a winner and her team is the recipient of patience, prodding and practicing. She is part of the winning team.

>> Be accountable for mistakes and learn from them. This makes you more valuable to the team

>> Hire people smarter than you

>> Spontaneously sing praises of each other and Doctor

>> Be generous with compliments to each other

>> Every patient has firm financial arrangements before receiving an appointment

>> Think about your actions, conversations, body language and how that reflects your leader's vision

>> Winning is a choice and there are many winners

>> Action may not always bring happiness; but there is no happiness without action

>> Practice, practice, practice

>> It's the fundamentals

>> You get out in front and you stay out in front

# 16

## KEEPING GREAT STAFF

## Dr. Paul DeCarlo

As an associate in Ft. Lauderdale, the new Dr. DeCarlo was looking for something on his own in the Fort Meyers area. His orthodontist friend told him of a practice for sale (Doctor died of heart attack) and Paul made a bid of $60K in 1974. This huge purchase was now his. The staff stayed making the transition easier and amazingly enough, three of those same staff have been with Paul for his 30 years. How does this happen? Paul said "the staff was very open-minded and flexible when I began and we all agreed to give it a fair shot at working before looking for something else. It worked out for the best for all of us."

Dr. DeCarlo knows it is unusual to have such devoted, talented and dedicated long-term staff. In trying to explain why this has occurred for him, "I really try to stand in someone else's shoes before making a decision or conclusion too soon. Everyone has strengths and knowledge that we don't have and if you listen long enough, you can learn every minute of your life. I like to couple this with being very patient, calm and flexible. This allows for new and varied relationships that may be lifelong."

On the other hand, Dr. DeCarlo describes himself as a perfectionist and over-achiever. "I also have to admit trying to be too precise or perfect can be a detriment to living in the 'real world.' Sometimes being too hard on myself creates a definite pitfall to my own success. This also made it more difficult to lead and communicate because I didn't allow the full spectrum of possibilities to develop. It is times like this when it is invaluable to have those around you like family and a close-knit staff to point out reality."

Initially, Paul knew little about office management. His staff knew the patients and town well and he thought, with their help, they could keep it going without big changes. Their personalities and philosophies blended quickly. "We were all instant leaders or followers at different times. I do feel this was instrumental in being successful with staff. We all looked at the initial situation as a challenge but we all agreed to go on the journey together to see what might happen."

Paul recognizes the tightrope of leadership and friend. "I was fortunate to have self-starters that loved their profession. From the very beginning, we agreed to talk over important decisions and it was understood, even after the discussions, I had the deciding vote. They respect the final decision is mine. Once the decision was made, like it or not, the entire team would stand behind it and make it work. I do believe employers would be further ahead if they believe they don't know ALL the answers. I like to hear all the knowledge and expertise before making choices. This develops natural trust and respect in team building."

He does believe a sense of humor is invaluable. Paul feels he was very deliberate and focused growing up; admired others who could have a sense of humor no matter the situation. "I tried to emulate this behavior and invite humor into my life more often. It seemed those who could laugh often had an easier journey through life, no matter what happened. Couple that with our working team having a fabulous sense of humor and we rely heavily on that, especially doing dentistry. Patients can't believe how loose and fun loving we are at work and yet, know when to get serious. I find my sense of humor is only as strong as those around me so I make it my goal to be around those kind of people at work, at home, at Church, or vacations."

His communication with staff has always been "open door" and no idea is thrown away without discussion. "We think outside the box as often as we can and I try to delegate all I can to various staff members. This makes them more accountable but also more creative in their individual ways. This allows for things to happen and keeps me from worrying about trivial details all day."

Over the years, they have recognized some patients who do not seem to fit. Shifting from trying to be "Dr. Everything to Everybody," Paul and team now work on people who have a mutual admiration society. If it is not a match, "we invite them to join another practice."

The staff's motivation has come from being important, feeling appreciated and having a very comfortable, safe place to work. They are truly part owners of the practice. "Together, we have had many life experiences. By using our combined resources, we have grown tremendously over the past 30 years and have had good financial gains, too. In 2004, each staff made $12K in bonuses and are on the same path for this year. But even more important is the fact we think, act and perform like a close-knit family that loves what we are doing."

Paul admits not everyone can make it in their office but "the right combination is a wonderful sight to see." He has six cross-trained staff plus an associate with assistant two days a week.

Paul's artistic wife, Linda Kay, has been a part-time staff member on and off over the years. She does not run the practice. All team are close friends as well as co-workers so Linda Kay was able to come and go without stepping on anyone's toes.

At 60, Paul is aware of choices. "Life is about choices and we all make them constantly but sometimes we don't slow down enough to make good choices for ourselves." In 1998, at age 53, Paul had prostate surgery for cancer. He did a lot of reading and reflecting on past, present and future. He made lists on legal pads of his practice likes and dislikes at the time. He was successful by the numbers but "very frustrated to his inner being." He wanted the practice to get to the point where "I could enjoy walking in the back door each morning, rather than have more frustrations than I could handle. The two issues that really bothered me were insurance issues and the fact that patients didn't seem to want what we had to offer."

When he discovered what he wanted to change, "I found a coach to lead me there and the rest was a matter of time and dedication. Bill Blatchford was the person who showed me how to get it done. Both of those issues were solved in less than a year and we haven't looked back. I now have a practice of my dreams along with some of the tangible rewards like a home in North Carolina that makes my family life totally enjoyable. The only loss I can think of in my practice life is the fact that it took me so many years to realize that with the right guidance, I could have any practice I wanted. Fortunately, that did happen and now I see nothing stopping us."

"Specifically, the insurance frustration was handled by getting out of the insurance rat race. We no longer accept assignment nor do pre-estimates. Our patients understand our position and don't have a problem paying us for their work and getting reimbursed. We thought it would drastically affect our practice but it has made no difference. In fact, patients tend to agree with this while seeing what a farce it is with medical insurance."

A thirty-year anniversary party with patients did occur the whole month of June. On June 15th (the actual day) the DeCarlo team were 'limozeened' to a shopping day in Sarasota. Special gifts were exchanged and a photo album of all team trips and happy occasions is now in their welcome room for patients to enjoy.

Goals for the future include doing much of the same, but being able to have more time as the years go by. "The practice has been more fun than ever and we all want to keep that goal at the top of our list. Who knows what will come during the next few years, but whatever it is, we are ready and willing to keep it going. I really don't want to retire. This is the exact opposite of seven years ago."

Thirty years ago, Paul selected Fort Meyers on Florida's West Coast because it was small and growing with families. Offering the best general dentistry, he felt there was room for growth and maturity. Studying with giants in dentistry, Dr. DeCarlo gives credit to L. D. Pankey and his cross of life, Peter Dawson and in the last five years, many trips to Las Vegas Institute. He also learned efficient systems from Mike Schuster of Phoenix.

"When I joined Bill Blatchford, he taught me how to integrate techniques, systems and patient motivation. As a result, we've made the largest strides over a shorter period of time than with anyone else." Dr. DeCarlo's practice has two major components. It still is a very strong general practice as well as a very strong cosmetic practice. "Because of our thirty years in Fort Meyers, we have children and grandchildren of our original patients of 1974. Being able to learn cosmetic procedures with confidence and integrating communication skills has taken the general practice to a more sophisticated cosmetic practice when it was the right time for different patients. When someone is not interested in more comprehensive or cosmetic work, it only means 'no' at that present time. History shows me anyone can change their mind at anytime depending on the right time for them. Learning to communicate with patients (listening, too) and have patience with myself has paid off many times over, with end result being happy patients about their cosmetics and dental function."

"Our 'A' game is easy to identify. It is when the entire office has a hand in taking either a phobic patient with a simple composite filling or a full mouth restoration case and has them stand up and hug us with tears in their eyes. It is then the true satisfaction comes through, knowing this was accomplished without focusing on persuading someone to do something they weren't ready to do."

Profitability has taken on new meanings for Paul and staff over the years. "We all want to be profitable, especially when we're young and starting out. Once a family, spirituality and spare time enter the picture, the meaning and emphasis on profitability changes. Since the recent birth of our grandchild, profitability has become much more emotional than financial. Anyone can be profitable in their own way. They must form a vision for themselves, work toward that vision while working within their comfortable pace."

A large hurdle for Paul early on was learning which local dental meeting stories to believe and which were "smoke and mirrors." The hardest decision Paul had to make was to not pretend to be like another clinician. "I was frustrated for years thinking I had to be like others in mannerisms and their practices. I gave myself permission to get off the dental tread mill and develop my own 'pace.' It may be faster or slower than others but it doesn't matter. As long as we can fit our practice into our vision and accomplish our main goals, we don't have to mimic anyone else. Our practice is very special and we all enjoy it immensely."

One of Paul's best decisions was to "perfect my dentistry and continue improving while 'pros' in other fields guided me with their expertise to the practice of my dreams." Paul's advice is to be the dentist and let others do the accounting, financial planning, investing and business advising. "I am the practice leader. I found it much more efficient and satisfying to develop a team of experts around me to coach me with their expertise."

Marketing is an ongoing work in progress. Dr. DeCarlo has two websites—www.pauldecarlodds.com shares a great staff picture filled with enthusiasm and out of the box. Internally, Paul said they have tried different things. They ask for referrals and the best marketing, he feels, is superior customer care. Externally, they have done newspaper ads, television, newsletters, radio and flyers. After all is said and done, Paul says, "I really believe taking care of someone and really caring for them during every minute of treatment and after has given us our best and longest lasting referrals. People know they are safe in our office and we will do our best to meet their needs and wants.

Numbers: Starting with Blatchford in 1998, our yearly P/C was $800K with a 61% overhead, 25 new patients a month and 7.5 staff. In 2004, production/collection was $1.55M, overhead was 57%, 25-30 new patients a month and six staff. Presently, a unit fee is $1,000.

"I found much of the reading material Bill suggested being extremely helpful. One of the biggest struggles towards profitability is making the constant changes. In reading of Ed Deming in _Out of the Crisis_, who influenced the rebuilding of Japan in the 1960's, Dr. Deming taught them a different work philosophy of 'constant never-ending improvement.' Instead of being content with the present, the reality of constant change is always in play. Being able to make those changes makes the goal of constant never-ending improvement an easier struggle."

Profitability and success have had different meanings at different times in Paul's life. "Most important, they now offer a very positive and complete feeling."

www.pauldecarlodds.com

_Team DeCarlo has 233 years of combined dental experience and still counting._

## Blatchford Game Plan: A Winning Staff

Dr. DeCarlo has been blessed with winning staff and longevity, a successful combination.

Relationships with patients are stronger, emotional ties to each other are invaluable and the team feels they have a higher calling.

Contrast this with the "revolving door" which occurs in some practices. Case acceptance is more of a struggle, team bonding is challenged and the bigger picture gets lost. What are the factors which allow the team to dedicate their professional lives to this practice? Is it luck or a factor of his leadership skills and a life filled with grace?

We dream of THE team! How do you gather people who will hold your vision as precious and treat patients special? From 8 to 5, we need a team with no "I" in it. We need enthusiasm, sophistication, warmth, brains and an internally motivated work ethic.

An average dentist can continue with an average staff where conversations and logistics are gathered from previous average dentists and the cycle continues. As dentistry has changed from crisis care to optional choices, the staff composition must change, also.

Upon driving into their lot, Les Schwab, the largest independent tire dealer in America, has staff run to your car to help. The building and store is immaculate and the staff all wears clean white shirts. How does he find such great workers? Les Schwab says "you cannot train people to have a good attitude. You have to select them."

If you want your staff to shine, you must select people who have the internal qualities you desire. You can train them in the technical dentistry. Of course, there are no guarantees in life, however, ask the questions and observe the structure of responses.

I would want self-confidence as a quality. Can they look you in the eye with warmth and shake your hand? Do they stand tall and dress with proper decorum? Is there enthusiasm and optimism present? Are they givers or takers? If they ask you a benefit question before they share what they are willing to do for you, this may be a clue.

Dentistry is now a people game. Are they comfortable being in a conversation with you? Do you use proper grammar and speak clearly in complete sentences? Would this person be able to relate to all ages? There is not a position available in good dental offices where you have no patient contact or important conversations. Everyone must be comfortable with different people.

Curiosity is an excellent trait. Do they ask questions? Business guru Tom Peters says "Hire curious people." Staffs that are willing to step outside the box are usually willing to go beyond routine and be accountable for the results.

Discover their ability to be multi-dimensional by asking what book they are currently reading or what is their latest hobby? People are more interesting to others (your guests) when there is something going on in their life. Would you take this person on a trip across West Texas in an unairconditioned VW bus?

Find out their picture of accountability by asking what they are responsible for now? How do they feel about owning their results? What is being "responsible" on a team?

Of course, cleanliness and order are very important. Personal grooming can be a reflection. Purses, cars and wallets are other indications of order and cleanliness. Check in the parking lot and have them use a pen from their purse during the interview.

Because dentistry is changing, determine their flexibility by asking some hypothetical questions like learning a new computer program or remodeling to work in a different area. Find people with a sense of adventure. Someone who cannot change will be like an anchor in your office.

Because dentistry is a business, your staff needs to be comfortable dealing with money and fees. Find out their own deserve level by asking questions. Is it ok with them for a guest to choose to spend $20,000 to improve their smile? Would you consider it for yourself?

A personal deserve level is an invisible floor and ceiling which we feel we could not penetrate in material goods, relationships, fun or our lives. We need teams who believe in your product.

You would follow the interview with a working interview. Have them work in your office for a day or two. If the basic characteristics that are important to you are present, you may find an excellent team mate. If after 10 days you discover they really interview well and there are some basics that concern you, consider finding a new staff member. Brian Tracy in Maximum Achievement said, "We know at least a year before we actually let someone go." This is costly in terms of your leadership as your team already knows who is playing the game well."

Finding the right team is a continual game. Keeping them is another story.

Bill Blatchford, DDS

# From the Blatchford Play Book: Character Counts

We have heard others say, "Dr. DeCarlo is a fine person." In building a practice and team, his basic character shows and it does count.

>> Look for honesty, respect and unselfishness

>> Look for people who stand for something

>> Surround yourself with positive people, get rid of negativity

>> Don't live in the "gray areas." An issue is either black or white, right or wrong

>> Never compromise what you think is right

>> To live a perfect day, you must do something for someone who will never be able to repay you

>> Keep your promises

>> Take care of your reputation

>> You are in charge of your attitude

>> Be real; walk your talk

>> Be the best you can be

>> Never compromise your integrity

>> Remember, no one makes it alone—have a grateful heart and be quick to acknowledge those who help you

>> Step up to the plate and be accountable for your actions. Take responsibility for the good things you do as well as the mistakes and failures

>> Become the most positive and enthusiastic person you know

>> Never cheat, lie or steal

>> Look people in the eye

# 17

# THE HIGHLY NICHED PRACTICE

## Dr. Rhys Spoor

What makes Dr. Spoor different is his passion, his intensity, his desire to keep learning and sharing plus his commitment to excellence. Rhys and his team will produce $1.5M in three 11 hour days a week, has a credit balance at all times working with three full time staff. His is a highly niched cosmetic and TMD practice on the 46th floor of a Seattle high-rise filled with lawyers and financial institutions. Thus, his marketing budget is nearly 10%; his patients arrive looking for a smile change.

They average 15-20 new consults a month, depending on the success of external marketing. He has one day a week of hygiene as his guests come into the practice for aesthetics or are referred for a specific reason.

Some Doctors desire to have a cosmetic practice like Rhys' and easy is what it might appear. A cosmetic practice without a general dentistry base can have great fluctuations in time and money based on patient entry, acceptance, delivery and completion. Rhys has basically eliminated general dentistry for smile design and complex restorative cases.

Seattle has many fine clinicians in a drawing population of a million plus. Branding, advertising and marketing are at a high level in Seattle.

He does not compromise in his treatment. He treats people exactly as he and his team would like to be treated. "I don't offer anything I wouldn't offer to my wife, Margaret, our children or my parents. My standards don't change based on the fact they pay for what I suggest. Ultimately, it is up to the patient to decide 'yes' or 'no.' I practice at the best level I know to do for everyone and I'm continually learning. The dentistry I do next year will compare differently from what I am able to do today. As technology changes, techniques are better and I get better. I want to keep incorporating all these changes for every patient, just as I do for my family."

Dr. Spoor's style of leadership reflects his intensity, excellence and passion. "I have been known by a number of people who work with me to be extremely demanding. I make no excuses or apologies. I am demanding on myself and I'm demanding of the people who work with me. However, I am fair. I expect their best efforts constantly. I expect each of them to strive for excellence as I do myself. I expect them to be honest, trustworthy and punctual. I'm direct and tend not to sugar-coat things. For some people, this is great. For others, this doesn't work at all."

"I have worked hard to assemble a team that truly sees their professional world as I do. We all have similar goals, standards and great communication. I do well with people who are proactive, take responsibility for themselves and are willing to take some risks."

"There have been times in my career when I worked with staff that had much different goals than mine. My hardest decision was firing a staff member for the first time. She was my receptionist, had worked with me for ten years and I liked her. I realized she just didn't have the ability to create the relationship with patients that we wanted to be there for the type of practice we were building. We had training sessions, workshops and scripting but she just didn't have the characteristics to make it work. I really liked her and wanted her to make it. I finally had to tell her we couldn't work together any more. It was the hardest thing I ever did."

"My definition of success has changed over time. When I first started, success meant making money. Therefore, very successful meant making a lot of money. Now, I feel success is based on how happy you truly are. Since we're at this job so many waking hours and days of our lives, being happy at work is a real definition of being successful to me. When I am happy at my work, we make more money which can buy us more time off. As much as I love what I do, I love the time off. Margaret and I love to travel, experience new cultures, do lots of things; that is where success really comes through. Recently a number of individuals in our lives have passed away. Never did I hear, 'I wish I would have spent more time at the office.' The time we do spend at work needs to be happy so you do not regret that time. You cannot buy that time back no matter how much money you make."

The three full time team members are cross trained which make for a very efficient team. They all assist, can make every piece of equipment hum, interview guests, make financial arrangements, speak highly of Dr. Spoor's clinical excellence and are purveyors of consideration and positivity.

"When we are on, we're on and everyone can feel it. In our 'A' game, things just flow. It feels good to be there because you know you're prepared and patients are receiving optimal care. Everyone is having a good time and the guests can feel it. There is a definite plan and it is like watching ice dancers. It is all choreographed. You have to know your part of the routine; it is not random. You also have the clinical ability to allow yourself to take divergent paths to reach the end point. Obstacles are challenges to go around but they do not halt the process. Every case has these challenges in some form or another. Even when the flow is going, you have to expect obstacles. Part of playing your 'A' game is having a plan of what you'll do when it becomes your 'B,' 'C' or even 'D' game."

Rhys feels he is profitable because he now sets long range and short term goals. He feels that is a natural progression of being older and seeing a finite time for your own life. He feels strongly anyone can be successful and profitable no matter your practice location. "You must define who you are, decide what is important to you and set your own goals. As much as I enjoy my career, it's not the primary thing I do in my life. It's an avenue I use to get the things I enjoy—time, travel, choices. Yet, I want to be happy at work and that is where we are now. We really enjoy the three 11-hour days at work and we are happy to be away from it."

Interestingly enough, when Rhys cut his days to three, his profitability increased. "I don't know if this means we should just work one day a week or not at all but it seems when you work less, you become more efficient. It is a balancing act of serving your client base and buying time away."

Many dentists want to duplicate Rhys' staff. Collecting a team of excellence requires a leader who is focused; willing and skilled in communicating expectations with clarity and praise. One young dentist recently told Blatchford, "I want my staff to praise me like Rhys' team members do. I want them to sell me." Rhys would tell you, "the team road is a long adventure. I have been blessed and I have done my share of replacing. I have been guilty of holding on, hoping it would work out. I have created a high level practice of choice. Therefore, I must have a team who is able the play the game full out for as Brian Tracy says, 'Everything counts.'"

What motivates his staff? Certainly money as this is a job. "The people I work with are well paid but stay because of many other factors like respect, satisfaction and a sense of making a positive difference. My current team enjoys a condensed work week and 8-10 weeks of time of with pay. They truly enjoy their jobs even though it is hard work."

Bottom line, Rhys warns the pitfalls of all this is if you can't communicate well; lack direction with leadership skills and keep the wrong staff around for your unspoken goals, your job as a dentist can be miserable and you can actually destroy a practice. "A successful dental practice is a small group of individuals and you have to do all the things effectively so that everyone can be happy."

Ever the perfectionist, Rhys works hard to communicate with his lab. Photography is used for his laboratory to achieve an excellent result. "There are such subtleties to this whole process. Photography is the key to transferring those subtleties to the laboratory to get the exquisite results. You have to be an excellent photographer to get the excellent photograph. Ultimate success is built on sequential steps, all performed at an unwavering level of quality that can't be missed or short changed. Practices that try to do aesthetics without photography are not giving the patients the results they could give."

Rhys candidly says, "over the years, most of the patients have said 'no.' In the first few years of aesthetics, the closure rate was 5-10%. Now it is much higher as people are coming in pre-selected from marketing or referrals. They arrive knowing more; it is not uncommon now at the initial appointment to close the case and collect the fee. We had one patient write us a check for $8500 before he walked in the door." Another recent consult we had the patient approved for $20,000 in financing before we ever met, thanks to excellent telephone skills of Maria Brown, the practice chief closer.

Up until recently, the majority of cases took two years to significant treatment. Now, no one walks in totally unprepared. "It has to do with how much they think they know about you before they come in. Now, when someone says 'no,' my attitude is 'not right now.' 'No' is an emotional decision; very changeable. Circumstances change; it can become a 'yes.'" Rhys' advice is to always be gracious in accepting their decision as it is their right.

Though it appears easy in the Spoor world, Rhys says, "I examine my overhead and make adjustments where possible. Some overhead cannot be cut; raising your fees is the alternative. Maximizing profitability is a balancing acts of fees, procedures and time as well as knowing your marketplace. On comprehensive cases on a new patient, they do not have anything to judge on; there is more latitude here. You want to have a fee structure designed to provide optimal care with flexibility to redo as the patient desires, as this is going to happen."

"What we do is so emotionally based, you can have a perfectly sound clinical and technical case which is a 'failure.' A patient can be greatly influenced by what others say, especially if it is a friend or relative. One negative comment can and does set off a cascade of events that ultimately may result in replacing much if not all of the recently placed work. A recent example involves a case where the patient was perfectly satisfied with her result until a co-worker thought her teeth looked gray. The patient previously lived with severe tetracycline stained teeth and is indeed hypersensitive to the shade. Even though the guest approved the color of her teeth several times during the process, she is now dissatisfied. If you want to have "the customer is always right" type of service, your fees have to support the occasionally redo of a case. You also have to remember that patient satisfaction is the biggest key to long term growth and success of an aesthetic practice."

Rhys' grandfather's advice for career was dentistry as he observed the dentist had respect, control of his income and time for vacations. While Rhys was in graduate school at U. of Washington, the funding for his master's thesis in fisheries was cut by the federal government. He remembered his grandfather's advice, did a 180 degree turn (literally, dentistry was across the street) and feels now it was the best decision he could have made as it has been a terrific career.

Not a planner as a young person, Rhys started in a friend's empty office space with "a chair, some instruments and an attitude." Finding it "a bit slow," he associated for a year and purchased a practice in Ballard, with marine repair and building as the main industries in this blue collar part of Seattle. The retiring dentist had practiced 24 years and 90 days in the year of purchase. In three years, Rhys tripled the production working 200 days. He had become insurance-free, converted an operatory to a photography studio and had a 24-hour Smile

Channel in his reception area covering the shared parking lot of several restaurants in the evening.

"As I studied aesthetics with Dr. David Baird (a very enjoyable and eye-opening experience) of Seattle and sought the council of Bill Blatchford (great systems and solid concepts), I realized I had reached my full potential in Ballard. To do the kinds of dentistry I wanted, I needed a downtown location and in 1996, sold my Ballard practice purchasing a downtown practice doing $800K a year in 190 days. I thought the practice would be a good base for transition. What I realized later, I really purchased the location. It turned out to be an insurance based general practice and within two years of purchase, I had less than 20% of the original patients. I actually had to rejoin Delta to gain the trust of my patient purchase."

Numbers: In Dr. Spoor's practice, collection is the same as production; they have a credit balance at all times. They have not sent statements in years. His projected gross for 12 months is $1.5M and he is working 126 days of 11 hours making 1386 hours worked for an hourly gross of $1,082. His overhead is 55%. He is demanding with his laboratory results as he is himself and primarily uses John Lavicka of Dental Ceramics (Garfield Heights, Ohio) for $300 a unit. Rhys does between zero and 32 units a day, depending on the day.

Rhys and his team see internal marketing as most important. "It's about being nice and treating people like family; being honest and making the client always right. People can see when you are really focused on them and giving your best. They will tell others." Team Spoor's goal is to have no or minimal discomfort, both physical or psychological. Painless local anesthetic techniques, sedation if necessary and keeping the guest truly comfortable through the process is Spoor internal marketing.

Lead assistant Jamie Purnell has developed her company, www.yourcomfortsolutions.com to lessen the psychological stress for dental care. These create a calming effect; well received. Rhys is not a real fan of sedative techniques because of the level of risk so these techniques Jamie has developed create a similar effect without the risks of sedation. "I was a skeptic at first but now I can see the difference it makes and that is the key point of internal marketing. We do deliver."

Dr. Spoor spends more on external marketing (8% going up to 10%) and they have tried almost everything. They have an excellent website, www.rhysspoor.com and steer everyone to their website which is always evolving. Rhys' advice on external marketing:

- Develop yourself as a brand
- Select a delivery medium and be consistent
- Study what others are successfully doing in your area.
- If no one is doing anything, start with the least expensive and easiest.
- Be first or different, be consistent and patient
- Market to your market
- Make marketing match you—-hard to be a veneer practice with 80% kids.

Other valuable continuing ed programs have included Las Vegas Institute and eventually instructing there. According to Dr. John Kraskowski of Wausau, WI, "Dr. Spoor was a most sought after instructor." Rhys has been on the faculty at U. of Washington operative department.

About his courses, (see www.rhysspoor.com for information and schedules), Rhys says "many of the Doctors tell us our courses are some of the best, if not the best of any continuing education they have ever taken. I take great personal satisfaction in getting those kinds of reviews. Our process shows the doctor how to comfortably and predictably create a great looking and functioning smile. We talk about how to do it in a timely manner, minimize the complexities and difficulties and probably most importantly, how to psychologically carry the patient from desire to result. And they have a great time doing it."

Rhys is a natural teacher and loves sharing with others. "I enjoy the interaction with people and seeing them grasp new ideas, seeing that little light bulb come on in their heads, realizing they have control over their destiny and they are truly artists who can add value to society. Once they see themselves that way, their patients see them in that light, too. I enjoy being a part of that."

"I tried to be successful from the day I started. I had a high desire to do three things:

- Be honest
- Do the right thing
- Do the best I could possibly do

There is a lot of question as to what is the right thing when it comes to dentistry. The right thing is what is correct for you as the dentist and what is best for the patient. Only you and the patient can decide this. No one else was there. Rule #3 requires a commitment of time and money to continuing education.

Being successful is an attitude followed by actions that support that attitude. You have a lot of control as to where your career will go and it starts right now."

www.rhysspoor.com

*Dentistry can give you so many options. The wonderful part of being a dental professional is it gives you the opportunity to control your time and environment so you can pursue your passions, like trying to find perfect powder, making the perfect landing or traveling to France to find the perfect little French Bistro.*

## Blatchford Game Plan:
## Business Decisions: A Cosmetic Transformation

Location and community composition are important in the success of a cosmetic practice. Because cosmetics is optional treatment, the success ratio is lower and it takes more marketing to specific people of value to continue success. Dr. Spoor was in a solid part of Seattle and knew to be highly niched, he needed to move uptown. He purchased a general practice in an excellent location. Much focus and hard work were needed to transform to a strictly cosmetic practice.

Achieving a successful cosmetic practice has become the dream goal of the American dentist. In moving toward that goal, there are real decisions and consequences which will be felt economically. Every general dentist would love to believe he either possesses or is rapidly moving towards a practice of cosmetics. As we all know, there is a huge gaposis between having "veneers" listed in your Yellow Page ad and the reality of presenting and performing the artistry to which every dentist aspires.

Are you and your practice financial and emotional candidates for a successful conversion to cosmetics? Can one mix cosmetics with TMJ, implants and pedodontics and become known in your community for aesthetic choices? What is the financial impact of moving from a general practice to a cosmetic, restorative practice? These are serious questions to contemplate in today's rapidly changing dental marketplace and the financial impact of those choices can be great.

Cosmetic dentistry is now one of the many discretionary items our patients can choose to purchase. We are competing with many other goods and services so we must have a clear and excellent reputation. Seventy-two million boomers want to look good, feel good and last a long time. It is not a given that a beautiful smile is even on the boomer's 'want list.' Patients are at choice here, too.

Choice is the operative word here. There are many choices, each creating a different economic consequence.

**Step One.** The first and most important area of choice is creating a solid vision of what you want your dream cosmetic practice to look like, financial results, reputation in the community, extent of cosmetic skills, etc. Practice vision is a personal extension of who you are as a dentist. What are your important standards and values in life? A strong vision demonstrates itself in every move you make as a dentist. Your actions speak your vision.

When a solid vision is articulated, it is very motivating for yourself and staff to see a dream picture of the future without barriers of time and money. You must have a clear picture of the end result. Otherwise, needless motion and money is wasted in making sideways decisions. You must stand for something strong or you become a meaningless victim of every fad. In Proverbs, it says, "The people without vision will perish." This vision will be tested continually by you, your staff, patients and other dentists.

Why cosmetics? Are you prepared to have a community reputation of high fees, catering to a select clientele and possible loss of former patients who only want to continue to do what their insurance covers?

One of the reasons you selected dentistry was to make a difference in people's lives. Be clear and strong in defining why you want to be a cosmetic dentist as the success of this exercise will greatly influence your cosmetic results. Your vision and action will show how committed you are to having a cosmetic practice. Your vision must be well defined and be a burning passion for you.

**Step Two.** Another business choice in the path to a cosmetic practice is the important technical skill courses. One weekend veneer class does not a cosmetic dentist make. Excellent clinicians, the "dentist's dentist," offer on-going hands-on courses to be on the leading edge of cosmetic artistry. This is an on-going process. Continue to take courses from the best. Expect to spend time and money in acquiring the skills and reputation necessary to be known as an excellent cosmetic dentist. Demonstrate your commitment by becoming an accredited member of the AACD.

Take the high road on these courses and become the best of the best. You owe it to yourself, your patients and your dental peers to do the very best cosmetic work possible.

**Step Three.** Another huge choice on the path towards a cosmetic practice is to have your own mouth completely restored to today's standards. Select one of the top Doctors and expect to pay for it. How can you present cosmetics if don't see the value for yourself? Your staff also must have the most beautiful smiles. This is a great opportunity to listen and handle your own objections as well as your staff concerns. Objections might be, "no time, don't NEED it, what will it look like?" If you cannot show value for your staff to have cosmetics at little charge, how do your presentation skills rate in working with your patients objections.

There are many advantages to a cosmetic update and one is it demonstrates to yourself your level of commitment to cosmetics. Your staff and patients will notice with much mutual admiration and motivation exchanged. You set the pace for your office. I so admire dentists who "walk their talk."

**Step Four.** Another choice is for you to define cosmetic dentistry as well as define how extensive cosmetic and restorative treatment will be in your practice. Some Doctors will be dabblers, some desire a 50% mix and others are looking at a pure cosmetic and restorative practice, perhaps in conjunction with other appearance specialists of plastic surgeons and orthodontists in a boutique or spa setting. All are choices.

It is very possible to change the nature of some practices from a general practice towards a cosmetic practice in 36 months. If a general practice is large with too many patients, a strong cosmetic practice can result in 24 months.  If a general practice is small and not financially strong, a pleasing cosmetic practice will not be the result or it will be a most difficult road.

If you see a strong cosmetic practice in your future, are you currently offering and presenting cosmetic treatment?  If you have an advanced skill level in cosmetic technique and cosmetics still represent less than 30% of your practice, ask yourself one more question—why?  It is one thing to have learned excellent technical skills but if you and your team have not mastered the presentation skills in asking needs development questions and really listening to patients, your cosmetic skill will remain academic and indeed, a dream.

Questions 5 through 9 are for you to determine the present financial strength of your practice.  In moving towards more comprehensive treatment, some of your general patients will leave your practice.  A small practice, deeply in debt, cannot handle that potential financial dip. Cosmetics is not the Great White Hope.  It will not bail out a bad practice.

In moving towards a cosmetic practice, choices are made eliminating some services as endodontics, periodontics and referring these to specialists.  However, before eliminating services, you must add and increase cosmetic services or your income will definitely drop.  Tom Peters in _Thriving on Chaos_ mentions when the overhead is high, it is difficult to impossible to make changes.  If there is a healthy margin of 40-45% profit, change is easier (general to cosmetic).  In other words, dentists need to have their practice in order before making drastic changes.

You may have too many patients at present and can afford to eliminate some by dropping insurance and eliminating services other than cosmetics.  If you learn to present cosmetics, the nature of your practice can quickly change.

## Cosmetic Practice Potential For Success

| | Present | 36 Months |
|---|---|---|
| 1. % of cosmetic income | _____ | _____ |
| 2. % of overhead | _____ | _____ |
| 3. % of collection from insurance | _____ | _____ |
| 4. % of staff expenses | _____ | _____ |
| 5. % of laboratory expenses | _____ | _____ |
| 6. Practice debt | _____ | _____ |
| 7. Personal debt | _____ | _____ |
| 8. Retirement Investment | _____ | _____ |
| 9. Age | _____ | _____ |
| 10. Cash at end of month | _____ | _____ |

**Step Five.** Just Do It! The best way to build a cosmetic practice within a general practice is to just do it. Decide to what extent you want to be known as a cosmetic dentist and let the world know. By having your own work done by the best, you become excited and motivated to continue. Do your staff's cosmetic dentistry. Have before and after picture albums in every room with framed pictures in the reception area. Dr. Spoor sends a strong message of cosmetic enthusiasm and skill to his patients in his reception room by showing framed after pictures of his patient's beautiful smiles. Dr. Spoor also has a photo studio in his consult room demonstrating to patients his emphasis, competency and commitment to appearance artistry.

Use the very best dental labs with the possibility of three to four day turn around for special clients. Eventually talk with every patient about the possibility of more long term care, looking good and avoiding problems. Ask questions and keep asking questions.

A cosmetic dental practice is about choices. Your patients also have the opportunity to choose. How would your patients even know you do great cosmetic work? What is the reputation you have in the community? Are you known for anything special? How committed are you and your staff to breaking out of the paradigms of the old dental model and creating something new called a cosmetic practice? You are always at choice and there are economic consequences to each choice. Which do you choose and how committed are you to making it happen well?

Bill Blatchford, DDS

# From the Blatchford Play Book: Courage to Succeed

When things are not going as you planned, it does take persistence, courage, focus and commitment to succeed.  Dr. Spoor has used much energy, focus and hard work to have a highly niched cosmetic practice.

>> Easy to be ordinary, takes courage to excel

>> Takes courage to stand by your convictions

>> Takes courage to keep fighting when you are losing

>> Takes courage to stick to your game plan and the unrelenting pursuit of your goal when you encounter obstacles

>> Takes courage to push yourself to places you have never been before, to break through barriers.

>> We are here to be tested, to be challenged with adversity, to see what we can accomplish

>> Takes courage to look deep within your soul

>> Courage is not how a person stands or falls, but how they get back up again

>> All glory comes from daring to begin

>> We cannot discover new oceans unless we have the courage to lose sight of the shore

>> There is no substitute for 'guts'

>> JFK said, "the stories of past courage can define that ingredient—they can teach, they can offer hope, they can provide inspiration.  But they cannot supply courage itself. For each man must look into his own soul."

>> Winston Churchill said, "Courage is the first of human qualities because it is the quality which guarantees all the others."

# 18

## PURCHASING A PRACTICE

## Dr. Chris Mueller

Dr. Mueller is a very young looking dentist producing $1M only four years out of dental school. He is smart, personable and definitely not slick. The most important thing in Chris' life is his family. He wants to be successful yet the three practice opportunities and decisions really "just happened" and he was in the right place at the right time.

He is surprised to find himself in the company of profitable dentists. "One of the reasons you may have selected me is that I was able to do between two to three times my production without significant overhead increases due to sound management principles and acquiring a patient base large enough to allow block booking plus minor fee increases."

To be near their families, Chris and his wife selected Port Orchard. It is a working town in Washington's Puget Sound, supplying labor for Bremerton Navy Shipyards and now becoming a growing bedroom ferry commute to Seattle.

Chris says, "I graduated in 2001 from U. of Washington and there are still moments when I am not 100% sure I will be successful. I purchased a practice that produced $250K the year of purchase, choosing it over another practice producing $600K. My decision was largely based on personal meditation and was against what logic would have dictated. Starting out was very intimidating and success was far from assured—I couldn't even get a bank loan, eventually having to ask my father for the $180K purchase price."

This practice had produced $450K. The owner was a skilled practitioner who had several personal issues preventing his full time attention for the last several years. He had walked away in Oct. 2001 leaving his two staff to keep it running without his input. Chris was able to work there two days a week for seven months and keep the practice open. He became attached to the small, comfortable setting. His first goal upon purchase was to return it to the historical production, reintroduce a hygiene program and eventually grow to $600K.

"In 2003, we collected $433K on $480K production and I felt we had reached a comfortable level and life was going smoothly. In Nov. of 2003, the dentist across the street unexpectedly passed away and life got complicated again. I was absolutely sure I wanted nothing to do with his practice and tried to convince a friend of mine to purchase. Weeks passed and Bill Blatchford heard of my possibility. How could I, a relative rookie, handle the patient load of two mature dentists? I worked slower so it seemed logical I couldn't produce more than I was currently doing, let alone the production of two faster dentists. It seemed overwhelming—-not to mention the pending staff issues, having to move offices, paper work headaches, etc. There were times where I firmly decided it would be too much work and chose not to rock the boat. Finally after much consultation, I put my hat in the ring. By this time, five months had passed. The daughter of the deceased Doctor felt I was the one her father would have wanted and chose me. His practice had collected $450K in 2003. The selling price was $260K for the practice and $250K for the building. I hoped to at least bring my production up to my $600K goal."

In retrospect, he feels definitely "the best business decision I made was buying the second practice and having Bill help me manage it. I never thought I would be this successful this early on." Chris is 33 years old.

The second practice challenges included the deceased dentist's wife being office manager and running the business on a peg board system with several helpers. She died six months before her husband.

Other pitfalls on the path to excellence for Chris include:

- "Holding on to staff too long once it was apparent they weren't sharing your vision. I kept hoping they would suddenly change, thinking, 'we can make this work.' If you have to MAKE it work, then you are spending energy instead of becoming profitable. I can't emphasize this one enough—by lacking the courage to make uncomfortable choices, I limited the heights to which we could rise. Once these choices were made, it was like cutting a hot air balloon free from its moorings. The interesting thing is that I knew in my gut that everyone of these people was not going to work out but my mind kept hoping they would change. People may change but not very much."

- "In the same vein, avoiding difficult situations for long periods of time by occupying myself with less important tasks. Technically, this is probably called 'risk avoidance.' It's much easier to tinker with a faulty handpiece than to have a frank discussion with your receptionist about how you're not happy with her performance. Essentially I had subconscious procrastination in the tough areas which just prolonged the problem."

- "Thinking busy was being profitable. This is coming more clearly to me as I have to write off large amounts of accounts receivable from bad accounts. I treated patients with the notion we'd get the money someday and I'd rather stay busy than not. In retrospect, I should have had a staff meeting, gone home early or read a book."

- "Not having a clue what the receptionist was doing and assuming she was doing what I envisioned regarding AR management, scheduling, recall, etc. I found out this was not the case most of the time. I was too busy with teeth and home life to actually check on it. I also did not know the computer system like she did and felt I could not match her experience. The solution was to purchase a new system where we were on equal footing. I should have had weekly meetings to discuss the numbers from the start."

- Trying to save pennies on supplies. Chris graduated from dental school with $15K debt by scrimping plus marrying a wife with a steady job after his freshman year with the MRS Scholarship. He is mindful of money.

On the other hand, Dr. Mueller's practice highlights have been "purchasing his first practice, purchasing the second practice, acquiring a team that supports my vision and is loyal to me while implementing techniques learned from Dr. Blatchford."

At the merger, Chris brought two full time staff plus one part time hygienist and he inherited four full time staff. Staffs were less than enthusiastic in joining together and making changes. In fact, "at the first staff seminar, the groups began forming 'camps' and would team up on me. It wasn't long before most departed or were shown the door. With that mess behind me, I realized what a burden I had really been dealing with every day."

In 2004, Dr. Mueller and newly reorganized team collected $797K, besting his goal of $600K. He had between three and seven staff the year he combined practices. Overhead was 71%. In 2005, his production/collection finished at $1.1M and overhead of 51%. His team is four full-time staff. Currently, they are attracting 30 new patients a month and working 180 days. In his first practice, a crown was $796. Currently, it is $850 plus $175 buildup.

Moving into a five op., fifty-year-old building with the last remodel in 1971 was not the most fun. Because the dentist had not moved out, there was thirty years of dental junk. Chris found equipment he had no idea it's function. The first phase of remodel was to be paint and carpet but evolved to renovating the welcome area, larger hygiene rooms and lighting, new door with Chris' logo, new floors and more. Phase 2 will be the rest. "It is starting to feel like I'm an established dentist rather than a new guy in someone else's office."

Chris had signed with a management consulting firm prior to Bill but they were "unable to motivate me to make any of the tough choices—firing staff members, etc. They still use me as a reference and I tell them to call Bill."

Chris feels Dr. Spoor's anterior courses "really changed the way I practice and enable me to offer treatment I had never considered before." When Chris purchased his second practice, he started addressing periodontal disease in the hygiene department, offering posterior bonded ceramic restorations, promoting veneers and referring time consuming extractions. "Some in my area cannot afford optional care or aren't interested but I know they will not say 'yes' until I ask."

He and his team are all involved in sales. Now that they have met all the patients, they are role-playing with receptionist asking questions on the phone, hygienist doing an excellent job of asking questions and setting Dr. Mueller up for the details."

"When we are playing our 'A' game, the day flows by without hardly noticing—all of a sudden, it is 5 PM. You're happy and your dinner conversation is not about work. You feel good about the services you have provided and your patients express that as well. You do not dread going back to work after the weekend."

"My staff is really motivated by the Blatchford bonus. The first one was just a couple hundred dollars, then the first one over $1000 really got them moving. They have more ownership of the practice now. My vision statement also has helped motivate them. Having one key team member who is on fire also has been very helpful for the others—kind of like a lead horse. Chris is amazed and impressed with staff on salary, they even want to come in on their day off for team meetings so as not to lower the bonus."

The biggest struggle along the profitability path for Chris has been staffing. "Getting a group around me who respected me as a dentist and a person and really saw my vision of what we stood for and where we are going has by far been the hardest part. This really has taken over two years and we still aren't perfect but much better." Now, Chris feels his leadership allowed him to create a vision statement. The team with the vision tends to address the issues themselves. "I do provide the final word but often times, I don't need to. Don't get me wrong—we still have plenty of room for improvement."

The next biggest struggle for Chris was feeling he did not have enough patients or accepted treatment to block book effectively. "To be honest, we were scared to try it and never did. We let fear keep us from knowing if it would work. This was solved by acquiring another practice which gave us enough patients."

Chris' practice goals are to increase the quality of new patients (those people who elect for ideal treatment) from below 15 a month to at least 30 by Dec. 2005. He wants to be consistently producing $120K a month which would result in $1.5M by Dec. 2006. He wants at least one anterior case per month and eventually one a week by Dec., 2006.

Internally, Chris and team started asking for referrals but when they did not see results, it slowly stopped happening. "Mostly, we have tried to secure as many patients of the former dentist as possible by providing superior customer service and quality dentistry. I try to make anesthesia as painless as possible to generate word of mouth. We take pictures of our larger cases to display."

Externally, "we offered free whitening with Valpak and received a handful of quality patients but most just came for the free whitening.

We have a small yellow page ad which has brought in a few. The bulk of our growth has been acquiring older practices and we are securing the charts from a third office. It is much easier for me and available in my community."

Chris and his wife are saving so he can be in a position to retire at age 45. Though not actually intending to retire, he would like to do a service mission to a developing country or Navajo nation. "My immediate goal is to be done with diapers by 2009." Chris feels profitability is allowing him to spend more time with his family, travel, have a waterfront home with view of Seattle, being able to help those I feel could use it and being able to help with part of my children's college funds.

Chris was always a voracious reader and this helped him to perform well in school. Thus he was able to study whatever he wanted in school and go to the dental school of his choice. He was originally a marine biology major. During his junior year, he did a semester at Hopkins Marine Station in Monterey, CA. He loved what he was doing but "Clinton was slashing government spending on research and many post-docs were hanging around looking for work. I didn't want to go to that much school and not be guaranteed a job in the end. Many of my classmates were pre-dent and pre-med. I didn't want medicine so dentistry it was."

During undergrad, Chris served two years on a mission to Zurich which gave him insight into what he wanted from life. He chose a wife to be a great partner and support. He sought advice from those who had done this before and found Bill Blatchford through them. "I didn't know what life would bring but I feel this has laid the foundation upon which success has followed."

e-mail: chrismueller@hotmail.com

*Mueller family.*
*A masterful feat to take a picture. Thanks Dad, for being home more.*

## Blatchford Game Plan:
## The Mathematics of Cosmetics —
## Multiplying Your Opportunity

Dr. Mueller is the prime example of taking advantage of several local practice sales and incorporating them into a $1M practice by the time he is 33 years old. Purchasing an existing practice is a guaranteed way to multiply your opportunities. Are you looking for that opportunity in your community?

How to increase your practice, that is the question. Most practices have the capacity and technical skill to produce much more which would dramatically increase the net. We want to increase the number of fee-for-service patients who sees value in a new smile. We need more non-media generated and non-coupon generated patients. As technical skills increase, so should production.

In many practices, new patient numbers are changing. The old fee-for-service insurance model offering practices a steady flow of newly insured patients for their free six month cleaning and exam may no longer be in the majority in your area. Alternative delivery systems of managed care initially are attracting those patient numbers. This has created a concern for private care practices who have the technical skill to deliver much more excellent dentistry.

In a strong general practice, healthy new patient numbers should approach 15 to 20 adults a month. When the focus of the practice is to present every patient with ideal treatment, a 50% case acceptance rate can be achieved if verbal skills of Doctor and staff are excellent. This number of new patients will result in $500,000 to $600,000 gross production.

If your new patient numbers have reached a plateau in the last several years as your ability to deliver cosmetic and better dentistry has increased, you have cause for concern. There are several solid answers to the concern over declining new patient numbers. One solution is to create a program of niche marketing. This is deciding the direction of your practice, building a reputation within that niche (cosmetics, reconstruction, mercury-free, etc.) which will garner new patients who see value in your excellent care. A marketing budget should be established and a professional marketing expert should be hired who understands niche marketing and the desired reputation for your practice.

The second solution is to purchase an existing practice in your area and merge it with your present practice to create the potential of an excellent strong practice. The benefits to patients, the selling Doctor and your bottom line are very positive if the purchase is structured correctly with a win/win for all. A practice merger is a perfect opportunity to create a new image in niche marketing with a dental marketing expert.

In fact, marketing with a practice acquisition is a must.

One win is for the patients of the purchased practice. With warm welcome letters and increased verbal skills of staff, the patient retention is high. Patients feel well served. The new energy level is high and newer technology might be offered. The selling Doctor wins when the financial structure of the sale supports his goals and is able to move onto his next project. The new Doctor wins when the contract structures the sale so there is financial reward from the beginning. He must be in control and able to see benefits from the beginning rather than strictly a payback for the first five years  Avoid costly pitfalls in purchases and sales by having a coach who represents you.

Another benefit to the buying Doctor is these patients are already established patients who see value in regular dental care. It takes more effort and funds to attract new patients than to geometrically reproduce established patients. A practice merger brings established patients.

A successful practice purchase really requires the help of a smart practice broker. His goal is a win/win for both parties. We coach our Doctors to avoid the heartbreaking pitfalls of practice purchase with strong guidelines. A few are:

- purchasing the practice outright and avoid any "partnership" situation
- seller leaves the practice with a non-compete covenant
- purchase price is definite at time of sale
- 100% financing through a bank as a total buyout is the best.

|  | Your Practice | New Practice | Combined |
|---|---|---|---|
| Prod. | $400,000 | $250,000 | $650,000 |
| Staff | $80,000 (20%) | $50,000 (20%) | $130,000 (20%) |
| Lab | $40,000 (10%) | $25,000 (10%) | $65,000 (10%) |
| Supplies | $20,000 | $12,500 | $32,500 |
| Rent | $40,000 | (Close office, | $40,000 |
|  |  | pay rent for 6-12 mo) |  |
| Equip | $40,000 | (Sell or donate to charity) | $40,000 |
| Misc | $60,000 | $60,000 | $60,000 |
| Total | $280,000 | $87,500 | $367,500 |
| Net | $120,000 |  | $282,500 |

The ADA average overhead is 73%.

NET AFTER PAYMENT $232,600

FINANCING  $250,000 New Practice Production
$200,000 Estimated cost

Nothing Down with 100% financing. Finance for five years at 10% Annual payment is $50,000 prior to taxes.

There are practices for sale within a five-mile radius of your office which could nicely merge with your existing practice and satisfy the new patient craving. Some of these practices are smaller and are overlooked by recent graduates as they perceive they could not make a living on just that practice.

Practices may be for sale because the Doctor is going back to graduate school, has family needs in a different area or feels it is just "time to sell." Some practices may be listed with a broker while others are not officially for sale. This is where networking with your peers works well as there are dentists who are either frustrated with the present system, nearing retirement age or perceive a different practice environment would be best but have not definitely made a decision yet. By lunching with possible candidates, you can offer your support should the decision be made. Be first in line.

Almost all practices can qualify as eligible for a cosmetic transition. If the seller was an adequate dentist with a loyal following, it is very possible for you to have a high patient retention rate and after several hygiene cycles, to see the fruits of your communication skills create good results. If the seller has a small high end cosmetic practice where most work is completed, this practice has value for you, too, as the reputation is already established and these patients see value in cosmetic work. They will continue to refer their family and friends to you.

With a desired result of 10 to 15 adult new patients a month, a practice merger is a great solution. Depending on the patient base, new patient flow can increase from 10% to 50%. There are several important keys to having the results show well—-

- use a smart broker representing the buyer (you)
- develop strong relationships with patient so treatment is not perceived as overwhelming
- learn and master skills in communication and enrollment
- broker represents the one paying the fee

I have seen excellent cosmetic practices produce incredible work on five or less new patients a month. What this means is that Doctor and team have learned how to form lasting, trusting relationships and have mastered sales skills which create value with the patient.

Without these sales skills, your excellent technical cosmetic work will unlikely be in someone's mouth.  Therefore, purchasing a practice and doubling your new patient flow is not the whole answer.  You must be able to convert those new patients into dental missionaries for your cosmetic work.

Once the  practice purchase has been made, your "new patient" flow has been increased to meet your goals.  The next immediate step is learning and mastering new skills in enrollment to make certain these new patients are asked questions to discover their needs, really listened to as never before and treatment is actually completed.  This then is the real value of purchasing a practice.  Do you and your staff have the excellent skills necessary in today's market to present and have accepted ideal treatment?

Bill Blatchford, DDS

## From the Blatchford Play Book:
## Pre-Game Preparation

Dr. Mueller is the coach for their morning huddle where all team members are present. Here are some points to make that meeting effective.

>> Morning huddle run by the coach

>> Team arrives early, focused and finished with breakfast

>> Who is ready to play?

>> Who knows the score today?

>> How will best service be delivered today?

>> Start huddle on a positive note, welcoming your team for another good day

>> Scheduling blocks are set to goal

>> Whole team starts at the same time

>> Team has copy of today's schedule in hand

>> Select referral requests, long-range planning conversations with recare guests

>> No personal talk during huddle, focus on serving guests well

>> Doctor starts at 8 AM with one great "A" patient

>> People notes on guests are shared so all know current information

>> Team is playing their 'A' game today

>> Coach asks and receives team commitment to make and exceed goal next four days

>> Complete huddle five minutes before first guest

>> High fives all around

# 19

# RELATIONSHIP BUILDING

## Dr. Curtis Chan

Curtis is successful in San Diego for many reasons and one he shared is his ability to connect with people. His physician father was in private practice, then in emergency room medicine (was fed up with insurance and never seeing his family) and when Curtis was 13 years old, his father joined the US Air Force. The family lived in Germany for five years and continued moving. Curtis feels this forced him to make friends quickly, to connect with everyone on some level and he accepted this as a personal challenge to build relationships.

"Being raised in different cultures forced me to hone my natural skills in relationship building. I became a good listener. At our practice, we exude caring and connect with people. We feel 99% of sales is building those relationships."

He has mastered these skills well enough that it basically serves as his marketing program. He virtually has no formal external marketing program and still attracts 20-25 new patients a month, mostly from happy client referrals.

None of the following Curtis does is part of his marketing program for his practice, yet these are skills and beliefs he personally holds: 20 year member of the LaJolla Symphony as a cello player, accomplished pianist, very active member of his Christian church and weekly host to a couples Bible study on marriage, and a member of a very large well networked family in San Diego. Curtis co-chairs the San Diego Dental Golf Group. Mae heads up several outreach ministries at church: Women's Outreach, Children's Ministry, and an Adoption Support Group.

Curtis is the fourth of five boys, all involved in the health care field. Four are dentists and one is an optometrist. When Curtis joined the Blatchford program 13 years ago, he wrote three goals: to get out of debt, to get married, and to live on a golf course. All of course have come true and the very best of all of these, was finding Mae and getting married at 36. They have two natural children and have adopted two babies from China; Grace and Matthew. They recently have decided to home school their children because of strong core values in the Chan family. It will be successful.

How do five boys all enter the health care field? Curtis' father was one of four brothers and two sisters orphaned in British Guyana, an English settlement. Their aunt was a Seventh Day Adventist and she urged them to emigrate to the US. All were high-achievers as the sisters became nurses and three of the boys went to medical school in California. The "cool" youngest uncle dropped out his second year of med school and later entered dental school at Loma Linda where he went on to specialized in orthodontics, greatly admired by the five nephews.

When the elder Dr. Chan joined the Air Force and was stationed in Germany for five years, one of his sons mastered the German language and graduated No. 1 at his dental school in Universität Tübingen, near Stuttgart. In the father's 23 years of service time, he served in the First Gulf War and was a commander of the largest mobile US Air Force hospital in Ryad, Saudi Arabia.

Mae, Curtis' wife, has a interesting family journey to the US. When the Chinese Revolution was occurring after WWII, her grandparents fled mainland China to Korea. With nine children, they eventually came to US. Two of Mae's aunts are dentists. Her father is a chemist who immigrated to Japan. In 1957, when he was 18 years old, he came to Abilene, Texas to study at Hardin-Simmons University.

All five Chan boys are high achievers. Clayton is the neuromuscular expert at LVI. He is an accountant by training and then a dental lab tech. He worked for Kerr as a dental lab tech and developed shade guides for composites along with a chemist and a physicist. After two children, he graduated from Loma Linda School of Dentistry and began his search for the "elements of occlusion." He was still not convinced of the Pankey occlusal direction. He was searching for an answer and found Myotronics. He became a passionate advocate and according to Curtis, "couldn't sleep and even gave up surfing."

Curtis decided by his junior year in high school to be a dentist so he "could help people improve their health." He had always been successful in setting goals and being the best he could be in school, in cello or piano. He feels success is not about money, for that will come.

In an associate position, he did hygiene during the week and some dentistry on weekends. Eventually there was a Del Mar practice for sale but Curtis had already invested in a new car and home. The practice was six months behind in rent and had 200 charts. A local dentist helped him put the financing together. He continued as an associate as he built his practice. He had to clear $4500 a month to break even.

In his fourth year, his brother Clayton graduated and they needed to start working more hours. They found a better location to share office space. They followed the Pride model of bigger is better with 1.5 assistants per operatory, two hygienists and two in front. "I knew I was digging a big hole." Clayton had a Blatchford tape and Curtis felt "it just couldn't be true." Eventually he heard Bill at an evening program. "I needed to do this but I felt badly doing something different than my brother."

"I arrived with eight staff and one by one, they excused themselves." Gradually he selected people who could see his vision and others came back, some driving 1-2 hours to work with he and the team. "All the things Bill said made sense and we moved to new levels. The 'right-sizing' took two years, while building with the right staff and systems. As we improved, we weeded out the low end of patients and created opportunities for better patients to find us. Bill also encouraged me to discover what I liked to do, thus I dropped endo, amalgams and most children."

The hardest thing Curtis has done in dentistry was to make the change to refine his practice. "I just had to jump in and do this. It was a 90 degree turn from the direction we were headed and it was tough." On the other hand, "doing Blatchford was the best thing I ever did. He became my mentor in dental business, made me accountable and is a good coach."

Curtis' team this year is really fired up and on track for $1M production/collection for 2005 by producing $85K every 15 day work period. Curtis and his family are making a point to vacation every 6 to 8 weeks. His goal is to work three days a week, doing one to two patients per day and 100 units a month.

His porcelain lava crown fee is $1500 and he uses an excellent laboratory at $200 a unit. Posterior crowns are $1200. He is focusing on his top 20% of patients. They collect in advance and have no Accounts Receivable. In July of 2005, he quit Delta, which constituted 20% of his collection. Curtis and staff had been speaking with his patients for a long time, positioning them well for Curtis becoming a non-provider with Delta.

Curtis' style of leadership is to find key people who are leaders and give them the latitude of making decisions. The leader's clear vision guides them and this eliminates the micro-managing. Regular communication is key with a focused morning huddle, weekly staff meetings, evening meetings and BMW 4x4 which is four hours every four weeks set aside for training and mastering conversations and systems. www.curtischandds.com

*The Chan Boys:*
*L to R: Clayton,*
*Carlton (baby),*
*Clifford, Craig*
*and Curtis.*

*The Curtis Chan Family—Mae, Grace, Jonathan,*
*Michelle, Curtis and Matthew.*

*Curtis smiling knowing*
*he's going in the right*
*direction.*

## Mints on the pillow, bugs in the bed

Dr. Curtis Chan has a stellar reputation. He is known for kindness, service, and excellence. His guests return and new clients arrive because of positive buzz in the community and personal networking. The continual challenge is to serve your guests to the highest standards at every moment. As the great sales trainer Brian Tracey says, "Everything counts, and everything counts."

Hold a victory celebration when you complete treatment on a guest and your conversations are focused, listening is keen, timeliness is observed, finances work, and the guest is overjoyed with the technical results. Do you take time to recount all the "everythings" that allowed this guest to be ecstatic? Do your systems ensure every time your guests visit, your treatment will go smoothly? Do you have qualified staff members who understand each system? Do your staff members sing your praises and the reasons they are happy to be working in your office?

Patients depart because of unfulfilled expectations, usually in the administrative area. It's the bugs in the bed that create ruffled feathers, not the technical work. Our systems of communication and follow-up are critical.

An office culture can develop haphazardly. With little direction or distinction, staff members do what they did in other offices. We remain average. With each staff member working independently, we miss opportunities for great conversations with patients, guests slip through the cracks, and we achieve excellence in a random manner. Strong systems form a practice culture when the leader is clear and communicates the bigger picture. Great staffs are drawn to clearly communicated passion and share the vision. Deep thought, clarity, and communication are the keys to invigorating your staff and being accountable. Where are the bugs in your bed that patients will notice?

- **Timeliness** — Unfulfilled promises of time. Running late is a symptom of a lack of direction from the leader. Are you Dr. Everything to everybody?

- **The waiting game** — Guests who have accepted treatment wait and wait for the doctor to appear, while they observe a flurry of activity elsewhere. Pareto's law of 80/20 indicates 80 percent of your profit comes from 20 percent of your patients. Do you know who they are and is their visit filled with exceptional care?

- **Random scheduling** — This creates chaos, little production, and an emotional void by the end of the day. Learn block-scheduling and schedule each day the same. Schedule to a daily goal by knowing your overhead per hour. Make that a figure to exceed.

- **The insurance game** — If you leave the patient out of the insurance loop, you make your office the center of insurance knowledge. Instead, collect upfront for most patients and give them the insurance form to submit for reimbursement. Quit creating work and trouble for yourself.

- **Order-taking** — Your first question to your patients should not be, "What is your biggest concern?" If it is, your diagnosis and treatment result in "small-picture" items. In the sales world, this makes you an "order-taker," rather than a creator of opportunity. Learn modern sales skills and begin with, "How may I help you? How would you like your smile to look in 20 years?" The result of order-taking is your patient's assumption that your treatment mix is limited and "if I want to beautify at 55, I should seek that care elsewhere."

- **Promises, promises** — When you say you will do something, do it! Connect with patients and staff. Excellent communication with your lab and specialists and networking in your community all lead to excellent results. Do you have solid systems in place to keep promises?

- **Layered staff** — A common "bug in the bed" complaint I hear from airplane seatmates is, "I seldom see the doctor, because the staff does all the work." Consider using skilled treatment coordinators who see the guest through to a happy completion. "It's not my job" is a bug in the bed. Hygienists should know all fees, assistants should know the schedule and how to do complete financial arrangements, and the doctor should know how to handle patient phone calls. What systems do you need to implement to make sure you clearly hear your patients and they feel complete and special?

Mints on the pillows are wonderful, yet momentary. Bugs in the bed are stories that are repeated to friends and family in the community. Solid systems will eliminate the bugs. Is it time to get some help ... or do you want to continue to be average?

Bill Blatchford, DDS

## Blatchford Game Plan: Playing your 'A' Game

Dr. Chan works at being a good coach for his team. Relying on internal marketing as he does, the team must be playing their 'A' game at all times.

During the final games of the NBA playoffs series several years ago, the Los Angeles Lakers lost very few games. However, after one particular loss, Shaquille O'Neal shared his simple explanation that "we didn't bring our 'A' game. We have an "A" game but we didn't play it tonight. We played our 'B' game, instead. We're bringing our 'A' game next time."

The L. A. Lakers benefited greatly that year from excellent, strong coaching. Phil Jackson took already talented individuals and honed them into a focused, lean and mean team to deliver results. A good coach, who is passionate about the game, plus already-skilled players who come together to play the "A" game, result in a winning combination.

What is your "A" game in the business of dentistry? Do you and your team know the game plan and come prepared to play hard all day, every day? Like the Lakers, a dental staff (including the Dr.) must arrive with all the up-to-date skills, sharp focus, mental balance and passion to deliver the best.

Tiger Woods, in his stunning win of the US Open, shared that he played his "A" game all week. He demonstrated skills, unbelievable focus, passion and practice with his coach, which resulted in a record win. He also spent five important hours practicing on Wednesday before the Open. Tiger Woods practices! If we were as good as Tiger, would we practice for five hours on routine skills?

What is Tiger's "A" game? How can a dental office play an "A" game like Shaq? The cheese has moved in dentistry and the need is great to reinvent ourselves. Instead of playing the old routine and thinking small, we must create an "A" game.

What has changed in dentistry? There has been a virtual clinical revolution with new products and techniques. This creates the possibility to deliver exceptional service and results, thus branding yourself in the marketplace as special and different. Dentistry has become truly optional and dentists who play their 'A' game, believe they are in the elective health care field. Patients also have become more sophisticated, realizing they do not NEED our services, but choose to have a more beautiful smile that works well and lasts a long time.

Another important aspect of change in dentistry is the people part of the 'A' game. For years, dentistry has been a product-driven industry. We are a service industry and are evaluated by the public by our level and focus of service. An 'A' practice sees dentistry as a people game and hires staff who genuinely enjoy people.

To play the 'A' game, the players, including the Doctor, need to present themselves with the highest skills possible. Taking the latest, greatest courses like the Las Vegas Institute, becoming accredited with American Academy of Cosmetic Dentistry or a national equivalent and continuing to reach for the next level is an important part of the "A" game.

An attitude of curiosity on the part of all players must become part of your practice culture. An "A" team has a sense of curiosity about life, others and the workings of things. At work the curious man finds an opportunity to learn while he earns. Having mastered the often-routine requirements of the job, his curiosity demands more, seeking answers to questions raised not by others but by his own desire to know. At play, myriads of questions bombard the mind. Every aspect of existence stimulates a question to the curious man. It is this drive to know everything, this drive that sustains the curious mind. Strange to say, the satisfaction is not the answer, but in the search itself. Be curious and hire curious people.

What is the game plan for implementing this curiosity and skill? It takes action to make your dream plan a reality. A vision in your head is dead. You must dig deep inside to discover your "hot buttons" and inner passion for excellence and making a difference for others. You must be able to communicate that picture to an already talented team. They must see what you see with possibly even more intensity.

The "A" game plan must include practicing of learned business and communication skills. Just because you have been in dentistry for twenty years does not mean you have developed the listening skills to allow a patient to dream. Learn the skills and practice asking questions, then really listen.

An "A" game must include reading of books on business, sales and marketing. What is your current book to put you in the "A" game? Audio and videotapes are available for stimulation. Phil Jackson of the Lakers has selected philosophy books of required reading for his talented team.

Be curious to the point of taking classes seemingly unrelated to the field of dentistry. Classes could be on self-esteem, psychology, web design and graphic artistry, stocks and financial planning as well as a physically demanding class. How does this connect to the "A" game? A person who has stretched to learn new ideas and skills is a much more enthusiastic person with others. Enthusiasm is the basis for sharing dreams and creating value for others.

An "A" game is one of constant improvement. Don't accept the status quo. Turn your weakness into a strength by practicing to constantly improve. Do not accept that your numbers have stopped growing and you have reached a plateau. The 'A' team reinvents themselves and breaks out of the doldrums.

Select a coach who pushes you. The coach can see things from a different point of view. Metaphorically, you are inside of your own leadership box and the instructions for getting out of the box are written on the outside. A coach has to be able to see what is happening, because you can't. The 'A' team finds a solid coach.

All these are skills and attitude to develop on your own time and bring your "new" person to the office team. At the office, the "A" game is being on time, creating dreams with patients and delivering excellence. A highly skilled, mentally focused team is thinking positive thoughts, complimenting each other's work, seeing the big picture with a vengence, self-starters (including the dentist) and real team players who boost each other and patients. They are excited about today, tomorrow and possibilities. Their dreams are coming true.

Everyone likes to think they play an "A" game because they are tired at night. When the Lakers lost, they were really tired and had given 110%. A checklist for the "B" game would be a practice culture of micromanaging, not so silent complaining, relying on reasons—not results, stars with little teamwork, a lack of curiosity and reliance on the status quo.

We all have a choice in the matter. Put on your game face and play your "A" game. Make the "A" game your practice culture.

Bill Blatchford, DDS

## From the Blatchford Playbook: Game of Life

A balance is what we are after. Dr. Chan and his wife Mae have a happy family life, an active spiritual being, are givers in the community of life and his practice supports all this.

>> Keep on playing the game

>> Never retire and hide; you are needed somewhere

>> What is your plan for a meaningful retirement?

>> Never deprive someone of hope. It might be all they have

>> Dentistry supports your life; life comes first

>> Develop passion in life

>> Be interested in others

>> Be curious about your surroundings

>> Always play full throttle, live each day

>> Say "yes" to opportunities even when you do not know the outcome

>> Demonstrate happiness

>> Enthusiasm is contagious

# 20

## A FAMILY PARTNERSHIP–
## THE TRIUMVIRATE

## Dr. Dennis O'Brien, Dr. Stephanie Race,
## Dr. Jeff O'Brien

Surely not unique yet very special when two children join their father in a general and cosmetic practice and all works well, all survive and all are thriving. Waukesha is a suburb of Milwaukee, WI and yes, a wealthier part of Milwaukee but certainly not Rye, NY or Palm Beach. Waukesha is the fastest growing area of Wisconsin, a city of 70K in the county seat, headquarters for GE Medical, foundries and auto accessories. It has actually become a destination for workers from Detroit traveling to Waukesha.

Dennis is the father, an accomplished dentist who started with a progressive partner, Dr. Pat Falvey and together they took courses from Drs. Omer Reed, Harold Wirth, Earl Estep and others.

Dennis feels the partnership just developed. "I always did like the idea of a family partnership. Of course, there are concerns of everyone getting along OK. It has worked out well."

Dr. Stephanie Race, his only daughter, knew she wanted to practice dentistry in the third grade. Jeff, his only son, started in dental school after one year of engineering at U of Wisconsin in Madison. The father, Dennis, was a pharmacist when he began dental school in 1970. In 1975, Dr. Falvey had a partner who left general dentistry for orthodontic school. Dennis became the associate and in 1977, a 50% partner.

The partnership ended in 1999 when Dr. Falvey retired. Five years prior to this time, Dr. Falvey had decreased his time in the practice by a certain percentage every year. Stephanie joined the practice in 1994 just as Dr. Falvey was cutting down. Dennis said, "Stephanie helped shape new life and new direction to the practice." Jeff did practice a few days while Dr. Falvey was here but there was a definite need for a new facility. The former office was in a multi-professional office building with six operatories in 2,500 square feet.

In 1996, Dennis and team took Walter Hailey's Dental Boot Kamp and it "opened our eyes to running our practice as a business, being more people oriented and involving our team in the process. In 1997, Stephanie and Dennis took Rosenthal and Dickerson's Baylor University Esthetic and Restorative Program, followed by second level of Boot Kamp and Advanced level Aesthetic courses at LVI.

Dr. O'Brien made a decision to gear up his practice, leadership skills and create a great opportunity for three dentists in the same family to practice well. He sought coaching from Blatchford to help create a bigger picture for long-term and make the challenges of multiple dentists be rewarding for all. Jeff joined the practice after a one year Veteran's Administration GPR. "Since taking Dr. Bill Blatchford's course in 1999, our practice experienced a much needed 20% increase in production for the year."

Dennis owned the land and borrowed a conventional bank loan to build the free-standing building. Jeff and Stephanie do not own part of the building yet. Dennis figures it could be an inheritance or a vehicle to help fund his retirement. The new building is 3000 square feet with seven operatories. Costs for the new building were $120K for the land, $80K in soft costs and $600K for the building.

Stephanie works 2.5 days a week, Jeff works four days and Dennis works three days (with more time off) for a total number of doctor days at 360. The only "evening hours" are Monday until 7 PM and Wednesdays, they start at 7 AM. They are all together on

Wednesdays, their staff meeting day. Their monthly production is $156K total which is $4100 a day. There are three hygienists who produce a total of nine days a week.

Their BAM for bonusing is $118,500 and 20% of production over BAM is shared with team. Bonus amount averages $7500 shared per month. This keeps the two receptionists, three assistants and three combined hygienists very eager to stay the course and play the game. They have bonused every month for the past three years. The team block books and does not deviate from that. They have found sedation dentistry to be such a boom for them, they have two set-ups. Oral sedation dentistry is where holding blocks of time really help for when there is fear and a person actually comes into the office, it is great to be able to accomplish as much dentistry as possible in one visit.

Their fees are the highest in the area. Crown fee is $1044, veneer is $1198 and Jeff enjoys doing cosmetic dentures at $3K a unit. They have a Cerec which they average about 20 units a month. They complete between 15-20 sedation patients a month.

In making the transition from a single dentist to three, some long term staff didn't make it. Dennis said those decisions were difficult and now, he realizes how important a great team is in making a practice a happy place.

As a team, their vision statement and subsequent actions are:

"It is mutually rewarding to do the dentistry we enjoy on those who value their health and well being and enthusiastically refer their friends and family. We accomplish our vision by partnering with our patients in a comfortable and personalized way to achieve their long term dental dreams. By exceeding expectations and being 100% committed, we add to the success and happiness of the people we touch daily."

Qualities that make a family of three dentists work well are:
- Dennis is a people person who is a good listener.
- Dennis has only two children, eliminating any possible inequality of power or money

- None of the spouses are involved in the practice as Stephanie's husband is an orthodontist and cannot be associated with one general practice too tightly

The practice is still owed by Dennis. The income is divided based on production as production and collection are virtually equal. Expenses are paid out of a general fund and the purchases are done by a committee of the three of us. Staff conflict resolution is generally done with all three present.

Presently they are working on a buy-in agreement with their accountant. "It will be spread out over time after I retire or work a much reduced schedule. Details and numbers are still pending."

*Sunset Dental Care in Waukesha, WI. What a thrill for Dr. Dennis O'Brien to practice with his two children, Dr. Stephanie Race and Dr. Jeff O'Brien.*

Sunset Dental Care is not a Delta provider nor are they signed for any plans. "We do not accept assignment of insurance below $250 which means the patient pays upfront. As we do larger cases, comprehensive dentistry and sedation dentistry, insurance becomes a smaller percentage. Our insurance collections account for about 20% of our work."

Different skills help with the mix of treatment. They have a Cerec and it works well with three practitioners doing a total average of 20 Cerec units a month. Jeff does most endo, extractions and sedation dentistry. They provide comprehensive dentistry with an emphasis on esthetics both posterior and anterior using Empress inlays, onlays and crowns, Cerec, porcelain fused to metal when appropriate. They have a decreased dependence on insurance and sedation allows more comprehensive dentistry as patients want treatment done in the least amount of appointments.

For continuing education, "we budget one major course a year with all three Doctors participating and one major course which involves the team. All three of us are in a mini-residency implant study club." Other courses which have made a difference are J and P Consultants for hygiene, Jim DuMolin, D.O.C.S. and becoming proficient in the administration of Oral Conscious Sedation.

Dennis sees the success in his practice as:

- Being the best husband, father, grandpa, son and father-in-law I can be

- Being able to inspire by example my son, daughter and team and for them to be the best they can be

- Being able to retire in my practice (Dr. Blatchford inspired) and to chose to work and to spend my extra time in pursuits other than dentistry.

Marketing is very low key with Chris Ads in the past, asking for referrals from every guest and ads in local newspapers. Those articles which have appeared in local paper have made a real difference. Two local periodontists refer regularly as they like what they see in cosmetics and sedation dentistry. They also show sedation dentistry in their yellow page ad as well as a website: www.sunset-dentacare.com

Dennis shared, "Thank you for the opportunity to share my story and my successes. Much of what I have learned about being successful and a profitable dentist is because of Blatchford coaching. I am grateful to have worked with both of you."

www.sunset-dentalcare.com

## Blatchford Game Plan: Dental Math

Dr. O'Brien knew the numbers needed to increase for his daughter and son to be successful in practice together. Making the numbers work successfully in your dental practice is not a skill taught in dental training. The business of dentistry eludes many dentists and they end up on a treadmill, running faster and faster and never able to catch that economic relief of which they dream.

Without returning to school to acquire a Master's Degree in Business, you, too, can learn to watch your numbers and make them grow in the direction you want. The result will be more joy in practicing and you can fall in love again with dentistry.

When you uncover how much it costs to deliver dentistry in your present mode, you can then make choices about the direction you want to pursue. You can change the mix of treatment presented and the manner in which it is delivered to produce.

Most practices schedule what ever treatment needs to be completed. There is no design or thought to cost per hour or overhead. If you could design your day so that your overhead is lower than present time and your treatment delivery was increased, would you be interested in making a change?

In this study of dental math, we are going to focus on the mix of treatment delivered and how it is delivered. In examining the mix of treatment, we are looking at three categories. We will label these "classes." This is not the technical diagnosis of treatment classes but rather a determination for dental math. The "class" we are discussing here has a monetary value. We are examining the money of the practice because it is a business and we want our business to work well.

Our three "classes" are defined in economic return. Class I are procedures that total $125 and under, Class II are procedures which total $126 to $300 and Class III are procedures that total over $301.

Why? The average dental office overhead per hour is around $250 per hour,** plus lab. With two providers (one dentist and a hygienist), overhead per provider is $125 per hour. No one else has studied your practice in this way to actually discover how you are spending your precious time and great skill.

*** Producing $500K with a 75% overhead and a lab bill of $7500, your monthly expenses are $30K a month and working 120 hours reached an overhead per hour of $250.*

Make a study of your appointment book for the last ninety days. Use Exhibit A as your study sheet. Reviewing your last three months of appointments, find the number of hours in your office that have Class I procedures done and what percentage of the total time is spent in Class I.

Do the same with Class II and Class III. With a $250 an hour overhead, the average dental practice spends 75% of time doing Class I procedures which you will note, does not cover the overhead. 75% of the time! No wonder you feel you are working hard but not producing much.

## EXHIBIT A
### Ninety Day Study

| Total number of hours _____ | Hours spent | % of Total Time |
|---|---|---|
| Class I ($125 and under) | _____ | _____ |
| Class II ($126 to $300) | _____ | _____ |
| Class III ($301 and up) | _____ | _____ |

The average dental practice spends 10% of time doing Class II procedures which is producing just enough to pay the overhead. In the average practice, only 15% of the time is spent producing procedures which total $301 or more.

What is the message and how can we make a change? Our goal is to flip the percentages around so that 75% of your time is spent producing procedures that are $301 and above and only 15% of your time on procedures that produce $125 and under per hour.

The difference between a practice producing $30,000 a month and $80,000 a month is the mix of treatment.  An $80,000 a month practice is spending 75% of the time doing procedures $250 and over and 10% of their time doing procedures under their overhead.

What are the steps that need to be taken to make this happen in your practice?  First, you must believe that your practice is not average.  What is average?  Are you an average dentist or an outstanding dentist?  Do you desire a practice of distinction or an average practice?  Are patients attracted to you because you are average?  I think not!

Determine what procedures you do that would be $301 and over.  Are you doing one crown at a time (the worst one) or is there a possibility the diagnosis and presentation could have been multiple units saving the patient time and emergency situations?  How much longer does it take to do two units as opposed to one?

Before you completely reject this idea of multiple units because we might be doing "unnecessary treatment," let's consider some possibilities.  Time is the most important commodity today to our patients.  They do not like to spend time in the dental chair and they definitely do not like to have three to four appointments for procedures.  Looking at the bigger picture for the patient, what value would there be for the patient to have you, the expert, see if there is other work to be done that could prevent multiple appointment and dental chair time in the future?

The second step is to create with your patients a long term treatment plan based on the three universal desires to look good, feel good and last a long time.  With a long term treatment plan based on what the patient wants, you begin to step out of the "patch" club and into more comprehensive dentistry.

Diagnosing multiple units requires some skill building with your staff.  Since looking good is one of the primary goals of patients, we need to learn to ask questions which bring out the values and desires of the patients. See Exhibit B for some possible questions staff and Dr. could ask. Showing pictures of beautiful smiles is a visual stimulation and addresses the patient question of "What will it look like?"

---

## EXHIBIT B

What would you like your smile to be like in 20 years?

What do you like best about your smile?

Looking at these pictures, is there anything you would like to improve about your smile?

What do you like best about the appearance of your teeth?

Whose smile do you most admire?

---

The next step in changing the mix of treatment is to examine your fees. Are your fees average or even below average? Studies show people purchase items because they desire them and see value in owning that item. Price, contrary to dental belief, is not the major factor 90% of the time. If your work and skill is above average, charge above average fees.

The next step which will allow a different mix of treatment is to block book your schedule. We want to develop an extraordinary reputation of service in our community. We want to deliver our excellent dentistry is a comfortable, non-hurried atmosphere. By block booking, you produce 80% of your daily goal by lunch. Block booking means you see only 2-3 patients in the morning, doing multiple units on each patient. Hold those blocks of time open to take care of the needs and wants of your patients.

When you have completed your appointment book study for the last 90 days and find the percentage of time spent on procedures, you will want to make changes. Change is difficult, yet, if your desire is to have a dream practice where patients see value in the excellent dentistry you have to offer and there is joy for you and your staff, change is necessary. You cannot keep doing things the way you have always done them and expect to achieve a different result.

Hopefully, this dental math is a real eye-opener for you and your staff. An awareness and belief in you is the first step. You can turn the numbers around in Class I, Class II and Class III. Dental math does make a difference.

Bill Blatchford, DDS

# From the Blatchford Play Book:
# Playing Your 'A' Game

>> Team is present and focused, no outside distractions or worries

>> Guest is number one priority

>> Team is on time

>> Doctor is technically skilled and can deliver quality

>> Guest drives the conversation when asked open ended questions

>> Staff listens as guest talks 80% of time, sharing their thoughts

>> No matter the direction of conversation, staff allows guest to feel heard and important

>> During treatment, guest has all creature comforts

>> Assistant and Doctor are symbiotic in procedures, organization and preparation.  There is a quiet confidence and all is well

>> Guest is overwhelmed with the results, thinks the temps are just right

>> Guest thinks whole team are magicians and walk on water, refers many

>> Team gifts guest with fishing magazine subscription and delivers gift basket of local products to his work

>> To quote Brian Tracy "Everything counts, everything counts, everything counts"

>> Systems are in place to assure success in procedures, no reap points to retake impressions or lab work not at office on time.

# 21

## REJUVENATION–
## IN SEARCH OF EXCELLENCE

## Dr. Robert Knupp

Dr. Knupp's dental highlight was meeting L. D. Pankey in 1970. Bob had attended a three-day Pete Dawson seminar in Detroit and spoke highly of Dr. Pankey. After listening to Dr. Dawson, "it didn't take me long to figure out Pete knew a lot more than me."

Bob was introduced to the cross of life—Work and Play, Love and Worship must be in balance. The more in balance these four are, the greater chance of happiness and peace. In addition, L. D. gave guidelines to set goals, the importance of setting goals and the encouragement to go home and practice the way we dreamed. "I'll never forget that he vowed to never, ever extract another tooth after he left Kentucky and went to Florida. He was driven by a moral conviction rather then the money."

Continuing education has been an important part of Bob's dental growth. Helping organize and participate in two study clubs; the Lake Cook focusing on perio and implants and the other is the Arlington Study Club focusing on TMJ disfunction. A valuable part of the Lake Cook Study club was the treatment study club discussing difficult cases meeting four to six times a year. An orthodontist, periodontist and general dentists shared their expertise.

"In 1993, I heard Bill at the MidWinter Meeting and I was restimulated and energized. Bill's approach to relating to patients was totally new to me and really gave me the spark. Yet, I was looking at the possibilities of another associate or partner because of my back. I went to an AFTCO Lecture and because of a long-term back problem, felt this was an answer. The lecturer assured me it would work and in fact, it was her brother she was promoting. Forget the details, I went into partnership in 1994, mainly because of my back problems."

Numbers for Dr. Knupp:

| | Pro. | Coll | OH | # of Staff |
|---|---|---|---|---|
| 2002 | $685K | $639K | | 6 (4 FT, 2 PT) |
| | | | | With partner |
| 2003 | $925K | $938K | 60% | 6 (4 FT, 2 PT) |
| | | | | First year with Blatchford |
| 2004 | $956K | $1.005M | 60% | 6 (2 FT, 4 PT) |
| 2005 | On track for $1.01M5 (3 FT, 2PT) | | | |

Bob is a Chicago boy through and through. As a high school sophomore, Bob was committed to being an outfielder for the Chicago White Sox. He was a pretty decent ballplayer, he thought and others were encouraging him. However, his dad who had always worked for AT & T, asked him,"what are you going to do with your life if you don't make it in baseball?" "I was really incensed that he had the audacity to ask me that question as I could really hit fast balls and 'yeah, dad, maybe I do have a little trouble with curve balls.'" But it got him thinking and at the end of that year, Bob got a clerking job at the local pharmacy which was part of a medical-dental complex containing two dentists and several physicians. The pharmacist's brother was one of the dentists. Bob thought they seemed like regular guys. The physician's seemed aloof (probably overworked).

The choice between medicine and dentistry for Bob was directly related to shots. Everytime, he thought, he visited the Doctor's office, he got a shot and passed out. His dentist never gave shots. Enter again his father who had quit school to take care of his mother and sister at 16 when his father passed away.  His father talked about the importance of education and that you could not achieve great success in a big corporation without a college degree.  After many dinner table discussions, Bob got the feeling that "there was no way I would work for anyone where they would be in control of my destiny."

Fortunately, Bob loved math and sciences and was a good student.  But he could not go into any field where needles played a part. He announced his plans to his parents one evening at the dinner table.  Calmly, he said he was going to Northwestern and Northwestern Dental School.  Silence.  Since this was only his junior year of high school, his parents thought it would pass.  It was the real deal when the acceptance to Northwestern arrived in his senior year.  Bob doubled up on languages and science as to save his parent's money and entered dental school after his sophomore year.  His mom went back work.  Bob did eventually find out that needles and anesthesia were an integral part of dentistry.  At his 25th dental class reunion of the Class of 1965, a classmate said he remembered the first week of school when Bob and classmates received 5-6 inoculations, Bob passed out 5-6 times and the smelling salts were right there.

Bob's goal after the Air Force was to have a general practice emphasizing reconstruction in a wealthy Northwest suburb.  He paid $6,000 for his practice in Arlington Heights.  At the only business course during Northwestern's senior year, they were told their dental degree was the only collateral needed for a practice loan.  Bob was very proud of his dental degree and his now pregnant wife, the sum total of all he owned.  He put his framed degree and his certificate from National Board in a shopping bag and went to the bank for a loan.  "What do you have for collateral?" asked the banker.  Bob again showed him his certificates and diploma.  The banker dismissed him and Bob was humiliated.  Enter Bob's fine dad again. He took Bob to his banker and with proper collateral, the practice loan proceeded.

Bob didn't even care about the practice numbers when he bought it. He just wanted to be a practicing dentist in Arlington Heights. It was a hole in the wall, one operatory, filthy and filled with smoke. He and his dad washed the walls one weekend and the patients thought he had painted the office. He discovered the prior dentist loved to take out teeth and do dentures. Bob had to rebuild.

Very soon after opening, several Doctors and dentists were building a professional building across the street from the hospital. Bob joined them, still with no money. Scared? Yes, but I knew I could do it. He built his present office in 1981. He remodeled five times, had four associates and one partner. The partnership ended in 2002.

Other mentors he has worked with: Drs. Niles Guichet, Jim Pride, Gordon Christensen, Nash and Lowe and Frank Spear. At the same time as I took Blatchford, he was encouraging me to take a hands-on course and I took from Dr. Ross Nash and Bob Lowe. "The face of cosmetics is so exciting and I really received a rejuvenation for dentistry."

"Dentistry has given me the lifestyle others would love to have. I have traveled a lot, I've taken a lot of time to "re-create." I really enjoy and love what I do for a living and enjoy living. I am very passionate about what I do, no matter if it's dentistry, photography, gardening or just living. I also have untiring energy to get what I want.

My biggest pitfall has been staff selection. For years, I did not feel confident in myself and looked to staff for affirmation and "love." My leadership and communication skills were lacking. I delegated responsibility for aspects of practice I needed to control. Now, after working with Blatchford, I feel I'm clear on my vision and therefore, it is easier to lead the staff rather than have them 'lead" me. I'm more capable of listening to their needs, wants and concerns. I've become a lot softer as years have marched on."

"About 75% of our practice has some insurance connection. I would much rather be doing much more extensive dentistry where insurance has no say."

"My wife, Judy, is a nurse and through her associations, I have many patients. She is a great marketer. We used to receive lists of new residents in Arlington Heights and I would send a series of letters to them. It worked well until other dentists started doing the same thing and diluted the pot. An oral surgeon and internist took a liking to me and referred patients. In addition, Judy and I were very involved in our church (like 4-5 nights a week). Very few knew I was a dentist as that was not our reason for being involved but eventually a lot of patients came because of our involvement. Yet, we had gotten into a business venture with people from church, including the minister. When it was all said and done, I was left holding the loans as everyone else bailed out or went bankrupt. That ended my association with the church and led to some very difficult times emotionally, financially, emotionally and spiritually.

This led me to finding a lot of peace in nature. I immersed myself in this aspect of photography. At a workshop of American wild animals, someone asked me if I had no fear, where would you go to photograph? Immediately, I said 'Africa.' Judy thought the first time I returned, I wanted to move to Africa. Each time I returned, I had learned more about animal behavior and movement.

My love and knowledge of photography has helped improve my dental photography. I have learned a lot from Rhys Spoor on four different occasions; one was totally dedicated to photography with the Hornbrook group. Kari on our team, takes the cosmetic pictures on our walls.

Having a nice personality or being able to relate to people is essential in practice. I feel it makes a huge difference in the success of the practice. In my case, I have incredibly loyal and quality patients. You can have the greatest skills but your patients are more concerned with how you and your staff relate to them. In all my years, it seems the most successful dentists are the ones with great personalities.

My dad got me started in photography.  I took my first pictures with a Kodak Brownie which Dad had given me just before I left for a Washington, DC trip with my high school classmates. I put aside photography until Judy bought me a camera for our first Christmas together. Within eight months, I was in the Air Force and had an opportunity to take travel pictures. In addition, I was introduced to intra-oral photography and my photographic journey had been rekindled."
www.drknupp.com

*Dr. Robert Knupp in the Jozani Forest of Zanzibar searching for red colobus monkeys on a photo expedition with eleven other nature photographers. "I love Africa because it offers unparalleled viewing of wildlife and the opportunity to capture a kaleidoscope of photographic images."*

## Blatchford Game Plan: Exit Right 4 U

When dentists become skilled working with new materials and techniques, often they feel a rebirth and rejuvenation about their profession. They can't believe how much more enjoyable practice is again. When a dentist keeps up with current education, there are ways to continue the enjoyment as well as the income stream from dentistry. Dr. Bob Knupp is one who got a "shot in the arm" and feels great about continuing to practice.

More than 31% of solo practicing dentists today are 55 years or older. Since most dentists have traditionally retired between 60 and 69, retirement is a "hot" topic. Financial advisors feel you will need around 70% to 90% of your current net in retirement. Yet, the baby boomers (now mid 40's to 60's) have reinvented each phase of their lives, never matching what has been customary. What will retirement be like for the boomers? What will be right for you?

Goal setters who have planned for retirement since the beginning have accumulated five times what a non-planner has saved. An ADA survey indicates dentists save 10.6% of their income which is below the federal limit of 15% contributions to a qualified pension fund.

The average dental net in 2001 was $173K. In retirement planning, eighty percent of that is $138,400 which is $11,500 a month. If you retire at age 60 and live another thirty years, your need would be $4.1 million from interest and savings.

The figures are staggering for the slightly unprepared. What are the choices for the today's boomer dentist? Sale? Partnership? Associateship? Practice in a different way?

A sale, if you can find a buyer, is worth about 18 months of net income which is then taxed for capital gains and deprecation. Although this will seem like a simple statement, you must be aware that a sale is final. You are now no longer a dentist in that location. There is no going back. The book is closed.

Partnerships in retirement have their own sets of pros and cons. By reviewing again the motivating factors for entering the profession, you may find independence and freedom on your list. Selling half your practice to an unknown partner means you have surrendered your freedom and half your net income in exchange for about nine months of net income. The staff will still look to you for leadership and details.

Becoming an associate after thirty years of private practice could be successful, if you have the qualities to be an employee. Will you be happy doing dentistry for someone else? Do you have the qualities to be a team player under someone else's leadership and rules?

Continuing to practice in a different manner is a viable alternative. You can continue to feel needed and serve others on your own terms. We call it "Retire As You Go," and the absolute to making this work is that you enjoy dentistry. This is a program for the optimist, the eager and the bright. This is for Doctors who want to learn the latest thing and continue to be involved.

There are some real advantages to keeping your practice viable. Presently, if you have a $1M practice, you are able to deduct about $50K of expenses which include a leased car, continuing education travel, entertainment and other. Upon selling your practice, these after tax expenses are now yours. Another big advantage is the psychology of your earned status in the community.

Why not take advantage of the qualities which drew you to dentistry in the first place? These might be independence, freedom from outside control, leading your own destiny and money, especially if you did not accumulate a bundle.

You design your ideal practice days, plan your continuing education around travel adventures and attract a staff to work your schedule. You may want to work three days a week for three weeks and take the fourth week off. If you can continue to work on your own terms, netting $150K and not having to use your retirement funds until you choose, count the advantages and your blessings.

It is true; the value of your practice may decrease. Weigh this; if you can continue to practice another 10 to 15 years, making $1.5M, against the original final selling price of 18 months net. I have a number of excellent boomer dentists who are reinventing "retirement" under their own terms. Are you interested in being one of them?

Dentistry offers the greatest possibilities for choices, even in retirement. If you enjoy dentistry and want to continue feeling needed and wanted, consider "Retiring As You Go."

Bill Blatchford, DDS

## From the Blatchford Play Book: Overtime

Of the 100+ plays in a football game, only four or five plays make a real difference. The challenge is that you do not know which play will make the "win." Dr. Knupp and team play full out.

>> Develop your sales skills

>> Shift your paradigm from education to listening

>> Shift from NEEDS to WANTS

>> Develop relationships by being interested

>> Ask questions to uncover wants

>> Ask deeper questions

>> Only present solutions when you have asked many questions about their dreams and desires

>> Write scripts for asking questions

>> Practice, practice, practice

>> Vince Lombardi says "every game is decided on one or two plays"

>> Play every play as though it is the one

>> Learn from your mistakes, don't repeat them

# 22

# A PASSION TO SURVIVE
# AND SUCCEED

## Dr. Steven Haywood

Successfully operating a model of two separate practices, Dr. Haywood works with the same great team in Pennsylvania and Maryland two days each. It works because he sees both practices as his "principle practice" as opposed to satellite practices. He and his team are full out four days a week. His thinking for two? "A specialist often has several locations. Why can't I?"

Dr. Haywood has energy plus and is a force to be reckoned. He is a solid visionary in action, enthusiastic, motivating and motivated. His practices are busy, successful and profitable, grossing $1.4M at 60% overhead. Even with two facilities, his rent is right at 5%. He is attracting 20-30 new patients a month and has 4.6 staff members.

His marketing is simple and direct. The same attractive ad in Baltimore magazine has been repeated to produce a presence and a branding of their product that attracts who they want. His ROI is about 12 to 1. In Pennsylvania, "we have a very affordable newspaper program which yields strictly implant cases and is very trackable at 20 to 1. He greatly reduced his Yellow Page ads "due to lack of solid return."

Some of his internal marketing "secrets" are:
- Be real and sincerely nice; call them by name. Everybody wins and it feels great.
- Do more than is expected and 'wow' with your treatment and skill with which you perform your task.
- Be an artist to them and they will refer everyone they know
- Make women feel attractive and men feel they have value and make a difference
- Get tears and hugs as your ultimate goal
- Treat your patients to a great office environment that is uplifting and elegant.  Our patients like what we do for them in this way; feel we are concerned about their comfort and tell their friends.

His first practice after the Air Force GDR ("too cool for words and better education than dental school"), was a downtown Baltimore practice for $20K which had been abandoned ten months earlier by a dentist with HIV.  Dr. Haywood found the city a difficult place to practice but liked the "thrill of being downtown."

While building his city practice, Steven was an HMO dentist… "top dog for skill level and training so I did all the cosmetic cases and fee for service patients. I was canned due to pressures at the HMO and was now in a position to earn a living for myself.  The strings were cut! I had to go it all on my own.  I had a great year and put in a ton of work."

"I realized I had tapped out the potential of this location and I needed something more.  A city practice is just too much work for the benefits.  I started to look for a new opportunity.  Through my participation with Paragon Management, I met Dr. George Trout who sold me his Pennsylvania practice and my income went up 500%. He pushed through a loan for me and personally financed 50%.  He stayed on three days a week for the next two years as my associate. Humbly, he took second place knowing the dreaded personnel issues were my problem as he hated the hassles and was ready to relinquish them to me."

"The income and second location allowed me to build a new office in Baltimore with no debt. I was not sure Pennsylvania would become my dream practice but I kept my options open."

Steven really did his demographic research for Baltimore. He studied the city, his first city practice and related locations to income. He observed where people were moving. He studied the housing trends in the area and surveyed perceptions of people with regard to certain locations that were in the running. "I wanted the best possible location for an ethnically neutral, acceptable, easy to get to, metropolitan location for the next 30 years. We scored a home run for a cosmetic/implant speciality practice in Baltimore."

"We are profitable because we have been planning to be very profitable for a long time, even when we were not profitable yet. The vision of achieving this was fundamental. I have felt that it was within my God given potential to achieve certain things and by not achieving them, I would not be the person I was supposed to become. Anyone can be profitable. A certain part of it is just a math equation. The rest is persistence."

Dr. Haywood feels he differentiates himself from others in three areas:

- **"I am willing to do anything.** I literally built the walls of the practice and installed the plumbing. I will come in for patient follow-ups even if it is not convenient. I have invested in my practice when others are following 'lean and mean' approach. We have always been better off for the investment in our practice."
- **"I will not give up and never have."**
- **"I have stayed as far ahead of my local peers as possible.** I have always offered more specialized cosmetic and implant care than anyone in the area and have taken tons of CE. The education

and business mentoring has given us confidence to present ourselves as different/better when our potential new clients are seeking a new dentist or when we are presenting a costly treatment to a patient."

Dr. Haywood knew in the seventh grade he would be excellently successful. "I was always big for my age and was regularly and on schedule picked on by older kids. I decided at one point I would never let anyone get the best of me again. I would not lose. I would hold my head up and I would win whatever the cost. I did and have never looked back. I never understood what that moment meant in my life. I could not let these people be obstacles to me physically and emotionally for the rest of my life. I could not explain to the school administrators why it happened but I knew my life had changed. My family knew I was capable, intelligent and hardworking. They had faith in me and showed me who I was. Now I just had to be true to myself."

Lest you think Dr. Haywood is all about success, he actually is very introspective and shares his pitfalls. "When I was dating, some book said, 'people usually get exactly what they think they deserve' and my personal pitfalls are summed up in this statement. I did not feel I deserved better or did not recognize the impact of those people on my life and my future success. I did not have the discretion to make wise decisions and I did not. My staff has had a good laugh at my expense several times. My hiring was neither well planned nor was it professional. I have lost a fortune because of this."

On his leadership, "I am immediate with praise and reprimands. I lead by example and help at all levels. I may do too much as I will succeed even in spite of the failings of my team members. I tend to carry them too often. I am direct and not blunt. I am a better communicator in writing and tend to do SOPs, checklists and office memos to communicate more clearly. We are on a journey at all times and our office certainly does not feel stagnant, never a dull moment and no two days are the same. I am learning to expect more accountability but see people I am working with are motivated by reward and punishment. I tend to create incentives for results for which I am seeking."

He has struggled with a poor financial deal when second practice (in PA) was purchased which drained the practice of profits, associates who were divisive and non-productive and poor accounting which lead to a financial crisis in 1997. Yet, "the hardest decision I ever made was to buy the Shrewbury (PA) practice. I just sucked it up! $500K financed without a dime to my name!" And the best decision he ever made? To buy the Shrewbury practice.

As a young boy, Steve was motivated to be in medicine and he observed a neighbor's medical father with long hours, poor demeanor and behavior which inspired Steve to observe his happier dentist. Steve's father is an attorney and had always dreamed of medicine as a career. Yet, he feels his early motivating factor was "fear of failure."

What he loves about dentistry is "satisfaction and acknowledge-ment as an artist. I am getting this regularly from my patients and I feel my skills and results are at a high point. My office is a treat to work in and my team now brings me joy. On the flip side, I have lost sleep, have gray hairs and tension headaches all caused by my toler-ance of certain behaviors and poor employees; I have learned some great life lessons from this journey. Dentistry and the business of it has affected every aspect of my life. In many ways, it has confronted me with myself and forced me to work out the dilemmas I have worked myself into. Hard lessons."

Steve was part of the "Rosenthal-Nash" life changing experience in 1995. He studied with Peter Dawson "rock solid science that is time tested and works," and took implant courses at U. of Miami from Dr. Arun Garg, "a very skilled clinician without an oppressive ego."

"I am still doing family dentistry though it is not my focus. I real-ly enjoy dentistry as a whole and love the results. 'We can do that' is a great attitude. I was concerned about losing my base of support as we raised our fees and eliminated crisis focused patients. We have gotten a little cockey in a fun way. Some clients choose to 'go elsewhere' and have given us a 'no.' We feel so comfortable that we are offering the very best. We know that..'going elsewhere?' You're really going nowhere! That's OK."

"I am however, concerned with a "no" means we have failed to present ourselves in the right way and we have alienated a patient or have caused a person to doubt our capabilities or professionalism and they choose to go elsewhere."

www.flossem.com

*Dr. Haywood's passionate hobby is completely restoring muscle cars. He has the full facility at his home, including a rotisserie for ergonomically working on the underside of a car. He enjoys this hobby with his family at his Maryland home.*

# Blatchford Game Plan:
# Selling Made Easy

Dr. Haywood and his team practice their sales skills, especially working on their listening skills.

The necessary skills for selling in dentistry are:
- Shifting your paradigm from NEED to desire
- Enter the conversation with no dental agenda on your mind
- To give up being the dental authority during the sales process
- Be an incredible listener
- Make your guest right, no matter what they say
- Never put any pressure on your guest in any form

We have it wired that "sales" means talking someone into something. Today's successful sales are the anti-thesis of this. There can be no pressure to purchase what you may have in mind for them.

The reason people buy anything is they want it, they trust and like you. All decisions about anything in life are made permanently, instantly and emotionally. Think about most conversations with patients in dental offices. It is usually very technical and these are left-brained conversations. Dentists and dental staffs love to tech talk about possible treatments. The problem with this is:

- People make decisions emotionally which is right-brain talking.
- Dentists try to talk patients into a result by educating about the treatment which is left-brain activity. Decisions cannot be made in a left-brained conversation.

Building trust, an important part of successful sales, means engaging yourself in their shoes and active listening, not just nodding and waiting for the next time you speak.

What systems do you have in your office to create trust and build relationships? Do you still have a new patient sit alone in your "waiting room" completing the health history? Do you assume they just want something "fixed"? Do you make a real effort to become acquainted with people more than "bridge on 13-15"? Do you take the time to discover the real person connected to the teeth?

Learn to ask questions. Even in the initial phone conversation, you can make a friend. Learn to play the role of a friend, rather than an order taker. Conversations on the phone can sound like "two eggs over easy, bacon and rye toast, buttered." Try to engage them in a conversation to discover why they are calling, how you can help them, what do they have in mind, what might be motivating this call, where are they in their research and so much more. Because you do not know how the conversation will go, your script needs just an outline so the patient can lead you, not you lead them.

In today's sophisticated marketplace, many guests have done their homework on the Internet, asked colleagues and neighbors. Some have an idea of what they want. Let them talk. Ask them questions to draw out their ideas and findings.

Anyone on your team is capable of asking questions and building relationships. This is a perfect opportunity for hygienists, dentists, assistants and especially the initial contact people on your team. Everyone must be engaged and skilled in asking questions. You cannot hide in the lab or pretend you did not have "time." This can be on an initial phone conversation, a recare visit or as a new guest enters your practice.

Try starting with "How can I help you?" (Does that sound like pressure?) Depending on the answer, you could ask "When did you first notice this?" You might try, "How did you try to solve this?" Then keep asking, "What else have you tried?" "How did that work?" "How has this affected your life, work?" "How would this improve your life?" "Let me show you an example." "Have you thought about a budget?" "What do you want to do next?"

You will notice:

- We do not offer solutions
- Keep the guest engaged on the right brain.
- Avoid any kind of tech talk

Next is an exam, findings and proceed from there. After the guest has said "yes," you can enter the left-brained arena and tech talk. Sales is a life-long learning process. How can one master sales in one 650 word article? Dive in and get involved. Other consultants have good ideas, too. We just happen to know this works.

Bill Blatchford, DDS

## From the Blatchford Play Book: Goal Setting

Dr. Haywood is a real goal setter. He is a visionary who is focused and accomplishes much because he sets goals. Here are some pointers for setting goals:

>> Set goals for the long term first

>> Set goals to be the best in your area

>> Goals must be specific, measurable and have a time line

>> Set goals for all areas of your life

>> Constantly measure your progress

>> Share your goals with your team

>> Set high goals if you want to excel

>> Set low goals if you want to be mediocre

>> Be persistent

>> Visualize the successful outcome

# 23

## LEARNING TO LEAD

### Dr. Mike Kellner

A good self image is an important factor in practice success. Mike knew he would be successful in whatever he tried. He was always taught to have high expectations and when dentistry was the direction he selected, he wanted to be a great dentist.

And he was successful by any measure. He was involved in much continuing education, always pressing himself and reaching for the next level. But he found he was a revolving door for staff and that really bothered him. What were the factors that caused staff not to stick with the practice and how could that be eliminated?

Dr. Kellner has demonstrated self-confidence by making some major decisions in his professional life, decisions that would rattle most dentists, like moving. He makes decisions easily compared to many dentists. He is more the 'ready, fire, aim' dentist not the 'ready, aim, aim, aim, aim.' Yet, keeping great staff eluded him.

When he originally applied to several medical schools and wasn't accepted, it really didn't concern him because at the same time, he had applied and was accepted at NYU dental school. During his junior year of college, his own dentist (also his Scout leader) "educated" him on the benefits of dentistry.

He wanted to practice in New York or New Jersey and was a Navy dentist stationed in Maryland. He was accepted into the Periodontal program at Boston University yet confusion reigned and he was placed on the wait list. He became aware of a Baltimore practice opportunity due to a dentist's sudden death and Mike purchased the practice for $13,000.

Mike's reading in 1972 had included Bob Leroy's book on the *$100,000 Practice*. This, then, became the goal. The equipment was old but the office was impressive and the production had been close to $100,000. "I knew if I hired a dental assistant, I could be more productive." And it came to pass, Mike produced $10K the first month and $100,000 the first year. "I was immediately successful because the practice was much better than I had expected. The patients had a high appreciation for dentistry and had the ability to afford good dentistry." The patient population included many of the "movers and shakers" in town including the presidents of four of the largest banks in Baltimore.

Realizing a golden opportunity, he decided to improve his skills. The PBP type consultant led him to Pankey Institute where Mike took all the Continuums and learned a lot about dentistry. The Pankey Institute confirmed that a high quality practice was the best way to proceed "and it established a framework for my success." He tried to be a "Pankey dentist" working on missionary type dentistry where a practice is built by referrals only. Mike couldn't make it work fast enough for him. He has made his professional life work by the purchase of seven different practices!

In some of these practices, he inherited or hired associates but that was short-lived because "they were not a good match for me or I was afraid to give up control." He started to recognize the staff revolving door "due to a lack of leadership skills. I was successful by most standards but I was frustrated because this success required so much unnecessary effort."

"My practice hit a plateau in the early '90's and my frustration was greatly increasing. At this point a patient introduced him to network marketing and Mike jumped in thinking this was a great avenue to achieve future security. In his 'networking' year, he earned nothing but benefited greatly in learning to appreciate dentistry more and now wanted to put his efforts towards improving his practice. "I realized that I spent many years being trained to be a dentist and should put my efforts towards improving my skills and taking better care of my patients."

The cosmetic movement was just starting and Mike "jumped in eagerly and rekindled my enthusiasm for dentistry." He took courses by Larry Rosenthal and Ross Nash and eventually taught for each in separate programs.

He participated in a 20-week program of IV Sedation and general anesthesia in 1975 but found he was not comfortable doing the dentistry AND monitoring patients at the same time. He took courses in implant dentistry and he now surgically places and restores many implants. He has received a Mastership from AGD in recognition of taking over 600 hours of CE including 400 hours in hands-on programs. He took Dental Boot Kamp and other consulting programs with minimal success.

"By working hard, taking risks, investing in my business, taking a lot of continuing education and being good at delivering quality dentistry, I am profitable and always felt that I deserved to be. My staff is well paid, too. Bonuses average $1,500 a month per staff member. I actually feel anyone can be profitable in dentistry if they are willing to pay the price to achieve success."

"I try to learn from my mistakes and not repeat them. I always try to maintain a positive attitude not matter what occurs. I have become an effective leader through very hard work and the right attitude. Staff selection and retention had been a problem for many years. I was learning the cost of retraining was very high. My solution was to pay them more then the prevailing rate. My lack of leadership cost me dearly for many years. I was just not able to retain associates or to build on effective staff."

To become a more effective leader, Mike has:

- Dug deep to format and communicate his vision
- Let team know they are valued
- Staff dinners, staff lunches, constant reinforcement, staff meetings, complimenting staff in front of patients.
- Weekly staff meetings with encouragement for participation, suggestions for improvement without fear of reprisal, developing an element of trust
- Implementing the Blatchford Bonus system which promotes accountability, ownership and motivation
- Staff participation with continuing education and expanded functions
- Working together to increase productivity

To become more productive, the Kellner team has been very active in internal marketing. "My staff delivers Five Star Service and they are constantly being complimented." Before and After photos are all over the office. New patients are shown a video from two Dramatic Makeover shows and are given a DVD copy with their new patient packet. They offer a full juice bar, warm cookies and fancy teas. They have paraffin wax, aromatherapy, warm facial wipes, massage pads, ceiling mounted movies and various music selections. They ask for referrals and then receive a hand written note. Every day, each staff sends a handwritten note to a patient seen the previous day. "I call my patients at night." Post treatment, they send flowers, restaurant gift certificates, Elizabeth Arden spa certificates and glamour photos.

Externally, Dr. Kellner's marketing has been massive and on the edge. Some has worked, some has not. "The best results have come from talk show radio which we have done for five years. I have also been successful in attracting patients in return for spa services as well as offering products in our office. We are initiating a relationship with Elizabeth Arden's Red Door Salon. This will start in September and includes seminars by us at the Salon and referring completed cosmetic patients to the Red Door Salon for a service paid by us."

"The hardest decision I had to make was to move my office after 22 years from downtown Baltimore to Baltimore County, a ten mile move. For five years, I continued to operate out of both offices, finding it increasingly difficult to acquire quality patients as my office environment was going downhill. My natural optimism kept telling me things would get better. I was practicing with 'one foot out the door' which made it impossible to make the necessary changes to my office."

"The second hardest decision was to do two Dramatic Makeover television shows, a $65K investment. It was a gamble. Yet, ultimately, it returned $400K to date plus the benefit of having a professionally recorded video which is shown continuously, especially to new patients."

"I have advertised for years in local magazines with good results. Lately, more are advertising so results are diluted. I have done booths at various shows with limited success although it brought recognition."

"I have recently hired a public relations firm and have a number of projects which are starting soon. One is a charitable project which should generate a lot of publicity and the other is an exclusive partnership with Red Door Salon where we will give presentations to their clients and they will market us in the salon in return for our office sending patients for services to be paid by our office, facials, makeup, etc......"

"The decision that allowed me to take my practice to the present level and where it will go in the future was the decision to market the practice. It started with radio and I did it with a lot of trepidation since dentists are 'professionals' and it was considered 'unethical' to advertise. However, by marketing my practice as being different from others by delivering a quality service, I have achieved tremendous name recognition in the area. This has allowed myself and my team to truly enjoy coming to work, knowing that we are helping a lot of patients to look and feel better and at the same time achieving an excellent income." Talk show radio—this is broadcast several times throughout the day. There are five commercials. I am introduced by a local personality. The cost is $30,000 a year and last year we grossed over $220,000.

Playing our 'A' Game is "complete euphoria. Our self-esteem is so much higher and our stress level is less. It almost seems the days go so quickly."

"I've always been optimistic about the future, due to real encouragement from my parents, especially my father. In dental school, I didn't know how but I knew I was going to be successful. I used to think about the fact I didn't want to wake up one morning and hate the thought of going to work. I had to find a way to make dentistry rewarding emotionally and financially. My first week at the Pankey Institute solidified my thought. I was given a model I could attempt to emulate and a recipe for success. Pankey talked about how he visited Dr. B. Holley Smith in Paris and he told him that there are dentists for Kings and Queens as well as for the general population and it was his decision to be the dentist for the Kings and Queens. I knew from then on I could only be happy if I could be known as one of the best dentists in our profession and be financially successful as well."

"I want to practice actively until I am 70 years old (nine more years) and then continue on some part time basis. I would love to lecture on cosmetic dentistry and possibly offering hands on programs to share my knowledge with colleagues. I would like to set up charitable foundations with contributions going to research in prostate cancer and cardiac care." These are both conditions experienced in the Kellner home. "I have been successfully treated for prosate cancer, and my wife had an aortic valve placed in 2000."

"I chose Blatchford Solutions after one year of deliberation with monthly phone calls and one face to face meeting with Dr. Blatchford. I called several dentists who were in the program and that convinced me that this was the right program for me. I was looking for a program that would not treat my practice like every other and try to improve my practice by some generic formula. Bill continued to ask me what I wanted and not tell me what I should do. I felt that he was committed to make the program work for me."

www.kellnersmiles.com

*Dr. Mike Kellner has earned his handsome smile and grey beard. He is a cancer survivor, has successfully merged seven practices, and is happily married with two grandchildren. He is active in Jewish charities and patriarch to a large family. Mike is a skier, plays tennis, runs and golfs. He has completed 18 marathons.*

## Blatchford Game Plan:
## Five Star Service Scheduling

The successful private practice must be known for serving patients well. The goal of this 'on-time' practice is to stand for excellent service. Patients will perceive outstanding service when appointments are fewer and more treatment is completed at each visit. Outstanding service in the patient's eyes is their perception they are the only patient and full attention is paid to their needs.

This Five Star Scheduling greatly benefits the busy dental patient. Reluctance on the patient's part to accept larger treatment stems from the old method of scheduling multiple patients in a triple booking schedule. A single crown took two-and-one-half appointments from their busy lives. They perceive a whole quadrant would take ten appointments. "Let me think about his, Doc,' is usually the response.

Holding large blocks of time open in the morning for longer and more demanding treatment creates a boutique practice, a practice of choice. If you had a two hour, three hour or four hour block of time and no other operative patients, how much treatment could be completed? What would be the benefits to the patient? The patient, who has accepted treatment receives individual attention, unrushed and focused. The doctor doesn't wear rollerblades in trying to see three other patients at the same time. The dental office is elegantly quiet and the doctor can focus on technical excellence. The staff loves this scheduling because each relationship is stronger with Five Star Service Scheduling.

What benefits are there for the practice? Five Star Scheduling creates an opening for larger diagnosis and acceptance with immediate treatment. When a doctor is so busy with smaller appointments, the subconscious does not want to diagnose a large case. If the patient accepted, the patient would have to be literally squeezed into an already exhausting schedule. The doctor then places this patient into the "Watch and Wait" Club. With larger diagnosis and acceptance, the production per hour increases, matching and even exceeding the overhead per hour, which increases the net return to the practitioner. Wow!

The Five Star Service Schedule is further enhanced by evaluating the most productive procedures and scheduling those patients in the morning blocks. To help evaluate your most productive work, the doctor and receptionist can do a 90-day study of the practice.

First, determine the overhead per hour in your practice. Eliminate the items which are legal to deduct but do not directly impact a practice-a leased car, continuing education/vacation, etc. Determine the true overhead per hour of the operation.

If the overhead in a practice grossing $500,000 a year is 75% (ADA statistics for average overhead), the overhead is then $30,000 a month, divided by 15 working days is $2000 of overhead per day. The daily overhead is divided into 8 hours and $250 an hours is the overhead. We will use this figure of overhead.

Review the appointment books starting three months ago to present. You will be marking each hour in Class I, Class II, or Class III. The following chart will help in your discovery if your overhead is $250 per hour.

Class I appointment is any hour spent producing from No charge to $200.

Class II appointment is any hour spent producing from $200 to $300.

Class III appointment is any hour spent producing $300 and over.

Ninety days is enough time to see trends developing. What you will find is a vast majority of time spent producing work under overhead, which are the Class I appointments. These are the smaller appointments, which eat into productive time. In many practices, 75% of time is spent producing work which does not even pay for overhead. A noteworthy portion of the 75% are Class II potential procedures which are squeezed and mashed into a triple booking arena which creates multiple short appointments for procedures which should take one hour when treated as a solo patient.

What percentage of your time was spent in Class III appointments? If the Class III patient had been the only patient (no triple booking), what could the income per hour have been? If, during this 90 day study, Class II procedures were booked simultaneously with other patient's treatment, how much extra time was spent to accomplish the Class III procedures? What would have been the total time of treatment if that patient were the only patient being treated?

If you are spending 75% of time on Class I appointments and 15% of your time on Class II appointments, the challenge for the future security of this practice is to change the mix of treatment and the manner in which the treatment is scheduled.

The goal of Five Star Scheduling is:

1.  Take care of patient's needs by being aware of their time, diagnosing lifetime dentistry and working from that plan.

2.  Achieving a daily production goal by deciding in advance what the production goal is and schedule accordingly.

3.  Provide a stress-free environment which means staying on time, completing treatment scheduled, no interruptions and having a pattern to each day.

Say "Goodbye" to multiple patients being scheduled simultaneously for treatment, which does not cover overhead. Rather than filling every line in the appointment book, Five Star Service Scheduling refers to a planned day which is actually repeated every day where blocks of time are held for larger and more optional treatment. Develop a template for perfect scheduling which allows the patient maximum time with the doctor, fewer and well-planned appointments, being seen on time and released on time while receiving the smile of their dreams.

Rather than having the dentist see many patients each day and do a little on each patient, we are going to start to serve patients well by seeing fewer patients while doing more treatment on each patient. We are going to be creating value for appearance and longevity rather than patching and doing one crown at a time.

Five Star Scheduling is easy to institute and has a great result for the patient. In the morning and every morning, the doctor sees no more than three patients. We have reserved a two-hour block from 8AM to 10AM and two one-hour blocks from 10AM to 11AM and from 11AM to noon. Notice even though we have more than one operatory, we book only one chair. Remember, this is a Class III patient and they definitely deserve their time of excellence. Surgeons do not make house calls during scheduled operations.

By changing the mix of treatment and how it is scheduled, we serve our patients well. Increasing the percentage of time spent doing Class III procedures where the practice is actually exceeding the overhead creates a situation of financial compensation. By block booking, the morning schedule facilitates 80% of the daily production goal. The doctor can sit with one patient and feel fine about it. The running days are over.

Five Star Service continues in the afternoon. Right after lunch, two co-diagnosis appointments are held for new patients returning after their initial cleaning and exam last week or it can be a recall patient to whom you are now speaking with about a long-term treatment plan.

From 1:30 to 3:00 in the afternoon, we have scheduled shorter appointments when your patients need a single surface filling, a quick check, suture removal, etc. This is also the only time emergency patients are seen. Five Star Service means declining an emergency patient if the only time they can be seen is during productive Class III time. As you start to speak to your patients about more long-term care, your emergency demands diminish. During this aerobic stretch in dentistry, your motto is "Start, Finish, Stop" as opposed to "Start,

Stop, Start, Stop, Start, Finish." In other words, even in shorter procedures, sit down and complete that patient before moving on.

Our Five Star Service Scheduling allows you to complete the day by seating the same number of units prepared in the morning. Patients look forward to this appointment so it is a relaxed, happy celebration of completed work, rather than squeezed between three patients. You have time to celebrate the beautiful final product by having your laboratory tech visit or taking final pictures. Patients love the attention.

Block booking creates an impression of excellent service to your patients. They feel they are receiving the best treatment from the best office when their needs are met with timeliness. Block booking is very simple but it does take effort and commitment to change from your present system. Do not change any appointed  patients. In your appointment book, draw a line when you are no longer solidly booked. Design a template of blocks and what treatment you want in the blocks.

Commit yourself to making it happen. Change your mix of treatment from 75% of Class I to 50% of Class III appointments. Encourage your staff to speak optimistically about the opportunity for individual attention from the doctor when you and he are fresh in the morning. Work on effective scheduling with scripting like—

"Congratulations! Your new smile is going to look great. This is Dr. Blatchford's favorite thing to do. To maximize your time and have the doctor when he is fresh we reserve time in the morning for these types of procedures. You will be the doctor's only patient during that time. We have time at 8AM on Wednesday. Will that work for you?"

Five Star Service Scheduling allows you to start your first patient on time, complete on time, and still have a quality conversation with your patients. Being unrushed and on time is one of the best ways to spread your reputation of excellent and timely service.

Bill Blatchford, DDS

## From the Blatchford Play Book: Practice Drills

The Kellner team practice in regularly scheduled BMW 4x4 skill building sessions.

>> Create phone skills, tag line and message that set you apart. It is your first opportunity to impress. Be bold, be different

>> Cross train each team member including the Doctor. Learn to answer the phone, make firm financial arrangements, having meaningful conversations about patient dreams, clean a room, run a day sheet, sharpen instruments, make appointments and operate the computer.

>> Practice introducing guests to staff members, sharing what you have learned and make your guest feel special.

>> Analyze some plays that have not worked in your office. Make changes, build skills and reconstruct confidence to move forward

>> Join Toastmaster's to learn confidence

>> Always practice harder than you expect to play

>> Video tape your role play sessions

>> Analyze your video tapes

>> Study what worked and duplicate that behavior

>> Create plans for every situation, follow the plan

# 24

## A REAL SURVIVOR

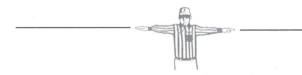

## Dr. Susan Weyers

Surviving two breast cancer diagnosis and treatments without missing a day of work marks a true survivor. Susan and her two staff have been to "hell and back. We all see the practice and our lives with 'new eyes.' Profitability no longer simply means achieving a certain financial goal at the end of each month. Profitability is now defined as by how I live my life each and every day, whether I am at work or not. I am learning my practice is simply an extension of my life. I have been blessed beyond belief in every aspect of my life. My practice is simply another way to touch people's lives and by doing so, enriching my own."

Dr. Weyers practice, started from scratch 16 years ago, is in the Carefree area of Scottsdale, AZ. For the first two years, she worked alone; living with her sister and brother-in-law and borrowed money to make it. She remembers those first two years as "a lot of really hard work."

Susan's demographic study for Carefree's growth was actually done by her architect sister who became a City Planner for Phoenix and her sister's husband, a landscape architect. They needed to find a place where population was going to grow and they could prosper. Their projection showed Carefree and North Scottsdale was the area to focus with subdivisions and growth to happen within five years. Amazingly enough, Carefree did grow just as projected. Dr. Weyers was just named #3 in the "Top 50 Dentists" as published in "101 North" magazine. This honor is especially meaningful to her as the results come from reader surveys. "These results actually come from patient input, not dentists surveys as is the case with other surveys."

Susan is actually a nurse by training and after two years as a private scrub nurse for an otorhinolarygoligist and his dermatologist wife, she decided this was not her life long path. Friends and family were in wonderment and very skeptical for her to enter school again. Dentistry appealed to her because of being the primary care giver and focus on preventive care, as opposed to medicine at the time. During dental school, she worked part time as a nurse doing insurance life insurance exams. She stayed at UMKC for a year teaching in the oral surgery department and one of her students was Howard Farran. She followed this with a two-year associateship that was 90 miles from Phoenix in Payson, AZ.

As she started in Carefree, three of the busiest dentists told her "too many here, don't need you." She knew the ratio numbers from Paxon and just knew she would be fine in Carefree. At that time, Carefree was more seasonal and the talk in the office was, "when it slows down." Now, Dr. Weyers hears patients saying, "It is more convenient to have the work done here."

Never thinking she might not make it, she feels the turning point for her was taking Blatchford Coaching which was recommended by her friend, Dr. Brian Dolberg of Scottsdale. Through Blatchford, she met Drs. Joe Harris and Rod Gore who encouraged her to take PAC-live with David Hornbrook and she was in their first continuum. Until that time, she was still doing amalgams and extractions. The combination of technical and business coaching "really changed the way I practice dentistry."

With her cancers, Susan feels she has faced the biggest fear of life.

The fear of a patient says 'no' simply does not have the sting it once had. "There are still things in my life that I am fearful of, however, they aren't the same things I used to lose sleep over. Cancer truly helps you gain perspective. There is really very little in your life you have control over. Frequently those things you control really aren't that important anyway. Don't, however, confuse 'control' with 'choice.' The most powerful thing in your life is to be able to make choices. Especially about the way you deal with the little things—like your attitude and which battles you are willing to fight." She is living life fully. She knows fear and profitability cannot go hand in hand. She has the blinders taken off and is going for it, full out.

Her first breast cancer diagnosis came from a mammogram showing Stage 0 with resulting lumpectomy and five days of radiation. Ten months later, she had three positive lymph nodes and Stage 2B reoccurance at the lumpectomy site. This time, the medical group treated it with a vengeance by mastectomy and three weeks later eight chemo treatments every other week, all arranged so Susan did not miss a day of work. This was followed by 6 1/2 weeks of radiation every day. She worked 3.5 days a week and Doctors made the schedule work for her. Doctors say the first 36 months are critical with scans every six months. Her first one showed "a complete remission at this time."

Dr. Weyers indicates there are a number of reasons she was able to continue her dentistry during her treatment:

- Her desire to continue with established pattern for continuity and hope
- Her staff of two were extremely supportive to make that happen
- All systems in place, thanks to Blatchford Coaching
- Susan had already established the vision and direction of the practice
- Patients relate on some level and wanted to be a part of her recovery

"It was important for me to continue. Cancer was very transparent in my practice and I am now so much closer to my patients and I think they feel that, too. Everyone wants to love you. Patients would say, 'you are so positive, so upfront.' You do not know how you will react or those around you. I just live my life and it seems to draw people in."

"My staff was called to do things they were never prepared to do. Twenty times a day, we recounted the 'cancer tale.' As difficult as it was, I think it was somewhat cathartic for the team as well. Two months after Dr. Weyers second diagnosis, Sherry Nelson, Dr. Weyer's hygienist and Barbara Salcedo, Dr. Weyers chairside assistant, raised $1800 for the Susan G. Komen Race for the Cure. Barbara has raised the necessary $2100 for the 2005 Breast Cancer 3-Day Walk in less than four months, mainly from friends and patients. "They have lived breast cancer for two years. We have bonded together more like sisters. They are loyal and genuine."

Dr. Weyers is married and has a very supportive mate, Matthew (Matty) who is a SWAT team leader for the Phoenix Police Dept. She was 41 and he was 43 when they married six years ago, both for the first time. An undercover policeman patient actually introduced them. This marriage is very special for when Dr. Weyers initially started her practice, relationships were sacrificed with all the hard work. Susan said, "the cancer scare brings depth to our wedding vows. Going through something like this will do one of two things to a relationship. It will totally destroy it or it will allow you to grow in ways you never dreamed possible. Fortunately, my husband and I feel that although it was a tremendously difficult experience, our relationship has taken on depths that we probably wouldn't have experienced otherwise. A great relationship is even better. This was probably more difficult for him as there really wasn't anything he could physically do to make me better."

They are taking more time off and actually finding dentistry to be even more profitable with time away. Our goals for the future have taken on a new perspective. Every year, Matty and I have a 'strategic planning session,' basically goal setting for the upcoming year and accountability for the goals set the previous year. We were unable to have them the past two years and it shows. We look at five areas: Financial, Growth in Marriage, Spiritual, Jobs and Travel. Each year it takes less and less time to set the goals. This year, we are spending more time in the Travel, Spiritual and Marriage categories and by so doing, are actually excelling in the other areas as well. I guess it is true that if you 'make the main thing the main thing,' the rest works itself out well, too."

Dr. Weyers has been asked several times to share her business model by local magazines. She is truly a "Better Is Not Bigger" model. It is small and profitable for her. Team produces $50-60K a month. Bonus level is $33K in a 13 work day cycle. She has hygiene three days a week and Dr. Weyers works 3.5 days a week. Her laboratory expenses are at 13% which means she is doing between 4-6 units of crown and bridge per day. Current crown fee is $1010 and new patients flow in about one a day.

Susan has chosen to have quiet elegant marketing in her area rather then television radio or magazines which are seen in the greater Phoenix area of six million. When she moved offices ten years ago, she arrived with a new logo and new branding. She uses several local newspapers, HOA newsletters and promotionals. "Maybe the _Tipping Point_ is happening. I have lots of people coming in to meet me. I have several people calling to do articles about my business model and dentistry. Usually we have a number of charts to purge at year end. Not so lately, not as many transients. Her success may be due to fifteen years of credibility, some mystery and breast cancer.

www.carefreesmile.com

*Dr. Susan Weyers
defines life with her
three S's —
Service, Survivor,
Success.*

# Blatchford Game Plan: Rightsize for Profitability

Many dentists feel they walk a tightrope between caring for all the patients who seek better dental health vs. having meaningful, productive days. They feel there is a balancing act between having adequate and fully trained staff and profitability. How can a dentist diagnose ideal dentistry and not become a financial institution for many patients?

Staffing a practice with committed partners, operating at 55% overhead, providing care for quality "A" patients who see the value of treatment you have to offer and feeling satisfaction or even delight at the end of the day for a job well done—can actually occur. A dentist can have a profitable practice and perform ideal dentistry with a plan to reach those goals.

When a dentist and staff do not fully understand the economics of a small business, a roller-coaster effect results with vast differences in monthly production and collections. Dental practices are many times staffed, equipped and supplied for producing between 50% and 100% more than is actually produced. This results in a practice constantly chasing their overhead which creates stress emotionally, physically and in the checkbook.

Why not staff for the present production, gather and serve "A" patients who see value in your excellent dentistry and all can be produced at 55% overhead, leaving a net of 45% every month. What is the plan? It is called "rightsizing."

Rightsizing a practice reduces overhead immediately to produce a profit whatever size you are now. How can some doctors net $150,000 out of $3000 gross production and other doctors must produce $450,000 to $600,000 to net $150,000? The smaller practice is "rightsized." A larger practice with multiple doctors is not always the most profitable. In fact, the profitability is more difficult to control as "bigness' creates layers of management which is not necessary in a smaller practice.

Many dentists operate their practices on hope. They are staffed to produce and collect what they hope. Many dental practices are actually staffed for double what they really produce and collect.

Rightsizing is operating a practice where the numbers work well no matter the outside economic factors or what the newspapers are shouting. A rightsized practice is profitable at whatever size. We work with doctors who have one staff member and their net return is 50%. We have practices with several doctors and their net return is 45%.

Rightsizing your practice is having the statistics work well for your practice now and laying concrete groundwork and goals for where you are headed in the future. Rightsizing your practice occurs when the leader of the practice takes a hard look at where he is headed, makes some assessments and clearly shifts to the direction for which he wants to be remembered.

What would be some benefits of a more controlled practice?

> An immediate increase in net income.
> By utilizing Block Scheduling, you perform more quality work on fewer numbers of patients, thus requiring a smaller staff.
> You determine the pace rather than being "Everything to Everbody."
> Team is easier to manage and direct with committed and highly skilled players.
> Overhead is reduced and productivity increases when number of staff is smaller.
> Team communication is greater with fewer, more focused staff.
> Dental office becomes as stressless as possible with the doctor seeing no more than 14 patients a day.
> Patients perceive quality care, quality time and quality staff.
> They refer patients with similar values.

More, bigger, bigger is no longer the desirable practice model for dentistry. It is difficult to have a favorable economic return with seven chairs, ten staff members and the doctor seeing 25 to 30 patients a day. A typical overhead in that office would be 80%. And the dentist and his staff worked hard! Yet, patients perceive this office as a dental factory with the doctor making rounds on his jet-powered roller-skates and the "girls doing all the work."

Instead of management out of control with too many underpaid staff members and an exhausted frustrated dentist, let's practice with a model which has the right balance for ease, quality treatment and net return for the doctor.

What is wanted and needed in dentistry is an efficient practice that can serve patients expediently. A smaller, efficient practice can be very rewarding and work well. It does require several important criteria to produce the results you want:

**LEADERSHIP:** The dentist needs to have a clear focus or picture of the standard of care he wants to deliver, the quality of patients he wants and the contribution he wants to leave in the community. He must be excited about the dentistry and patients he serves. His motivation and delight must show.

**TEAM:** When the dentist has a clear picture of where he wants to go in dentistry, staff members who want to make the same contribution will be drawn to the practice. In hiring quality staff, the attitude and the people skills weigh more heavily than the technical skills, which can be learned by a motivated person.

**SYSTEMS:** Business and technical systems must be in place (see checklist).

**CASE PRESENTATION:** The dentist and staff must become very skilled in the area of case presentation, acceptance and financial arrangements. This requires asking the patient questions and listening, rather than you speaking. Case presentation is a learned skill that must be practiced continually. You are presenting to patients the possibility of keeping their teeth for a lifetime.

**BLOCK SCHEDULING:** Implement a daily template of how you want your day to be with 80% of the productive work completed by lunch. Hold blocks of time open in the mornings for major procedures. Schedule towards a goal. Your patients receive undivided attention, you are "on time" and they perceive your impeccable asepsis techniques.

An argument could be made that the dentist could not possibly change the size and format of his practice because he needs all his staff to perform the work. This is true. You do need all the present staff if you continue to practice the same way when seeing 25 to 30 patients a day.

Rightsizing is an opportunity to look at the possibility of attracting and keeping "A" patients who appreciate you timeliness, quality and service. Analyze the "B" and "C" patients you continue to treat to have them show up as "A's" in your practice or encourage them to find care where they might show up as an "A" in the other practice.

Doctors might say, "Rightsizing sounds good but I just don't have the quantity of quality patients to fill the morning blocks with permanent work." Virtually every practice has a large number of "A" patients who are very loyal to you. What has been missing is a clear direction from the leader as to the standard of care for which he/she wants to be remembered.

Once that standard is established, the team needs skill building in the area of case presentation. Ask questions of your existing "A" patients which will have them visualize the kind of smile they would really like.

Present to your existing patients the opportunity for lifetime dental plans. Set goals with them for permanent quality dentistry. It may be accomplished a phase at a time and it will be appreciated.

The advantages of rightsizing your practice are many.

> With staff overhead at 20%, profitability returns for doctor and staff with a bonus plan.

> By focusing on quality more permanent work, the practice

attracts patients who want that work and refer their family and friends.

> With fewer team members, each is accountable for the result. Team members learn to work more efficiently.

> The dentist has the opportunity to focus the practice in the direction of choice rather than treating everyone.

> With block booking in place, patients receive the undivided attention of the professional team. No other patients are seen during those reserved blocks. Patients receive extraordinary service by unhurried professionals.

> By rightsizing your practice, you are attracting those patients who want the same type of dentistry being delivered. The team can be well-compensated and patients will be receiving the attention and service they want and deserve.

## CHECK LIST FOR RIGHTSIZING

**Leadership:**

1. Doctor has defined picture of practice in ten years, 20 years and has shared that with staff.
2. Doctor has set standard of care for his practice.
3. Doctor knows and shares the numbers in the practice.
4. Doctor is excited about dentistry and his patients.
5. Doctor is able to let go and delegate tasks.

**Team:**

1. Committed team players for staff.
2. Morning meetings to set the day.
3. Weekly team meetings which produce results.
4. Team participates in a bonus plan.

**Systems:**

1. Block scheduling in place for doctor and hygiene.

2. Office financial policy in place with agreement that no treatment is scheduled without financial arrangements.

3. Financial choices available to patient include outside funding sources.

4. Over the counter collection goal is 35% of production.

5. Establish a short call list, insurance profile notebook and pending treatment book.

**Case Presentation:**

1. Gather a library of books, audios and videos on sales and staff skill-building with team.

2. Ask the patient "open ended" questions (which cannot be answered with "yes" or "no".)

3. Avoid giving the Dentistry 101 lecture with pictures on each phase of treatment.

4. Include instamatic pictures of patient for your record taking. Patients get to see their own teeth and smiles.

5. Use before and after pictures to create interest with patients.

6. Present life-time treatment plans to all patients.

Bill Blatchford, DDS

# From the Blatchford Play Book:
# Turning Your Weakness Into A Strength

As Dr. Weyers can testify, a dentist can and needs to have their house in order to flourish, no matter the cause. Systems and skills need to be practiced and mastered. Facing your fears and evaluating your strengths before you need them is essential to keep a balanced life and successful practice moving forward.

>> Face your fears for they will keep you weak

>> One permanent emotion of the inferior man is fear—fear of the unknown, the complex, the inexplicable. What he wants beyond everything is safety.

>> Anyone can conquer fear by doing things he fears to do, providing he keeps doing them until he gets a record of successful experiences behind him

>> What are your weaknesses? Put yourself under a microscope.

>> How good do you want to be?

>> When the game is on the line, there is no substitute for skill

>> Eliminate your negative qualities

>> Do not let your weaknesses master you

>> Do not use your weaknesses as an excuse

>> Be willing to be uncomfortable

>> Work on your weaknesses

>> Always remember, behavior is a choice

>> Chose positive and productive behavior

# CONCLUSION

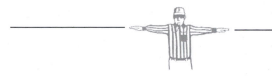

Over the last twenty years, I have coached over 1,800 dental offices for success. Each dentist's goals and aspirations determine their success. It is different for each person. Success is doing what you think is rewarding. The rewards are also as individual as the definition of success. Our society tends to measure success by material measurements yet, these stories of real people demonstrate each has their own measure. We selected stories from all parts of the country and various levels of income. Each story is unique and all are successful in their own way. Each has shared their personal story about their professional life and practice. They speak of what worked and shared pitfalls as well. They have shared what motivates them and their frustrations. Each is different. All have been my clients, some on a continuing regular basis and others, I have not had regular contact for some time. It is rewarding for me to see that I made an impact on their lives and practice. I enjoy seeing that they have kept on "keeping on" with the direction they set while working with Blatchford Solutions.

After observing many dentists in their offices, I have found several common characteristics which contribute to success. These are shared in all the stories and more importantly, by all success practices. I have always studied why some dentist are successful and make it look easy while others struggle and are constantly dissatisfied. I have found that behind all of those who make it look easy, there has been a lot of hard work and dedication. A wise man once said, "Successful people make a habit of doing those things that others know about and choose not to do." **There are no secrets.** Knowledge is valuable yet many do not put it into action.  Many dentists are very academic and study every situation until the opportunity goes away. It is also called "paralysis by analysis."

The first and most important trait I have observed in a successful dentist is a strong sense of **purpose or vision.**  This is known but few actually practice it. A study of *Man's Search for Meaning* by Victor Frankel illustrates how vision is a compelling force. Vision offers the bigger picture. It is the motivating force that gets one through hard times. One must have a bigger picture of life and what you want to accomplish in your short stay on the planet. People with vision have a positive outlook on life and exhibit this daily. For them, failures are just opportunities to learn.  They have failures but get over them quickly and move on with their life. For them, the glass is either full or half full. For them it is never empty or half empty.  As Helen Keller said, "Life is either a daring adventure or nothing at all."  Vision is what drives these people to always trying to improve. I observe each of these dentists has a living a vision many believe not possible. All believe  if it has been done, it must be possible. They even believe if it has not been done, it may be possible.

The next common characteristic is clear **goals** which are much more concrete than vision statements. Many people go through life with out any goals. They seldom accomplish much and are constantly dissatisfied. All of these doctors have very clear goals. They gain satisfaction by accomplishing a goal and moving to the next one. If they do not reach a goal, they keep trying. I believe that the happiest dentists are the ones who have goals in all areas of their life and have balance as a result of this. Goals must be specific. Can you measure it?

Goals that are not specific are not really goals but just passing thoughts. Nonspecific goals are also known as wishes. Goals must have a time line. A "by when" this will be complete. It is too easy to put off making things happen. There must be some form of affirmation. You must write them down and review constantly. Share them only with some one committed to your success. Do not share them with the naysayers for they will try to discourage you. Most people with out goals (95% of the population) do not share your enthusiasm for life and success. All of these stories share goals and how they were accomplished. They have also shared setbacks along the way.

All of these dentists share the third characteristic of **constant learning;** continually learning new techniques. They are reading and taking courses. They are willing to spend the time and money to seek the best teachers in our profession. They are not satisfied with the minimum. They take the comprehensive courses to master a topic; not satisfied with only a short course. Besides learning new techniques, they have learned you do not have to spend time trying to reinvent the wheel. The wheel is already invented and if it worked for someone it may work for them also. They are constantly striving to be the best. They are open-minded and are very willing to look at different ways to accomplish things. They are constantly reminded of Dr. Omer Reed's quote, "You do not know what you do not know." As soon as we think we know something, we stop asking questions. When we stop asking questions, we stop learning. When we stop learning, we die spiritually.

The fifth characteristic I see in all of these stories is **surrounding your self with great people.** It is not just mentors but also having a great team. There are several common rules for attracting and keeping great team members. One is the Doctor's clear vision and what will it take to get there. You must decide what the position entails and then hire to the position, not adapt the position to fit the person. Set high standards and lead by example. Always hire for attitude. You can train someone with a great attitude to do anything but you can not teach anything to someone with a poor attitude. Attitude is manifested as behavior and behavior is always a choice. Hire people with great behavior. Several of these stories indicate how they kept people with poor attitude too long.

They have all set up systems of accountability. All of the dentists have learned the value of rewarding the team well. All want their team to be the best paid in town. They constantly look for areas to compliment their team. There must be accountability in each area for their team to flourish. The successful doctors in this book are quick to acknowledge great performance. While it is fine to like your team members, you must remain the leader. You did not hire them to be a pal. There is a reason that in the military officers are prohibited from fraternizing with the enlisted personnel.

The sixth characteristic is an **awareness of the business** of dentistry. While they are not micro managers, they study the numbers and own them. They have discovered what numbers are important. They know their cost per hour. What does it cost to do a unit of Crown and Bridge? What does it cost to see a hygiene patient? What does it cost when a patient cancels or no shows? What procedures actually make money for the practice? They realize that by doubling hygiene production per day, it is less than one additional unit of C&B. they realize what a fee increase does for the bottom line. They know if they keep their staff overhead between 15-20% of their gross, the numbers fall into line. They know it is better to pay individuals well, but not have as many total staff. They understand they want their lab to be over 10% of their gross. If it is lower, they are not effective in showing value to their guests. They know their diagnosis to appointment ratio. What is their new patient per month flow? Where do these patients come from? They recognize the value of a marketing budget. These dentists do not receive their marketing advice from internet forums. They have a long-range plan by stablishing a budget and either hiring professionals or studying the local market themselves. One characteristic of these doctors is awareness of the bigger picture and not worry what percentage they spend on the dental supplies or lab. They understand quality and are willing to charge a fair fee not dictated by insurance companies. Several of the doctors in the book charge fee plus lab or fee plus implant for discretionary items.

The seventh characteristic is the **willingness to be courageous in marketing**. All are doing some form of marketing. They recognize they are in a discretionary form of treatment and must let the public know what they do. All but one has a website and they rely on it for new patient flow. They use it to inform and educate. They promote the website every way they can. Several are using radio on a regular basis. Several use print media. Some are using television. Several have filmed their own Extreme Makeover shows. All are doing some form of networking to let people know who they are and what they do. All of this has taken courage to break the mold from traditional attitudes about marketing. Several have grown by purchasing practices and merging with their existing patient base. In each case, they have had to establish a budget and act on faith. They are always looking for ways to promote their practice to the right people.

The eighth and last characteristic is the **development of superior communications skills**. They have learned how to first communicate with their team. By doing this, they do not have to micro-manage every detail. They are able to paint the big picture and stand back letting team members move forward. The doctors in the book realize team members have good ideas and allow them to be true team members. The leader's job is to create an environment for learning. They realize that the most important skill not only in their practice but in their life is communication. This is the ability to communicate their vision and to discover other people's vision. They realize they can not be all things to all people.

These characteristics seem to run common through out all the dentists in this book and are also common among all successful people. The main characteristic of all these people is the choice to do those things that unsuccessful people know about and choose not to do.

Bill Blatchford, DDS

*Loyola dental student Bill Blatchford practicing denture setup in his Chicago kitchen, 1967.*

# Blatchford Custom Coaching

- Just starting a practice and want to do it right the first time?
- Are you working too hard and not being rewarded?
- Do you feel your leadership is less than stellar?
- Are you tired of dentistry, management issues and ready to quit?

Blatchford's Custom Coaching allows doctors to reach their individual and practice goals. *Not* a cookie cutter approach, the goals achieved and resulting practice model occurs because Coach Blatchford helps doctors discover and clarify their own goals, values and dreams.

With 35 years experience in the dental field, Bill has a no-nonsense approach. His goal is your goal.

Custom Coaching is 12 months of one-on-one coaching with Dr. Blatchford personally. A full day summit with Dr. Blatchford is filled with personal discovery, introspection, revelation and commitment.

Two staff seminars (two days each) are packed with energy, systems, team accountability and skill building. Separate monthly conference calls on timely topics are held for doctor and team members. A Blatchford professional consultant has regular contact and in-house learning.

We limit Custom Coaching to 50 doctors a year. To discuss your participation, (800) 578-9155; www.blatchford.com; info@blatchford.com.

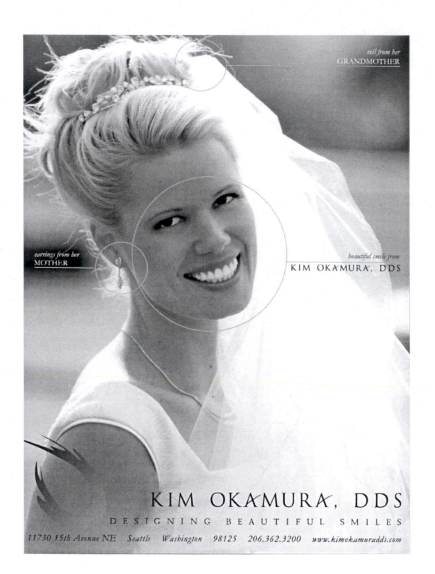